THE SHAKESPEARE PARALLEL TEXT SERIES, THIRD EDITION

Romeo and Juliet

by William Shakespeare

Perfection Learning®

Editorial Director	Julie A. Schumacher
Senior Editor	Rebecca Christian
Series Editor	Rebecca Burke
Writer	Janie B. Yates–Glandorf, Ph.D.
Design	Mark Hagenberg, Deborah Bell
Art Research	Laura Wells
Cover Art	Brad Holland

© 2004 **Perfection Learning**®
www.perfectionlearning.com

39588

PB ISBN: 978-0-7891-6087-4
RLB ISBN: 978-0-7569-1489-9

18 19 20 21 22 PP 19 18 17 16

Printed in the United States of America

Table of Contents

Juliet and Her Romeo

Romeo's name comes first in the play's title, but Juliet is the stronger character. She, not Romeo, makes all the important decisions in the play. She is even the first to propose marriage.

Two facts about Juliet tend to surprise today's audiences and readers. One is that she is only 13. The other is that her part was probably first played by a teenaged boy.

On Shakespeare's stage, female roles were acted by boys. One of the most famous was John Rice, who created the roles of Lady Macbeth and Cleopatra. These parts made him something of a celebrity. Rice was even invited to make a special appearance before King James I.

The part of Juliet was probably first played by Robert Goffe. He probably played Juliet opposite the famous tragic actor Richard Burbage. The older actor later created the roles of Hamlet, Macbeth, Othello, and King Lear. But in *Romeo and Juliet*, Goffe got the meatier role.

Juliet was first played by a woman in 1662. Since that time, the role has almost always been performed by a woman. During the 19th century, women sometimes even played the part of Romeo. The most famous female Romeo was the American actress Charlotte Cushman, who was also known for her Hamlet.

In Shakespeare's time, women were not allowed to play dramatic roles. However, they could marry at a much earlier age than is acceptable

Betrothal

today. In Elizabethan England, a girl could legally marry at the age of 12. For boys, the legal age was 14. Wealthy families sometimes arranged marriages to protect their fortunes, but, in fact, early marriages were not common. The average wealthy woman in Elizabethan England married at 20, the average wealthy man at 22. Still, nobles carefully guarded the legality of early marriage and sometimes arranged for their children to marry at ages even younger than the law allowed.

Early marriage was a common enough practice to be quite controversial. Certain scholarly and medical authorities decried the practice in words similar to those of Juliet's father: "And too soon marr'd are those so early made." The danger of childbirth at such an age was widely recognized. And early marriage often led to many children, something Elizabethan society discouraged for practical, economic reasons.

Charlotte Cushman as Romeo
and her sister Susan as Juliet

A Political Romance

Audiences often think of *Romeo and Juliet* as a love story and nothing more. In fact, the play has a political dimension that is too frequently overlooked. The politics of *Romeo and Juliet* have their roots deep in the story's earliest Italian sources.

The play's plot goes back to several Italian novels. All of these novels feature two lovers named Romeo and Giulietta, whose happiness is thwarted by their feuding families, the Montecchi and Cappelletti. The first of these was written by Masuccio of Salerno during the 15th century. During the 16th century, Luigi da Porto based another novel on Masuccio's, and Matteo Bandello based yet another on Luigi's.

Florence in 1490

During the Italian Renaissance, powerful families often quarreled violently. One feud was between the Cerchi and Donati families in Florence. They began fighting around 1300 and barely stopped for another 50 years. The Cerchi and Donati families represented two opposing political factions—the Ghibellines and Guelphs, respectively. The Ghibellines (or the White faction) believed in a large Italian empire. The Guelphs (or the Black faction) favored independent city-states under the direction of the pope. Italian fans of Romeo and Giulietta may have seen the lovers as tragic pawns in the struggle over the destiny of Italy itself.

Shakespeare learned their story through Arthur Brookes' narrative poem *The Tragicall Historye of Romeus and Juliet*, published in 1562. He may have used the story of the two Italian lovers to explore a controversy in his own time—the nature of marriage. Should marriages be arranged, or should young people choose their spouses? Is marriage simply a practical way to raise children, or should personal happiness be considered?

The controversy about marriage was influenced by religious differences. Catholics tended to see happiness in this world as less important than eternal bliss. Protestants, more concerned with worldly success, generally rated marital happiness highly—sometimes even as essential to salvation. But these divisions were by no means simple and clear-cut. The purpose of marriages and the role of parents in arranging them remained quite controversial in Shakespeare's Protestant England. Which viewpoint did Shakespeare himself hold?

Leonardo DiCaprio and Claire Danes get married in *Romeo and Juliet*. (Luhrmann, 1996)

Generations of English teachers have advised their students that Shakespeare and his audience were not as sympathetic to the actions of Romeo and Juliet as we are today. The play, they have said, is partly a cautionary tale about the importance of obeying one's parents. But as Shakespearean scholar Cedric Watts points out, the text itself does not support this interpretation.

The love between Romeo and Juliet is necessary to bring about peace between their families. And in the speech that closes the play, Prince Escalus does not place any blame upon the young lovers. Instead, he blames their families and even assumes some responsibility for failing to enforce the peace. If Shakespeare had felt that Romeo and Juliet were seriously at fault, surely he would have found a character to voice this viewpoint. Since he did not, we can only assume that, like Escalus, he blamed their families—and more sweepingly, a concept of marriage that did not properly value happiness. To a greater degree than is usually admitted, *Romeo and Juliet* is a play about gender politics.

There is even an interesting trace of feminism in Shakespeare's play. In most romantic stories of his time, a dashing hero actively woos a beautiful but passive heroine. The hero gets to behave heroically and also to speak splendid lines as he lavishes poetry on his rather witless love object. But Juliet is at least Romeo's equal as an initiator of action, and her poetry often surpasses his in beauty. Consider her breathtaking pronouncement in the balcony scene: "My bounty is as boundless as the sea, / My love as deep; the more I give to thee, / The more I have, for both are infinite."

Juliet's strength and assertiveness seem all the more remarkable because her life is so limited. Like a typical well-born Renaissance girl, she can't even come and go as she pleases, much less roam the streets at night as Romeo does with his pals Mercutio and Benvolio. Again and again, we are dazzled by her determination and resourcefulness.

Timeline

1558   Elizabeth I becomes Queen of England.

1562   Arthur Brookes publishes *The Tragicall Historye of Romeus and Juliet*.

1564   Shakespeare is baptized.

1572   Shakespeare begins grammar school.

1576   Opening of The Theatre, the first permanent playhouse in England.

1580   Drake sails around the world.

1582   Shakespeare marries Anne Hathaway.

1583   Shakespeare's daughter Susanna is baptized.

1585   Shakespeare's twins are baptized.

1588   Spanish Armada is defeated.

1592-94   Plague closes all of London's theaters.

1594   *Titus Andronicus* becomes first printed Shakespeare play.

1594   Shakespeare joins the Lord Chamberlain's Men.

1599   Lord Chamberlain's Men build the Globe Theatre; Shakespeare is part-owner of the building.

1609   *Shakespeare's Sonnets*, written in 1598, published for the first time.

         The King's Men acquire the Blackfriars Playhouse.

1610   Shakespeare retires to Stratford.

1613   Globe Theatre burns to the ground.

1616   William Shakespeare dies at the age of 52.

1623   Shakespeare's wife Anne dies.
         First Folio published.

Reading *Romeo and Juliet*

Using This Parallel Text

This edition of *Romeo and Juliet* is especially designed for readers who aren't familiar with Shakespeare. If you're fairly comfortable with his language, simply read the original text on the left-hand page. When you come to a confusing word or passage, refer to the modern English version on the right or the footnotes at the bottom.

If you think Elizabethan English doesn't even sound like English, read a passage of the modern version silently. Then read the same passage of the original. You'll find that Shakespeare's language begins to come alive for you. You may choose to work your way through the entire play this way.

As you read more, you'll probably find yourself using the modern version less and less. Remember, the parallel version is meant to be an aid, not a substitute for the original. If you read only the modern version, you'll cheat yourself out of Shakespeare's language—his quick-witted puns, sharp-tongued insults, and evocative images.

Keep in mind that language is a living thing, constantly growing and changing. New words are invented and new definitions for old words are added. Since Shakespeare wrote over 400 years ago, it is not surprising that his work seems challenging to today's readers.

Here are some other reading strategies that can increase your enjoyment of the play.

Background

Knowing some historical background makes it easier to understand what's going on. In addition to the timeline in the front, you will find information about Shakespeare's life and Elizabethan theater at the back of the book. Reading the summaries that precede each act will also help you to follow the action of the play.

Getting the Beat

Like most dramatists of his time, Shakespeare frequently used blank verse in his plays. In blank verse, the text is written in measured lines that do not rhyme. Look at the following example.

> He jests at scars that never felt a wound.
> But soft what light through yonder window breaks?
> It is the east, and Juliet is the sun.
> Arise, fair sun, and kill the envious moon.

You can see that the four lines above are approximately equal in length, but they do not cover the whole width of the page as the lines in a story or essay might. They are, in fact, unrhymed verse with each line containing ten or eleven syllables. Furthermore, the ten syllables can be divided into five sections, called **iambs**. Each iamb contains one unstressed (U) and one stressed (\) syllable. When the rhythm follows an unstressed/stressed pattern, it is called **iambic**. Try reading the lines below, giving emphasis to the capitalized syllable in each iamb.

U \	U \	U \	U \	U \
He JESTS	at SCARS	that NEV	er FELT	a WOUND.

U \	U \	U \	U \	U \
But SOFT!	What LIGHT	through YON	der WIN	dow BREAKS?

The length of a line of verse is measured by counting the stresses. This length is known as the **meter**, and when there are five stresses, as in the preceding lines, the pattern is known as **iambic pentameter**. Much of Shakespeare's work is written in iambic pentameter.

Of course, Shakespeare was not rigid about this format. He sometimes varied the lines by putting accents in unusual places, by having lines with more or fewer than ten syllables, and by varying where pauses occur. An actor's interpretation can also add variety. (Only a terrible actor would deliver lines in a way that makes the rhythm sound singsong!)

Renaissance Italian city

Prose

In addition to verse, Shakespeare wrote speeches in prose, or language without rhythmic structure. Look at the Servant's speech on page 46 (Act I, Scene ii). If you try beating out an iambic rhythm to these lines, you'll discover that it doesn't work because they're in prose. But once Benvolio enters and starts speaking, you'll be able to find the rhythm of iambic pentameter again. Shakespeare often uses prose for comic speeches, to show madness, and for characters of lower social rank such as servants. His upper-class characters generally do not speak in prose. But these weren't hard-and-fast rules as far as Shakespeare was concerned.

Contractions

As you know, contractions are words that have been combined by substituting an apostrophe for a letter or letters that have been removed. Contractions were as common in Shakespeare's time as they are today. For example, we use *it's* as a contraction for the words *it is*. In Shakespeare's writing you will discover that *'tis* means the same thing. Shakespeare often used the apostrophe to shorten words so that they would fit into the rhythmic pattern of a line. This is especially true of verbs ending in *-ed*. Note that in Shakespeare's plays, the *-ed* at the end of a verb is pronounced as a separate syllable. Therefore, *walked* would be pronounced as two syllables, *walk*ed*, while *walk'd* would be only one.

Speak and Listen

Remember that plays are written to be acted, not read silently. Reading out loud—whether in a group or alone—helps you to "hear" the meaning. Listening to another reader will also help. You might also enjoy listening to a recording of the play by professional actors.

Clues and Cues

Shakespeare was sparing in his use of stage directions. In fact, many of those in modern editions were added by later editors. Added stage directions are usually indicated by brackets. For example, [aside] tells the actor to give the audience information that the other characters can't hear.

The Play's the Thing

Finally, if you can't figure out every word in the play, don't get discouraged. The people in Shakespeare's audience couldn't either. At that time, language was changing rapidly and standardized spelling, punctuation, grammar, and even dictionaries did not exist. Besides, Shakespeare loved to play with words. He made up new combinations, like *fat-guts* and *mumble-news*. To make matters worse, the actors probably spoke very rapidly. But the audience didn't strain to catch every word. They went to a Shakespeare play for the same reasons we go to a movie—to get caught up in the story and the acting, to have a great laugh, an exciting adventure, or a good cry.

Cast of Characters

The House of Capulet

JULIET
LORD CAPULET her father
LADY CAPULET her mother
NURSE servant to Juliet
PETER servant to the Nurse
TYBALT first cousin to Juliet and nephew to Lady Capulet
2. CAPULET Capulet's kinsman
SAMPSON servant to Capulet
GREGORY servant to Capulet
POTPAN servant to Capulet
other **SERVANTS**

The House of Montague

ROMEO
LORD MONTAGUE his father
LADY MONTAGUE his mother
BENVOLIO first cousin to Romeo and nephew to Lord Montague
BALTHASAR servant to Romeo
ABRAHAM servant to Montague

Others

CHORUS actor who introduces Acts I and II
ESCALUS Prince of Verona
PARIS young nobleman and kinsman to the Prince
PAGE servant to Paris
MERCUTIO friend to Romeo and kinsman to the Prince
FRIAR LAWRENCE Franciscan priest
FRIAR JOHN Franciscan priest
APOTHECARY pharmacist from Mantua
MUSICIANS, CITIZENS, TORCH-BEARERS, GUARDS,
   SERVANTS, ATTENDANTS, WATCHMEN, KINSMEN from both houses

TIME the fourteenth century

PLACE Verona and Mantua, cities in northern Italy

Romeo and Juliet ACT I

Laurence Olivier and Vivien Leigh exchange a holy palmer's kiss during a production in New York. (1940)

"My only love sprung from my only hate!"

Before You Read

1. The Prologue to Act I suggests that the relationship of Romeo and Juliet is doomed from the start. Some people believe that things are fated to happen, no matter what. Others believe that your actions can change the course of your life. Explain your own beliefs about fate.

2. What role do you think a family should have in the selection of their child's wife or husband?

3. As you read, notice the opposites (love/hate; light/dark) that Shakespeare provides in his language and imagery. Think about what purpose opposites might have in this play.

Literary Elements

1. A **foil** is a character in literature who has qualities that are in sharp contrast to another character, thus emphasizing the traits of each. In *Romeo and Juliet*, the responsible and highly regarded Paris is a foil to the brash and emotional Romeo.

2. **Foreshadowing** refers to hints in the text about what will occur later in the plot. The Prologue to *Romeo and Juliet* forecasts that an old grudge is about to break out in renewed violence.

3. **Hyperbole** is exaggeration that is not meant to be taken literally. Lord Montague, describing his son's lovesickness, claims that Romeo locks himself up in his room "and makes himself an artificial night."

4. A **pun** is a play on words that have similar sounds but more than one possible spelling or meaning. For example, Romeo says Mercutio has "nimble soles," but he himself has "a soul of lead."

5. Good drama has **conflict**: struggle between opposing forces. In *Romeo and Juliet*, the Capulet and Montague families have been at war as long as anyone can remember. Their conflict creates problems for their families as well as Prince Escalus and the other citizens of Verona.

Words to Know

The following vocabulary words appear in Act I in the original text of Shakespeare's play. However, they are words that are still commonly used. Read the definitions here and pay attention to the words as you read the play (they will be in boldfaced type).

adversary	enemy; opponent
augmenting	adding to; enlarging
deformities	irregularities; disfigurements
discreet	showing good judgment; perceptive
disparagement	criticism; censure
nuptial	wedding; marriage
obscured [obscur'd]	hid; darkened
pernicious	harmful; destructive
portentous	ominous; threatening
posterity	future generations
prodigious	terrible; extraordinary
profane	dishonor; make impure
propagate	reproduce; increase
purged [purg'd]	got rid of; expelled

Act Summary

In the Prologue, a Chorus (or narrator) previews this play about two feuding families and the tragedy that occurs when their children meet and fall in love.

One day, in the public square in Verona, Italy, two servants from the Capulet household pick a fight with rival servants from the Montague household. The Capulets and Montagues have quarreled for so many years that nobody even knows how their feud began.

When the fight begins, a young Montague, Benvolio, tries to make peace. Instead, a fiery Capulet named Tybalt makes the tensions escalate. Soon, even onlookers and the elderly lords of the two warring sides are trying to join in the brawl.

Prince Escalus, the ruler of Verona, arrives and demands that the fighting stop. In the quarrel's aftermath, Lord Montague asks Benvolio, a friend of his son Romeo, why Romeo seems so depressed. Benvolio tracks Romeo down and learns that he is in love with Rosaline, who doesn't return his affections. Benvolio vows to make Romeo forget her.

Meanwhile, in the Capulet household, Lord Capulet and a nobleman named Paris discuss Paris's proposal of marriage to Lord Capulet's daughter Juliet. They discuss the masked banquet the Capulets will host that night and hope that Juliet will get to know Paris and agree to marry him. Of course, the hated Montagues are not invited to the banquet.

When Benvolio and Romeo catch wind of it, though, they decide to go in disguise. During the party, Tybalt guesses their identity and vows revenge on Romeo, whom he assumes has come only to mock the Capulets and cause trouble.

When Juliet catches Romeo's eye at the banquet, he instantly forgets Rosaline. By the time Romeo and Juliet realize they are from warring families, it is too late: they have fallen in love.

PROLOGUE

Enter CHORUS.

CHORUS

Two households, both alike in dignity,
    In fair Verona, where we lay our scene,
From ancient grudge break to new mutiny,
    Where civil blood makes civil hands unclean.
5 From forth the fatal loins of these two foes
    A pair of star-cross'd lovers take their life;
Whose misadventur'd piteous overthrows
    Doth with their death bury their parents' strife.
The fearful passage of their death-mark'd love,
10   And the continuance of their parents' rage,
Which, but their children's end, naught could remove,
    Is now the two hours' traffic of our stage;
The which if you with patient ears attend,
What here shall miss, our toil shall strive to mend.

      [Exit.]

PROLOGUE

The CHORUS *enters.*

CHORUS
Two equally respected families,
    living in lovely Verona, where our play is set,
break out in renewed violence due to an old grudge.
    The townspeople soil their hands with each other's blood.
The son of one enemy and the daughter of the other,   5
    victims of unfavorable fate, commit suicide.
Their unfortunate, pitiful deaths
    bury their parents' quarrel.
The sad story of their ill-fated love,
    and of their parents' continuing anger,   10
which nothing except their children's deaths could end,
    you will see acted in the next two hours on our stage.
If you will listen patiently,
our play will fill in what is missing from the Prologue.

Exit.

ACT I, SCENE I

[*Verona. A public place.*] *Enter* SAMPSON *and* GREGORY, *of the house of Capulet, armed with swords and bucklers.*

SAMPSON
Gregory, on my word, we'll not carry coals.

GREGORY
No, for then we should be colliers.*

SAMPSON
I mean, an we be in choler, we'll draw.

GREGORY
Ay, while you live, draw your neck out of collar.

5 **SAMPSON**
I strike quickly, being mov'd.

GREGORY
But thou art not quickly mov'd to strike.

SAMPSON
A dog of the house of Montague moves me.

GREGORY
To move is to stir, and to be valiant is to stand; therefore, if thou art mov'd, thou run'st away.

10 **SAMPSON**
A dog of that house shall move me to stand. I will take the wall* of any man or maid of Montague's.

GREGORY
That shows thee a weak slave; for the weakest goes to the wall.

SAMPSON
'Tis true; and therefore women, being the weaker vessels,

---

2   *colliers* coal sellers

11   *take the wall* A drainage ditch ran down the center of many streets. The person of superior rank was usually granted the privilege of walking closest to the wall since this was the cleanest route.

ACT 1, SCENE 1

A public street in Verona. SAMPSON *and* GREGORY, *servants of* CAPULET, *enter carrying swords and shields.*

SAMPSON
Gregory, I swear it, we'll not endure insults.

GREGORY
No, for then we would be insult-sufferers.

SAMPSON
I mean, if we get angry, we'll draw our swords.

GREGORY
Yes, and if you want to live, draw your head out of the hangman's rope.

SAMPSON
I strike quickly when I'm angry.   5

GREGORY
But you're not likely to get angry quickly.

SAMPSON
A dog from Montague's house makes me angry.

GREGORY
To be angry is to move, to be brave is to stand still. Therefore, if you're angry, you'll run away.

SAMPSON
A dog of that house shall move me to be brave. I will walk   10
near the wall if any of Montague's servants pass by.

GREGORY
That shows you're a weak slave, for the weakest is pushed to the wall.

SAMPSON
That's true, and therefore, women, being the weaker sex, are

15 are ever thrust to the wall; therefore I will push
Montague's men from the wall, and thrust his maids to
the wall. *messing with eachother*

GREGORY
The quarrel is between our masters and us their men.

SAMPSON
'Tis all one. I will show myself a tyrant. When I have
20 fought with the men, I will be cruel with the maids;
I will cut off their heads.

GREGORY
The heads of the maids?

SAMPSON
Ay, the heads of the maids, or their maidenheads;* take it
in what sense thou wilt.

GREGORY
25 They must take it in sense that feel it.

SAMPSON
Me they shall feel while I am able to stand; and 'tis known
I am a pretty piece of flesh.

GREGORY
'Tis well thou art not fish; if thou hadst, thou hadst been
poor John. Draw thy tool; here comes two of the house of
30 Montagues.

Enter two other serving-men, ABRAHAM *and*
BALTHASAR.

SAMPSON
My naked weapon is out. Quarrel! I will back thee.

GREGORY
How! Turn thy back and run?

SAMPSON
Fear me not.

rape the women

---

23 *maidenheads* Sampson is making one of many bawdy puns in his exchange with
Gregory. He means he will rob the girls of their virginity.

always being pushed against the wall. So I will push   15
Montague's men away from the wall, and his maidens to
the wall.

GREGORY

The quarrel is not only between our masters, but between us
and their servants, as well.

SAMPSON

It's all the same quarrel. I'll prove myself a tyrant. After I've
fought with the men, I'll be cruel to the maidens. I'll cut off   20
their heads.

GREGORY

The heads of the maidens?

SAMPSON

Yes, the heads of the maidens, or their maidenheads. Take it
in any sense you like.

GREGORY

They must take it in the sense they feel it.   25

SAMPSON

They'll feel me as long as I'm able to stand, and everyone
knows I'm a real man.

GREGORY

It's a good thing you're not a fish. If you were, you would
not give much satisfaction.—Draw your weapon! Here
come two of Montague's servants.   30

Two servants, ABRAHAM *and* BALTHASAR, *enter.*

SAMPSON

My bare sword is out. Start a quarrel! I'll back you up.

GREGORY

How will you back me up? By turning your back and running?

SAMPSON

Don't be afraid of me.

GREGORY

No, marry;* I fear thee!

(handwritten: Let the others start the fight)

SAMPSON

35   Let us take the law of our sides; let them begin.

GREGORY

I will frown as I pass by, and let them take it as they list.

(handwritten, left margin: they won't be provoked)

SAMPSON

Nay, as they dare. I will bite my thumb at them; which is disgrace to them, if they bear it.

ABRAHAM

Do you bite your thumb at us, sir?

SAMPSON

40   I do bite my thumb, sir.

ABRAHAM

Do you bite your thumb at us, sir?

SAMPSON

[*aside to* GREGORY] Is the law of our side, if I say ay?

GREGORY

No.

SAMPSON

No, sir, I do not bite my thumb at you, sir; but I bite my
45   thumb, sir.

GREGORY

Do you quarrel, sir?

ABRAHAM

Quarrel, sir? No, sir.

SAMPSON

But if you do, sir, I am for you. I serve as good a man as you.

ABRAHAM

50   No better.

SAMPSON

Well, sir.

---

35   *marry* originally meant "Virgin Mary," but by Shakespeare's day it had become an exclamation comparable to "really," "indeed," etc.

GREGORY

Afraid, indeed! Don't be ridiculous.

SAMPSON

We'll get the law on our side. Let them begin.   35

GREGORY

I'll make a sour face as I pass by, and let them take it as they choose.

SAMPSON

No—as they dare, I'll thumb my nose at them. That will insult them, if they notice it.

ABRAHAM

Are you thumbing your nose at us, sir?

SAMPSON

I'm thumbing my nose, sir.   40

ABRAHAM

Are you thumbing your nose at us, sir?

SAMPSON (*to* GREGORY)

Is the law on our side if I say yes?

GREGORY

No.

SAMPSON

No, sir. I'm not thumbing my nose at you, sir. I'm just   45
thumbing my nose, sir.

GREGORY

Are you trying to start a fight, sir?

ABRAHAM

A fight, sir? No, sir.

SAMPSON

If you do start a quarrel, I'm ready. My master is as good as your master.

ABRAHAM

But he's no better.   50

SAMPSON

Well—sir—

Enter BENVOLIO.

GREGORY
Say "better"; here comes one of my master's kinsmen.

SAMPSON
Yes, better, sir.

ABRAHAM
You lie.

SAMPSON
55 Draw, if you be men. Gregory, remember thy swashing blow.

[*They fight.*]

BENVOLIO
Part, fools!
Put up your swords; you know not what you do.

[*Beats down their swords.*]

Enter TYBALT.

TYBALT
What, art thou drawn among these heartless hinds?
60 Turn thee, Benvolio; look upon thy death.

BENVOLIO
I do but keep the peace. Put up thy sword,
Or manage it to part these men with me.

TYBALT
What, drawn and talk of peace! I hate the word
As I hate hell, all Montagues, and thee.
65 Have at thee, coward!

[*They fight.*]

Enter three or four CITIZENS *and* OFFICERS, *with clubs or partisans.*

OFFICERS
Clubs, bills, and partisans! Strike! Beat them down!
Down with the Capulets! Down with the Montagues!

Enter CAPULET *in his gown, and* LADY CAPULET.

BENVOLIO *enters.*

GREGORY
You should say "better." Here comes one of my master's relatives.

SAMPSON (*to* ABRAHAM)
My master is better, sir.

ABRAHAM
You're a liar.

SAMPSON
Draw your swords, if you're real men. Gregory, give him your   55
crushing blow.

They fight.

BENVOLIO
Stop it, you fools!
Put your swords away. You don't know what you're doing.

He strikes down their swords.

TYBALT *enters.*

TYBALT
Are you fighting with these cowards?
Turn around, Benvolio. I'm going to kill you.   60

BENVOLIO
I'm only trying to make peace. Put away your sword,
or use it to get these men away from me.

TYBALT
You have your sword drawn and you talk about peace! I hate
    the word peace,
as I hate hell, all Montagues, and you.
Fight, coward!   65

They fight.

OFFICERS *and three or four* CITIZENS *enter with clubs and
pikes.*

OFFICERS
Clubs, axes, and pikes! Strike! Beat them down!
Down with the Capulets! Down with the Montagues!

CAPULET, *in his robe, and* LADY CAPULET *enter.*

CAPULET

What noise is this? Give me my long sword, ho!

LADY CAPULET

A crutch, a crutch! Why call you for a sword?

CAPULET

70 My sword, I say! Old Montague is come,
And flourishes his blade in spite of me.

Enter MONTAGUE *and* LADY MONTAGUE.

MONTAGUE

Thou villain Capulet!—Hold me not, let me go.

LADY MONTAGUE

Thou shalt not stir one foot to seek a foe.

Enter PRINCE ESCALUS *with his train.*

PRINCE ESCALUS

Rebellious subjects, enemies to peace,
75 Profaners of this neighbour-stained steel—
Will they not hear?—What ho! You men, you beasts,
That quench the fire of your **pernicious** rage
With purple fountains issuing from your veins,
On pain of torture, from those bloody hands
80 Throw your mistemper'd weapons to the ground,
And hear the sentence of your moved prince.
Three civil brawls, bred of an airy word,
By thee, old Capulet, and Montague,
Have thrice disturb'd the quiet of our streets,
85 And made Verona's ancient citizens
Cast by their grave beseeming ornaments
To wield old partisans, in hands as old,
Cank'red with peace, to part your cank'red hate;
If ever you disturb our streets again,
90 Your lives shall pay the forfeit of the peace.
For this time, all the rest depart away.
You, Capulet, shall go along with me;
And, Montague, come you this afternoon,
To know our farther pleasure in this case,
95 To old Free-town, our common judgment-place.
Once more, on pain of death, all men depart.

CAPULET

What's all this noise? Give me my sword!

LADY CAPULET

You need a crutch! Why are you asking for a sword?

CAPULET

Give me my sword, I said. Old Montague is coming,   70
and he is waving his sword in defiance of me.

MONTAGUE and LADY MONTAGUE enter.

MONTAGUE

You're a villain, Capulet! (*to* LADY MONTAGUE) Don't hold me,
let me go!

LADY MONTAGUE

You shall not move a foot toward your enemy.

PRINCE ESCALUS enters with his followers.

PRINCE

Rebellious people, enemies to peace,
Abusers of your swords bloodied with your neighbor's blood— 75
Won't they listen?—Listen to me, you men, you beasts,
you who quench the fire of your destructive rage
with purple blood spurting from your veins.
Unless you want to be tortured, throw those angry
weapons you hold in your bloody hands to the ground   80
and hear this sentence from me, your angry prince.
Three fights arising from meaningless insults—
started by you, old Capulet, and you, old Montague—
have disturbed the quiet of our streets three times,
and caused Verona's old men   85
to throw away their proper, dignified ornaments
and carry old pikes, rusted with peace, in their equally old
hands to part your deadly hatred.
If you ever disturb our streets again,
you will have to die for breaking the peace.   90
For now, all of you go away
except you, Capulet. You'll go with me.
And you, Montague, are to come to me this afternoon
to find out what I am going to do in your case.
Go to my castle, Freetown, the common judgment place.   95
Once more, unless you want to die, all of you must leave now.

[*Exeunt all but* MONTAGUE, LADY MONTAGUE, *and* BENVOLIO.]

MONTAGUE

Who set this ancient quarrel new abroach?
Speak, nephew, were you by when it began?

BENVOLIO

Here were the servants of your **adversary**,
100   And yours, close fighting ere I did approach.
I drew to part them. In the instant came
The fiery Tybalt, with his sword prepar'd,
Which, as he breath'd defiance to my ears,
He swung about his head and cut the winds,
105   Who, nothing hurt withal, hiss'd him in scorn.
While we were interchanging thrusts and blows,
Came more and more and fought on part and part,
Till the Prince came, who parted either part.

LADY MONTAGUE

O, where is Romeo? Saw you him to-day?
110   Right glad I am he was not at this fray.

BENVOLIO

Madam, an hour before the worshipp'd sun
Peer'd forth the golden window of the east,
A troubled mind drove me to walk abroad;
Where, underneath the grove of sycamore
115   That westward rooteth from the city's side,
So early walking did I see your son.
Towards him I made, but he was 'ware of me
And stole into the covert of the wood.
I, measuring his affections by my own,
120   Which then most sought where most might not be found,
Being one too many by my weary self,
Pursued my humour not pursuing his,
And gladly shunn'd who gladly fled from me.

MONTAGUE

Many a morning hath he there been seen,
125   With tears **augmenting** the fresh morning's dew,
Adding to the clouds more clouds with his deep sighs;
But all so soon as the all-cheering sun

All leave except MONTAGUE, LADY MONTAGUE, *and*
BENVOLIO.

MONTAGUE
> Who started up this old quarrel again?
> Speak up, nephew, were you here when it started?

BENVOLIO
> Capulet's servants were here,
> along with your servants, and they were fighting as I came up. 100
> I drew my sword to separate them. At that moment,
> the hot-tempered Tybalt arrived, with his sword drawn,
> breathing defiance in my ears,
> swinging his sword about my head, and slicing the winds.
> But the winds, not being hurt, hissed at him in scorn. 105
> While we were exchanging blows,
> more and more people came to fight on each side
> until the prince came and stopped the fighting.

LADY MONTAGUE
> Where is Romeo? Have you seen him today?
> I am glad he wasn't at this fight. 110

BENVOLIO
> Madam, about an hour before the wonderful sun
> peered out of the golden east,
> a troubled mind drove me to take a walk.
> Underneath a grove of sycamore trees,
> west of the city, 115
> I saw your son walking at that early hour.
> I went toward him, but he saw me,
> and he slipped into a thicket in the woods.
> Sensing that he felt the same way I did—
> wanting to get away from everyone 120
> and feeling I was one too many by my weary self—
> I chose to pursue my own desire rather than to pursue him.
> I as gladly shunned him as he fled from me.

MONTAGUE
> He has been seen there many mornings,
> adding tears to the moisture of the fresh morning dew 125
> and adding more clouds to clouds with his deep sighs.
> But as soon as the sun, which cheers everything,

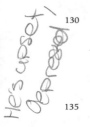

Should in the farthest east begin to draw
The shady curtains from Aurora's bed,
130 Away from light steals home my heavy son,
And private in his chamber pens himself,
Shuts up his windows, locks fair daylight out,
And makes himself an artificial night.
Black and **portentous** must this humour prove
135 Unless good counsel may the cause remove.

BENVOLIO
My noble uncle, do you know the cause?

MONTAGUE
I neither know it nor can learn of him.

BENVOLIO
Have you importun'd him by any means?

MONTAGUE
Both by myself and many other friends;
140 But he, his own affections' counsellor,
Is to himself—I will not say how true—
But to himself so secret and so close,
So far from sounding and discovery,
As is the bud bit with an envious worm
145 Ere he can spread his sweet leaves to the air
Or dedicate his beauty to the sun.
Could we but learn from whence his sorrows grow,
We would as willingly give cure as know.

Enter ROMEO.

BENVOLIO
See, where he comes! So please you, step aside;
150 I'll know his grievance, or be much deni'd.

MONTAGUE
I would thou wert so happy by thy stay
To hear true shrift. Come, madam, let's away.

[*Exeunt* MONTAGUE *and* LADY.]

begins in the far east to draw
the dark curtains from dawn's bed,
my sad son creeps home, away from this light. 130
He secludes himself alone in his room,
shutting his windows, locking the lovely daylight outside,
and creating an artificial night.
His mood will become dark and ominous
unless good advice can remove the cause of his sadness. 135

BENVOLIO
My noble uncle, do you know the reason for his behavior?

MONTAGUE
I do not know it, and I cannot learn it from him.

BENVOLIO
Have you pleaded with him in any way?

MONTAGUE
I have tried, and so have many friends,
but he is the counselor of 140
his own emotions, though I will not say how well he plays
counselor.
He is so secret and close-mouthed,
so far from being found out and cured,
that he's like a bud bitten by a deadly worm before
the bud can spread its sweet leaves to the air 145
or offer its beauty to the sun.
If we could just learn what causes his sorrow,
we would willingly cure it as know about it.

>   ROMEO *enters.*

BENVOLIO
Here he comes. If you will, please step aside
and I'll find out what's wrong with him. If I 150
don't, you can deny any connection with me.

MONTAGUE
Stay. I hope you'll be lucky enough
to hear his true confession. (*to* LADY MONTAGUE)
Come, madam, let's go.

>   LORD *and* LADY MONTAGUE *exit.*

BENVOLIO
Good morrow, cousin.

ROMEO
                              Is the day so young?

BENVOLIO
155   But new struck nine.

ROMEO
                         Ay me! Sad hours seem long.
Was that my father that went hence so fast?

BENVOLIO
It was. What sadness lengthens Romeo's hours?

ROMEO
Not having that which, having, makes them short.

BENVOLIO
160   In love?

ROMEO
Out—

BENVOLIO
Of love?

ROMEO
Out of her favour, where I am in love.

BENVOLIO
Alas, that love, so gentle in his view,
165   Should be so tyrannous and rough in proof!

ROMEO
Alas, that love, whose view is muffled still,
Should, without eyes, see pathways to his will!
Where shall we dine? O me! What fray was here?
Yet tell me not, for I have heard it all.
170   Here's much to do with hate, but more with love.
Why, then, O brawling love!* O loving hate!
O anything of nothing first create!

---

171   *brawling love, etc.* Lines 171–178 are oxymorons, in which contradictions are
stated. Oxymorons occurred in the "artificial" love poetry in Shakespeare's day.
Romeo's love for Rosaline is not deep, so he is speaking "artificially."

BENVOLIO

Good morning, cousin.

ROMEO

Is it still morning?

BENVOLIO

The clock just struck nine.   155

ROMEO

Alas, the hours seem so long.
Was that my father who left here so quickly?

BENVOLIO

Yes, it was. What sadness lengthens your hours, Romeo?

ROMEO

Not having something that, if I had it, would make the hours
   seem short.

BENVOLIO

Are you in love?   160

ROMEO

Out—

BENVOLIO

Of love?

ROMEO

The one I love doesn't love me.

BENVOLIO

It's too bad that love, so gentle in appearance,
should be so tyrannous and rough when being experienced.   165

ROMEO

It's too bad that love, whose sight is blindfolded,
can still see ways to work his will even without his eyes.
(*pause*) Where shall we eat? (*pause*) My, what fight happened
   here?
On second thought, don't tell me, for I've heard it all.
It has much to do with hate, but more with love.   170
Why, then, Oh brawling love! Oh loving hate!
Oh anything first created out of nothing!

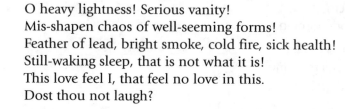

O heavy lightness! Serious vanity!
Mis-shapen chaos of well-seeming forms!
175 Feather of lead, bright smoke, cold fire, sick health!
Still-waking sleep, that is not what it is!
This love feel I, that feel no love in this.
Dost thou not laugh?

BENVOLIO

No, coz, I rather weep.

ROMEO

180 Good heart, at what?

BENVOLIO

At thy good heart's oppression.

ROMEO

Why, such is love's transgression.
Griefs of mine own lie heavy in my breast,
Which thou wilt **propagate** to have it prest
185 With more of thine. This love that thou hast shown
Doth add more grief to too much of mine own.
Love is a smoke made with the fume of sighs;
Being **purg'd**, a fire sparkling in lovers' eyes;
Being vex'd, a sea nourish'd with lovers' tears.
190 What is it else? A madness most **discreet**,
A choking gall, and a preserving sweet.
Farewell, my coz.

His love
has been
taken away

BENVOLIO

Soft! I will go along.
And if you leave me so, you do me wrong.

ROMEO

195 Tut, I have left myself; I am not here.
This is not Romeo; he's some otherwhere.

BENVOLIO

Tell me in sadness, who is that you love?

ROMEO

What, shall I groan and tell thee?

BENVOLIO

Groan! Why, no;

Oh heavy lightness! Serious frivolity!
Deformed chaos of outwardly pretty forms!
Lead feather, bright smoke, cold fire, sick health!   175
Ever-wakeful sleep, that is not what it is!
I take no joy from this love I feel.
Are you laughing at me?

BENVOLIO
No, cousin, I'm crying.

ROMEO
Dear, good-hearted friend, why?   180

BENVOLIO
Because of your good heart's grief.

ROMEO
This is love's sin.
My own griefs make my heart heavy
which will only increase if burdened
with your sorrow, too. The love which you have shown me   185
adds more grief to my own too heavy sorrow.
Love is a smoke rising from the fumes of sighs;
when the air is cleared, love is a fire sparkling in lovers' eyes.
When frustrated, love is a sea fed by lovers' tears.
What else is love? A very wise insanity,   190
a choking bitterness, and a lasting sweet.
Good-bye, cousin.

BENVOLIO
Wait! I'll go with you.
If you leave me, you'll do me wrong.

ROMEO
Nonsense, I've lost myself; I'm not here.   195
This isn't Romeo; he's somewhere else.

BENVOLIO
Tell me in all seriousness, who is it that you love?

ROMEO
Do you want me to groan and tell you?

BENVOLIO
Groan? No,

200   But sadly tell me who.

ROMEO
    Bid a sick man in sadness make his will—
    A word ill urg'd to one that is so ill!
    In sadness, cousin, I do love a woman.

BENVOLIO
    I aim'd so near when I suppos'd you lov'd.

ROMEO
205   A right good mark-man! And she's fair I love.

BENVOLIO
    A right fair mark, fair coz, is soonest hit.

ROMEO
    Well, in that hit you miss. She'll not be hit
    With Cupid's arrow; she hath Dian's wit;
    And, in strong proof of chastity well arm'd,
210   From Love's weak childish bow she lives unharm'd.
    She will not stay the siege of loving terms,
    Nor bide th' encounter of assailing eyes,
    Nor ope her lap to saint-seducing gold.
    O, she is rich in beauty, only poor
215   That, when she dies, with beauty dies her store.

BENVOLIO
    Then she hath sworn that she will still live chaste?

ROMEO
    She hath, and in that sparing make huge waste;
    For beauty starv'd with her severity
    Cuts beauty off from all **posterity**.
220   She is too fair, too wise, wisely too fair,
    To merit bliss by making me despair.
    She hath forsworn to love, and in that vow
    Do I live dead that live to tell it now.

BENVOLIO
    Be rul'd by me, forget to think of her.

ROMEO
225   O, teach me how I should forget to think.

but tell me, seriously, who you love.   200

ROMEO

You want a sick man, in seriousness, to make his will.
That's not good advice for someone who is so ill!
In all seriousness, cousin, I do love a woman.

BENVOLIO

I assumed that when I learned you were in love.

ROMEO

You're right on the mark! And the one I love is beautiful.   205

BENVOLIO

A bright clean target, cousin, is the easiest to hit.

ROMEO

Well, you missed the target that time. She won't be hit
with love's arrow. She has the same views as Diana, the moon
     goddess.
She's well-protected in her armor of virginity.
She's safe from love's weak, childish bow.   210
She will not listen to my loving words,
or let me look at her with love in my eyes,
or allow herself to be seduced.
Oh, she is rich in beauty; only poor
in that when she dies, her treasure will die with her beauty. 215

BENVOLIO

Then has she sworn that she'll live as a virgin for now?

ROMEO

She has, and in being stingy, she is horribly wasteful.
For when beauty is starved by severe attitudes,
it is cut off from all future generations.
She's too beautiful, too wise, too wisely beautiful   220
to earn her way to heaven by making me suffer.
She vows she will not love, and because of that vow,
I'm dead, though I live to tell the fact now.

BENVOLIO

Listen to me: forget her.

ROMEO

Oh, teach me how to forget to think!   225

BENVOLIO

By giving liberty unto thine eyes;
Examine other beauties.

ROMEO

'Tis the way
To call hers, exquisite, in question more.
230   These happy masks that kiss fair ladies' brows,
Being black, puts us in mind they hide the fair;
He that is strucken blind cannot forget
The precious treasure of his eyesight lost.
Show me a mistress that is passing fair,
235   What doth her beauty serve, but as a note
Where I may read who pass'd that passing fair?
Farewell! Thou canst not teach me to forget.

BENVOLIO

I'll pay that doctrine or else die in debt.

[*Exeunt.*]

- He not going to be able to get over her.

- He strucken in love
- He wonk get distracted by other women

BENVOLIO

Just set your eyes free
to look at other beautiful women.

ROMEO

That would just be another way
to make me recall her unparalleled beauty.
Those fortunate masks that kiss beautiful ladies' foreheads,   230
being black, make us remember that they hide the beautiful.
The man who is struck blind can't forget
the precious treasure of his lost eyesight.
Show me a woman who's surpassingly beautiful,
and I'll ask what good is her beauty except as a note   235
where I could read who is still more beautiful than that beauty?
Good-bye! You can't teach me to forget her.

BENVOLIO

I'll make you change your mind or die trying.

They exit.

ACT I, SCENE II

[A street.] *Enter* CAPULET, PARIS, *and the clown*
[a SERVANT*].*

CAPULET

But Montague is bound as well as I,
In penalty alike; and 'tis not hard, I think,
For men so old as we to keep the peace.

PARIS

Of honourable reckoning are you both;
5   And pity 'tis you liv'd at odds so long.
But now, my lord, what say you to my suit?

CAPULET

But saying o'er what I have said before.
My child is yet a stranger in the world;
She hath not seen the change of fourteen years.
10   Let two more summers wither in their pride,
Ere we may think her ripe to be a bride.

PARIS

Younger than she are happy mothers made.

CAPULET

And too soon marr'd are those so early made.
The earth hath swallow'd all my hopes but she;
15   She is the hopeful lady of my earth;
But woo her, gentle Paris, get her heart,
My will to her consent is but a part;
And, she agreed, within her scope of choice
Lies my consent and fair according voice.
20   This night I hold an old accustom'd feast,
Whereto I have invited many a guest,
Such as I love; and you, among the store
One more, most welcome, makes my number
     more.
At my poor house look to behold this night
25   Earth-treading stars that make dark heaven
     light.
Such comfort as do lusty young men feel
When well-apparell'd April on the heel

ACT 1, SCENE 2

A street. CAPULET, PARIS, *and the clown (a* SERVANT*) enter.*

CAPULET
 Montague is under bond, just like me,
 and facing the same punishment. It shouldn't be hard, I think,
 for men as old as we are to keep the peace.

PARIS
 You both have honorable reputations,
 and it's a pity you've been fighting for so long.   5
 But now, my lord, what do you say about my proposed
 marriage to your daughter Juliet?

CAPULET
 By saying again what I told you before:
 my child is too young to know the rules of society.
 She isn't quite fourteen years old yet;
 it will be two more years   10
 before I think she'll be ready to be married.

PARIS
 Younger girls than she have become happy mothers.

CAPULET
 Yes, and they were disfigured by that early childbirth.
 All of my children are dead except her;
 she is the only hope I have in the world.   15
 But go ahead and try to win her heart, gentle Paris;
 my wishes only partially guarantee her consent.
 If she agrees,
 I'll go along with her wishes.
 Tonight, I am going to give my annual masquerade banquet,   20
 and I have invited many guests
 who are people I love. You are invited, too.
 One more very welcome guest makes the company all the
    richer.
 At my humble house tonight, you'll see
 the most beautiful maidens of Verona that make the night   25
    bright.
 Such joy as red-blooded young men feel
 when well-dressed spring treads on the heel

Of limping winter treads, even such delight
Among fresh female buds shall you this night
30 Inherit at my house. Hear all, all see,
And like her most whose merit most shall be;
Which, on more view of, many, mine being one,
May stand in number, though in reckoning none.
Come, go with me. [*to* SERVANT] Go, sirrah, trudge about
35 Through fair Verona; find those persons out
Whose names are written there, and to them say
My house and welcome on their pleasure stay.

[*Exeunt* CAPULET *and* PARIS.]

SERVANT

Find them out whose names are written here! It is written
that the shoemaker should meddle with his yard* and the
40 tailor with his last, the fisher with his pencil and the
painter with his nets; but I am sent to find those persons
whose names are here writ, and can never find what names
the writing person hath here writ. I must to the learned.
—In good time.

Enter BENVOLIO *and* ROMEO.

BENVOLIO

45 Tut, man, one fire burns out another's burning,
One pain is lessened by another's anguish;
Turn giddy, and be holp by backward turning;
One desperate grief cures with another's languish.
Take thou some new infection to thy eye,
50 And the rank poison of the old will die.

ROMEO

Your plantain-leaf is excellent for that.

BENVOLIO

For what, I pray thee?

---

39 *shoemaker should meddle with his yard* The servant, a comic character, has
everything backwards. He means: the shoemaker's leather, the tailor's wool, the
fisherman's nets, and the artist's pencil.

of limping winter, just such joy
among the lovely young maidens will you find tonight
at my house. Listen to everything, look at everything,   30
and like the lady best who is most worthy.
My daughter will be among the ladies,
but she may not be the one you choose when you have seen
    them all.
Come with me. (*to the* SERVANT) Go, servant, walk about
beautiful Verona; find the people   35
whose names are on these invitations and say to them
that I will be pleased to welcome them to my house tonight.

> CAPULET *and* PARIS *exit.*

SERVANT

I'm to find those whose names are written here! I've heard
that the shoemaker should work with his wool, and the tailor
with his leather, the fisherman with his pencil, and the painter   40
with his net. But I have to find the people whose names are
written here, and will never find them because I can't read.
I must find someone who can read. Here's help already!

> BENVOLIO *and* ROMEO *enter.*

BENVOLIO

Come on, Romeo. One fire burns out another fire;   45
one person's pain is lessened by some else's misery;
become dizzy from spinning, and be helped by reversing
    the direction;
one terrible grief can be cured by someone else's pain.
Find a new infection in your eye,
and the poison of the old infection will die.   50

ROMEO

The plantain leaf is a good remedy for that.

BENVOLIO

For what, I ask you?

ROMEO

For your broken shin.

BENVOLIO

Why, Romeo, art thou mad?

ROMEO

55 Not mad, but bound more than a madman is;
Shut up in prison, kept without my food,
Whipp'd and tormented and—God-den, good fellow.

SERVANT

God gi' god-den. I pray, sir, can you read?

ROMEO

Ay, mine own fortune in my misery.

SERVANT

60 Perhaps you have learn'd it without book.
But, I pray, can you read anything you see?

ROMEO

Ay, if I know the letters and the language.

SERVANT

Ye say honestly. Rest you merry!

ROMEO

Stay, fellow; I can read.
65 [*Reads.*] "Signior Martino and his wife and daughters;
County Anselme and his beauteous sisters; the lady widow
of Vitruvio; Signior Placentio and his lovely nieces;
Mercutio and his brother Valentine; mine uncle Capulet,
his wife, and daughters; my fair niece Rosaline; Livia;
70 Signior Valentio and his cousin Tybalt; Lucio and the
lively Helena." A fair assembly: Wither should they
come?

SERVANT

Up.

ROMEO

Wither? To supper?

SERVANT

75 To our house.

ROMEO

For your wounded shin when I kick you.

BENVOLIO

Romeo, are you crazy?

ROMEO

No, I'm not crazy, but a madman is freer than I am. 55
I'm shut up in prison, given no food,
whipped, tortured, and—(*Sees the* SERVANT.)—Good evening,
good fellow.

SERVANT

And a good evening to you. Sir, can you read?

ROMEO

Yes, that's my one happiness in my unhappiness.

SERVANT

Perhaps you memorize. 60
Can you read anything you see?

ROMEO

Yes, if I know the letters and the language.

SERVANT

You're an honest fellow. Have a nice day!

ROMEO

Wait, fellow, I can read.
(ROMEO *takes the list and reads*.) *Signior Martino and his wife* 65
and daughters; Count Anselme and his beautiful sisters;
Vitruvio's widow; Signior Placentio and his lovely nieces;
Mercutio and his brother Valentine; my uncle Capulet, with his wife
and daughters; my lovely niece Rosaline; Livia; Signior Valentio and
his cousin Tybalt; Lucio and the lively Helena. 70
(*Returns the paper to the* SERVANT.) *This is a beautiful group of*
people. Where are they to go?

SERVANT

Up.

ROMEO

Where?

SERVANT

To dinner, to our house. 75

ROMEO

    Whose house?

SERVANT

    My master's.

ROMEO

    Indeed, I should have ask'd you that before.

SERVANT

    Now I'll tell you without asking. My master is the great
80   rich Capulet; and if you be not of the house of
    Montagues, I pray, come and crush a cup of wine.
    Rest you merry! [*Exit.*]

BENVOLIO

    At this same ancient feast of Capulet's
    Sups the fair Rosaline whom thou so loves,
85   With all the admired beauties of Verona.
    Go thither; and with unattainted eye
    Compare her face with some that I shall show,
    And I will make thee think thy swan a crow.

ROMEO

    When the devout religion of mine eye
90   Maintains such falsehood, then turn tears to fires;
    And these, who, often drown'd, could never die,
    Transparent heretics, be burnt for liars!
    One fairer than my love! The all-seeing sun
    Ne'er saw her match since first the world begun.

BENVOLIO

95   Tut, you saw her fair, none else being by,
    Herself pois'd with herself in either eye;
    But in that crystal scales let there be weigh'd
    Your lady's love against some other maid
    That I will show you shining at this feast,
100   And she shall scant show well that now seems best.

ROMEO

    I'll go along no such sight to be shown,
    But to rejoice in splendour of mine own. [*Exeunt.*]

ROMEO
Whose house?

SERVANT
My master's.

ROMEO
Of course, I should have asked you that before.

SERVANT
Now I'll tell you without your asking. My master is the very rich
Capulet, and if you're not a Montague, I invite you to come and 80
have a drink of wine. Bless you!

The SERVANT *exits.*

BENVOLIO
At this party of Capulet's,
the beautiful Rosaline that you love so much will dine
with all of the beautiful girls of Verona. 85
Go there, and with an unprejudiced eye,
compare her face to some of the others I'll show you,
I'll make you think your swan is a crow.

ROMEO
When the devout belief of my eyes
asserts such a lie, then my tears will turn to fires; 90
and these eyes, often drowned in tears, could never die.
transparent unbelievers should be burned for lying!
Someone more beautiful than my love? The all-seeing sun
has never seen my love's equal since the world began.

BENVOLIO
Ha! You think she's beautiful because, having no one to 95
    compare her with,
you only saw her balanced in each of your eyes.
But in your two eyes, those crystal scales of yours, weigh
your lady's love against another lady
whom I will show you at this party,
and your Rosaline will scarcely look good who now seems 100
    the fairest to you.

ROMEO
I'll go with you, not to find a lovelier girl,
but to rejoice in the beauty of my own Rosaline.

They exit.

ACT I, SCENE III

[*A room in Capulet's house.*] *Enter* LADY CAPULET *and* NURSE.

LADY CAPULET
Nurse, where's my daughter? Call her forth to me.

NURSE
Now, by my maidenhead at twelve year old,
I bade her come. What, lamb! What, ladybird!
God forbid—Where's this girl? What, Juliet!

Enter JULIET.

JULIET
5   How now! Who calls?

NURSE
                Your mother.

JULIET
Madam, I am here. What is your will?

LADY CAPULET
This is the matter.—Nurse, give leave a while,
10 We must talk in secret.—Nurse, come back again;
I have rememb'red me, thou's hear our counsel.
Thou know'st my daughter's of a pretty age.

NURSE
Faith, I can tell her age unto an hour.

LADY CAPULET
She's not fourteen.

NURSE
15   I'll lay fourteen of my teeth,—
And yet, to my teen be it spoken, I have but four,—
She's not fourteen. How long is it now
To Lammas-tide?

LADY CAPULET
A fortnight and odd days.

ACT 1, SCENE 3

A room in Capulet's house. LADY CAPULET *and the* NURSE *enter.*

LADY CAPULET
Nurse, where's my daughter? Tell her to come to me.

NURSE
Now by my virginity, when I was twelve years old
I told her to come. (*Calls to* JULIET.) Lamb! Ladybird!
Heavens above, where is that girl? Juliet!

JULIET *enters.*

JULIET
What is it? Who's calling?   5

NURSE
Your mother.

JULIET
Madam. I am here. What do you want?

LADY CAPULET
I'll tell you.—Nurse, leave us for awhile,
we must talk in secret. (*pause*)—Nurse, come back again.   10
I just remembered that you are to hear our plan.
You know my daughter is at the marrying age.

NURSE
Indeed. Heavens, I can tell her age to the exact hour.

LADY CAPULET
She's not quite fourteen.

NURSE
I would wager fourteen of my teeth—   15
and yet it is my misfortune to admit I have only four—
that she's not fourteen. How many days
until Lammastide?

LADY CAPULET
A bit over two weeks.

NURSE

20   Even or odd, of all days in the year,
    Come Lammas-eve at night shall she be fourteen.
    Susan and she—God rest all Christian souls!—
    Were of an age. Well, Susan is with God;
    She was too good for me. But, as I said,
25   On Lammas-eve at night shall she be fourteen;
    That shall she, marry; I remember it well.
    'Tis since the earthquake now eleven years,
    And she was wean'd,—I never shall forget it—
    Of all the days of the year, upon that day;
30   For I had then laid wormwood to my dug,
    Sitting in the sun under the dove-house wall;
    My lord and you were then at Mantua;—
    Nay, I do bear a brain;—but, as I said,
    When it did taste the wormwood on the nipple
35   Of my dug and felt it bitter, pretty fool,
    To see it tetchy and fall out wi' the dug!
    "Shake," quoth the dove-house. 'Twas no need, I trow,
    To bid me trudge.
    And since that time it is eleven years;
40   For then she could stand high-lone; nay, by the rood,
    She could have run and waddled all about;
    For even the day before, she broke her brow;
    And then my husband—God be with his soul!
    'A was a merry man—took up the child.
45   "Yea," quoth he, "dost thou fall upon thy face?
    Thou wilt fall backward when thou hast more wit;
    Wilt thou not, Jule?" and, by my holidame,
    The pretty wretch left crying and said, "Ay."
    To see, now, how a jest shall come about!
50   I warrant, an I should live a thousand years,
    I never should forget it. "Wilt thou not, Jule?" quoth he;
    And, pretty fool, it stinted and said, "Ay."

LADY CAPULET
    Enough of this; I pray thee, hold thy peace.

NURSE

Even or odd, of all the days of the year,   20
on the evening of July thirty-first she'll be fourteen.
Susan and she—God rest all Christian souls!—
were the same age. Well, Susan is with God.
She was too good for me. But as I said,
on the evening of July thirty-first, Juliet will be fourteen.   25
To think she might get married—I remember her birth well.
It is now eleven years since the earthquake
and since she was weaned—I'll never forget it.
Of all the days of the year, I remember that day.
I'd used a bitter herb on my breast to wean her,   30
and I was sitting in the sun next to the dovehouse wall.
You and my lord were in Mantua at the time—
I do have a good memory—but as I said,
when the baby tasted the herb on the nipple
of my breast and found out it was bitter, the pretty little thing   35
became fretful and didn't want to nurse any more!
Then the dovehouse shook from the earthquake. There was
      no need
for anyone to have to tell me to run away.
Since that time it's been eleven years,
for by then she could stand up alone—indeed, I swear by the   40
      cross,
she could run and waddle all around.
Just the day before, she'd fallen on her forehead,
and then my husband—God rest his soul,
he was a happy man—picked her up.
He said, "Did you fall on your face?   45
You'll fall backward when you know more,
won't you, Juliet?" And I swear,
the pretty child stopped crying and said, "Yes."
To see now how a joke turns out!
I swear, if I live a thousand years,   50
I'll never forget it. "Won't you, Juliet?" he asked.
And the pretty child stopped crying and said, "Yes."

LADY CAPULET

That's enough, Nurse. Please be quiet.

NURSE

> Yes, madam; yet I cannot choose but laugh
> 55 To think it should leave crying and say, "Ay."
> And yet, I warrant, it had upon its brow
> A bump as big as a young cock'rel's stone;
> A perilous knock; and it cried bitterly.
> "Yea," quoth my husband, "fall'st upon thy face?
> 60 Thou wilt fall backward when thou comest to age;
> Wilt thou not, Jule?" It stinted and said, "Ay."

JULIET

> And stint thou too, I pray thee, nurse, say I.

NURSE

> Peace, I have done. God mark thee to his grace!
> Thou wast the prettiest babe that e'er I nurs'd.
> 65 An I might live to see thee married once,
> I have my wish.

LADY CAPULET

> Marry, that "marry" is the very theme
> I came to talk of. Tell me, daughter Juliet,
> How stands your disposition to be married?

JULIET

> 70 It is an honour that I dream not of.

NURSE

> An honour! Were not I thine only nurse,
> I would say thou hadst suck'd wisdom from thy teat.

LADY CAPULET

> Well, think of marriage now; younger than you,
> Here in Verona, ladies of esteem,
> 75 Are made already mothers. By my count,
> I was your mother much upon these years
> That you are now a maid. Thus then in brief:
> The valiant Paris seeks you for his love.

NURSE

> A man, young lady! Lady, such a man
> 80 As all the world—why, he's a man of wax.

be lucky

NURSE

Yes, madam. (*laughing*) But I can't help laughing
to think that she would stop crying and say "Yes."   55
And yet, I swear, she had a bump on her forehead
as big as a rooster's comb.
She took a bad fall, and she cried bitterly.
"So you fell on your face?" said my husband.
"You'll fall backward when you are older,   60
won't you, Juliet?" And she stopped crying and said, "Yes."

JULIET

And you must stop, too. I beg you nurse.

NURSE

Enough, I'm finished. God bless you.
You were the prettiest baby I've ever nursed.
If I can live to see you married,   65
I'll have my wish.

LADY CAPULET

Indeed, marriage is the very subject I came to talk about.
Tell me, Juliet,
how do you feel about getting married?

JULIET

It's an honor I've never dreamed of.   70

NURSE

An honor? If I weren't your only nurse,
I'd say that you sucked wisdom from your nurse's breast.

LADY CAPULET

Well, think about marriage now. There are younger women
    than you,
ladies of esteem living here in Verona,
who are mothers already. If I count correctly,   75
I became your mother at the same age
you are now. So, in short,
the brave Paris wants you to be his love.

NURSE

A man, young lady! Lady, he's such a man
as the entire world—why, he's the handsomest model of a man! 80

LADY CAPULET

Verona's summer hath not such a flower.

NURSE

Nay, he's a flower; in faith, a very flower.

LADY CAPULET

What say you? Can you love the gentleman?
This night you shall behold him at our feast;
Read o'er the volume of young Paris's face
And find delight writ there with beauty's pen;
Examine every married lineament
And see how one another lends content,
And what **obscur'd** in this fair volume lies
Find written in the margent of his eyes.
This precious book of love, this unbound lover,
To beautify him, only lacks a cover.
The fish lives in the sea, and 'tis much pride
For fair without the fair within to hide.
That book in many's eyes doth share the glory,
That in gold clasps locks in the golden story;
So shall you share all that he doth possess,
By having him, making yourself no less.

NURSE

No less! Nay, bigger; women grow by men.

LADY CAPULET

Speak briefly, can you like of Paris' love?

JULIET

I'll look to like, if looking liking move;
But no more deep will I endart mine eye
Than your consent gives strength to make it fly.

Enter SERVANT.

SERVANT

Madam, the guests are come, supper serv'd up, you call'd,
my young lady ask'd for, the nurse curs'd in the pantry,

Handwritten margin notes: "She has no desire to get married" (lines 85–95); "Pregnant" (near line 99)

LADY CAPULET

There's not a summer flower in Verona that can match him.

NURSE

He is a flower, truly—a real flower.

LADY CAPULET

What do you say, Juliet? Do you think you can love the
gentleman?
Tonight you'll see him at our banquet.
Read young Paris's face carefully,   85
and you'll find delight written there with beauty's pen.
Examine each different feature
and see how one feature complements the others.
Read the concealed inner qualities of character
written in the margin of his shining eyes.   90
This precious book of love, this unbound lover,
only needs a wife to make him more handsome.
The fish lives in the sea, and it's wonderful that
something beautiful is hidden in something beautiful.
In many people's eyes, a book is also glorious   95
when golden clasps on the cover bind a good story.
You too will share everything Paris has.
By marrying him, you'll not lower your position.

NURSE

No less! No, you'll be even bigger! Women get pregnant.

LADY CAPULET (*to* JULIET)

Tell me, briefly, can you accept Paris as a lover?   100

JULIET

I will look at him with the intention of liking
him, if looking can make me like him,
but I won't look any further
than you wish me to look.

    A SERVANT *enters.*

SERVANT (*to* LADY CAPULET)

Madam, the guests have come, supper is served, you have been
called,
my young lady's presence has been requested, the nurse is   105
being cursed in the kitchen (because she isn't helping),

and everything in extremity. I must hence to wait; I
beseech you, follow straight.

LADY CAPULET
We follow thee. [SERVANT *exits.*]
Juliet, the County stays.

NURSE
Go, girl, seek happy nights to
happy days. [*Exeunt.*]

and everything is happening at once. I must go immediately to serve. I
beg you to follow me immediately.

LADY CAPULET

We'll follow you. (SERVANT *exits*.)
Juliet, the Count is waiting.

NURSE

Go, girl, find happy nights to go with your happy days.
> *They leave.*

ACT I, SCENE IV

[*A street.*] *Enter* ROMEO, MERCUTIO, BENVOLIO,
with five or six other Maskers, Torch-bearers.

ROMEO

What, shall this speech* be spoke for our excuse?
Or shall we on without apology?

BENVOLIO

The date is out of such prolixity.
We'll have no Cupid hoodwink'd with a scarf,
5   Bearing a Tartar's painted bow of lath,
Scaring the ladies like a crow-keeper;
Nor no without-book prologue, faintly spoke
After the prompter, for our entrance;
But let them measure us by what they will,
10   We'll measure them a measure and be gone.

ROMEO

Give me a torch. I am not for this ambling;
Being but heavy, I will bear the light.

MERCUTIO

Nay, gentle Romeo, we must have you dance.

ROMEO

Not I, believe me. You have dancing shoes
15   With nimble soles; I have a soul of lead
So stakes me to the ground I cannot move.

MERCUTIO

You are a lover; borrow Cupid's wings,
And soar with them above a common bound.

ROMEO

I am too sore enpierced with his shaft
20   To soar with his light feathers, and so bound
I cannot bound a pitch above dull woe.
Under love's heavy burden do I sink.

---

1   *speech* The custom at one time had been to give a formal introduction to
masqueraders.

ACT 1, SCENE 4

A street. ROMEO, MERCUTIO, *and* BENVOLIO *enter with five or six other masqueraders and torch-bearers.*

ROMEO

Shall I give a formal speech to introduce us?
Or shall we just enter without any introduction?

BENVOLIO

Those speeches are out of fashion.
We don't want a blindfolded Cupid,
Carrying his painted bow,   5
scaring ladies like a scarecrow.
And we don't want an impromptu prologue softly spoken
behind a prompter for our entrance.
Let the people measure us as they want to;
we'll dance one dance and be gone.   10

ROMEO

Give me a torch. I'm not for this leisurely dancing.
Since I'm so weighted down with sadness, I'll carry the torch.

MERCUTIO

No, gentle Romeo, we want you to dance.

ROMEO

Not me, believe me. You have dancing shoes
with light soles; I have a soul of lead   15
which holds me to the ground so I can't move.

MERCUTIO

You are a lover. Borrow Cupid's wings
and fly with them above an ordinary dance leap.

ROMEO

I'm too painfully pierced with Cupid's arrow
to fly with his light feathers, and so bound to the ground,   20
I cannot leap even an inch above dull sorrow.
I'm sinking under love's heavy burden.

MERCUTIO

And, to sink in it, should you burden love;
Too great oppression for a tender thing.

ROMEO

25   Is love a tender thing? It is too rough,
Too rude, too boist'rous, and it pricks like thorn.

MERCUTIO

If love be rough with you, be rough with love;
Prick love for pricking, and you beat love down.—
Give me a case to put my visage in, [*Puts on a mask.*]
30   A visor for a visor! What care I
What curious eye doth quote **deformities**?
Here are the beetle brows shall blush for me.

BENVOLIO

Come, knock and enter; and no sooner in,
But every man betake him to his legs.

ROMEO

35   A torch* for me; let wantons light of heart
Tickle the senseless rushes with their heels,
For I am proverb'd with a grandsire phrase:
I'll be a candle-holder, and look on.
The game was ne'er so fair, and I am done.

MERCUTIO

40   Tut, dun's the mouse, the constable's own word.
If thou art dun, we'll draw thee from the mire
Or, save your reverence, love, wherein thou stickest
Up to the ears. Come, we burn daylight, ho!

ROMEO

Nay, that's not so.

MERCUTIO

45   I mean, sir, in delay
We waste our lights in vain, like lights by day.
Take our good meaning, for our judgment sits
Five times in that ere once in our five wits.*

---

35   *torch* This is a pun on "carrying the torch" for Rosaline.

48   *five wits* common sense, imagination, fantasy, judgment, and reasoning

MERCUTIO

And to sink in it would burden love.

That's too heavy a burden for so tender a thing as love.

ROMEO

Is love a tender thing? It's too rough,   25

too rude, too rowdy, and it pricks like a thorn.

MERCUTIO

If love is rough with you, be rough with love.

If love pricks you, prick it back, and you'll beat love down.

Give me a mask to cover my face. (*Puts on a mask.*)

A mask for an ugly face! What do I care   30

if a curious eye notices my ugliness?

The beetlelike eyebrows on this mask shall cover my
    embarrassment.

BENVOLIO

Come, knock, and let's go in. And when we get in,

every man is to dance.

ROMEO

Give me a torch. Let mischievous, light-hearted men   35

dance over the floor coverings.

I take the advice of the old proverb which says,

"I'll be an onlooker and watch.

It's better to quit the game while it's still fun!"

MERCUTIO

Nonsense, like the sheriff says, be still as a mouse.   40

If you're a horse, we'll get you out of the mud,

or if you'll excuse me, out of love where you're sticking

up to your ears. Come on, we're burning daylight.

ROMEO

No, that's not true.

MERCUTIO

I mean, sir, that by delaying,   45

we waste our time in vain, like using torches by day.

Take it as I mean it, for judgment is found

in correct interpretation five times before it's found once in
    our five wits.

ROMEO

And we mean well in going to this mask;
50   But 'tis no wit to go.

MERCUTIO

Why, may one ask?

ROMEO

I dream'd a dream to-night.

MERCUTIO

And so did I.

ROMEO

Well, what was yours?

MERCUTIO

55   That dreamers often lie.

ROMEO

In bed asleep, while they do dream things true.

MERCUTIO   *fairy queen*

O, then, I see Queen Mab hath been with you.
She is the fairies' midwife, and she comes
In shape no bigger than an agate-stone
60   On the fore-finger of an alderman,
Drawn with a team of little atomies
Over men's noses as they lie asleep;
Her wagon-spokes made of long spinners' legs,
The cover of the wings of grasshoppers,
65   Her traces of the smallest spider web,
Her collars of the moonshine's wat'ry beams,
Her whip of cricket's bone, the lash of film,
Her waggoner a small grey-coated gnat,
Not half so big as a round little worm
70   Prick'd from the lazy finger of a maid;*
Her chariot is an empty hazel-nut
Made by the joiner squirrel, or old grub,
Time out o' mind the fairies'
        coachmakers.
And in this state she gallops night by night

what she looks like

69–70 *worm . . . maid* Maids were told that if they were lazy, worms would grow in
their fingers.

ROMEO

We have good intentions in going to this masquerade dance,
but it isn't intelligent to go.   50

MERCUTIO

Why, may I ask?

ROMEO

I dreamed a dream tonight.

MERCUTIO

And so did I.

ROMEO

Well, what was your dream?

MERCUTIO

That dreamers often lie.   55

ROMEO

In bed asleep, while they dream true dreams.

MERCUTIO

Oh, I see that the fairy, Queen Mab, has been with you.
She delivers babies for the fairies, and she is
no bigger than an agate for a ring
on the forefinger of a magistrate.   60
She's drawn by a team of tiny creatures
over men's noses as they lie asleep.
Her wagon spokes are made of long spiders' legs;   *Picture*
the cover is made of the wings of grasshoppers;
the harness is made of the smallest spider web;   65
her steeds' collars are made of the rays of watery moonbeams;
her whip is made of cricket's bone; the lash a spider's web;
her coachman is a small, grey-coated gnat,
not half as big as a little round worm
removed from the finger of a lazy maid.   70
Her chariot is an empty hazelnut shell
made by a squirrel, or an old worm,
who, ever since anyone could remember, have been the fairies'
    coachmakers.
In this manner she gallops night after night

Act 1, Scene 4

Through lovers' brains, and then they dream of love;
On courtiers' knees, that dream on curtsies straight;
O'er lawyers' fingers, who straight dream on fees;
O'er ladies' lips, who straight on kisses dream,
Which oft the angry Mab with blisters plagues,

80   Because their breath with sweetmeats tainted are.
Sometime she gallops o'er a courtier's nose,
And then dreams he of smelling out a suit; *aud*
And sometime comes she with a tithe-pig's tail
Tickling a parson's nose as 'a lies asleep,

85   Then he dreams of another benefice.
Sometime she driveth o'er a soldier's neck,
And then dreams he of cutting foreign throats,
Of breaches, ambuscadoes, Spanish blades,
Of healths five fathom deep; and then anon

90   Drums in his ear, at which he starts and wakes,
And being thus frighted swears a prayer or two
And sleeps again. This is that very Mab
That plaits the manes of horses in the night,
And bakes the elf-locks in foul sluttish hairs,

messes with their minds
95   Which, once untangled, much misfortune bodes.
This is the hag, when maids lie on their backs,
That presses them and learns them first to bear,
Making them women of good carriage.
This is she—'*wants him to know your*
dreams make no sense
All they dream about is death
—asumption

ROMEO

100   Peace, peace, Mercutio, peace!
Thou talk'st of nothing.

MERCUTIO

           True, I talk of dreams,
Which are the children of an idle brain,
Begot of nothing but vain fantasy,

105   Which is as thin of substance as the air
And more inconstant than the wind, who woos

when people stop ingaging in the world
i's when people start to dream
saying dreams arent real
—dreams are made when we fantize about

through lovers' brains, and then they dream of love.   75
She travels over courtiers' knees, and they dream of bowing;
over lawyers' fingers, and they dream of fees;
over ladies' lips, and they dream of kisses.
Often the testy Mab puts blisters on the ladies' lips
because their breaths smell of too many sweets.   80
Sometimes she gallops over a courtier's nose,
and then he dreams of finding someone whose cause he can
    support for a fee;
and sometimes she comes with the tail of a pig owed to the
    church
and tickles a minister's nose as he sleeps,
so that he dreams of being given another well-paying post.   85
Sometimes she drives over a soldier's neck,
and he dreams of cutting foreigners' throats,
and of invasions, ambushes, Spanish knives,
and drinking toasts from glasses thirty feet deep.
    Then soon he hears
drums and he awakens   90

and being frightened by the noise, he says a prayer or two
and goes back to sleep. This is that same Mab
who braids the manes of horses in the night,
and tangles dirty, unkempt hair
which, when untangled, means terrible misfortune.   95

This is the hag which presses maidens down
as they lie on their backs and teaches them to bear up
so they will have good posture. This is the
fairy woman—

ROMEO

Stop, stop, Mercutio!   100
You're talking nonsense.

MERCUTIO

True, I'm talking about dreams,
which are the children of an idle brain,
born from nothing but an empty fantasy.
Dreams are as thin as the air   105
and more likely to change than the wind, who is wooing

Even now the frozen bosom of the north,
And, being anger'd, puffs away from thence,
Turning his face to the dew-dropping south.

BENVOLIO

110 This wind you talk of blows us from ourselves.
Supper is done, and we shall come too late.

ROMEO *party is going to cause problems*

I fear, too early; for my mind misgives
Some consequence yet hanging in the stars
Shall bitterly begin his fearful date
115 With this night's revels, and expire the term
Of a despised life clos'd in my breast
By some vile forfeit of untimely death.
But He that hath the steerage of my course
Direct my sail! On, lusty gentlemen!

foreshadowing

BENVOLIO

120 Strike, drum.

[*They march about the stage.*]

[*Exeunt.*]

The gods will decide fate, the idea of self determination

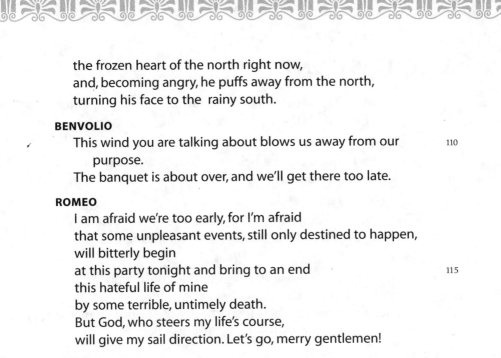

the frozen heart of the north right now,
and, becoming angry, he puffs away from the north,
turning his face to the rainy south.

BENVOLIO

This wind you are talking about blows us away from our   110
    purpose.
The banquet is about over, and we'll get there too late.

ROMEO

I am afraid we're too early, for I'm afraid
that some unpleasant events, still only destined to happen,
will bitterly begin
at this party tonight and bring to an end   115
this hateful life of mine
by some terrible, untimely death.
But God, who steers my life's course,
will give my sail direction. Let's go, merry gentlemen!

BENVOLIO

Beat your drums.   120

   They march about the stage and then leave.

ACT I, SCENE V

[*A hall in Capulet's house.* MUSICIANS *waiting.*] *Enter*
SERVING-MEN, *with napkins.*

1. SERVANT

Where's Potpan, that he helps not to take away? He shift a
trencher! He scrape a trencher!

2. SERVANT

When good manners shall lie all in one or two men's
hands, and they unwash'd too, 'tis a foul thing.

1. SERVANT

5   Away with the joint-stools, remove the court-cupboard,
look to the plate. Good thou, save me a piece of
marchpane; and, as thou loves me, let the porter let in
Susan Grindstone and Nell. Antony and Potpan!

2. SERVANT

Ay, boy, ready.

1. SERVANT

10   You are look'd for and call'd for, ask'd for and sought for,
in the great chamber.

3. SERVANT

We cannot be here and there too. Cheerly, boys; be brisk a
while, and the longer liver take all. [*They retire.*]

Enter [CAPULET, *with* JULIET, TYBALT, *and others of
his house, meeting*] *the* GUESTS, ROMEO, *and other
Maskers.*

CAPULET

Welcome, gentlemen! Ladies that have their toes
15   Unplagu'd with corns will walk a bout with you.
Ah, my mistresses, which of you all
Will now deny to dance? She that makes dainty,
She, I'll swear, hath corns. Am I come near ye now?
Welcome, gentlemen! I have seen the day
20   That I have worn a visor and could tell

ACT 1, SCENE 5

A hall in Capulet's house. MUSICIANS *waiting. The*
SERVANTS *enter with napkins.*

FIRST SERVANT
Where's Potpan? He's not helping us take the plates away. He
carries a wooden platter! He scrapes a wooden plate!

SECOND SERVANT
When household manners rest in the hands of only one or two
people—and their hands dirty at that—it's disgusting.

FIRST SERVANT
Take these folding stools away, remove the sideboard, watch   5
the silverware. Save me a piece of marzipan, and if you're
really a friend, tell the doorman to let in Susan Grindstone
and Nell (for our own party). Antony and Potpan!

SECOND SERVANT
Yes, boy, get ready.

The THIRD SERVANT *enters.*

FIRST SERVANT (*to* THIRD SERVANT)
We've looked for you, called for you, and searched for you   10
in the dance hall.

THIRD SERVANT
We can't be here and there, too. Be cheerful,
boys, and be quick. To the one who lives longest go the spoils!

They exit.

CAPULET *enters with* JULIET, TYBALT, *and others of his house to*
greet the guests, ROMEO, *and others in disguise.*

CAPULET
Welcome, gentlemen! Those ladies who don't have
corns on their toes will dance with you.   15
Ah, dear ladies, which of you
will now refuse to dance? If you hesitate,
I'll swear you have corns. Did any of you think that joke hit home?
Welcome, gentlemen! I remember the time
when I too wore a mask and   20

A whispering tale in a fair lady's ear,
Such as would please; 'tis gone, 'tis gone, 'tis gone.
You are welcome, gentlemen! Come, musicians, play.

[Music plays, and they dance.]

A hall, a hall! Give room! And foot it, girls.
25 More light, you knaves; and turn the tables up,
And quench the fire, the room is grown too hot.
Ah, sirrah,* this unlook'd-for sport comes well.*
Nay, sit, nay, sit, good cousin Capulet,
For you and I are past our dancing days.
30 How long is't now since last yourself and I
Were in a mask?

2. CAPULET
By'r lady, thirty years.

CAPULET
What, man! 'Tis not so much, 'tis not so much.
'Tis since the **nuptial** of Lucentio,
35 Come Pentecost as quickly as it will,
Some five and twenty years; and then we mask'd.

2. CAPULET
'Tis more, 'tis more. His son is elder, sir;
His son is thirty.

CAPULET
Will you tell me that?
40 His son was but a ward two years ago.

ROMEO
[to a SERVING-MAN*]*

What lady's that which doth enrich the hand
Of yonder knight?

SERVANT
I know not, sir.

---

27 *sirrah* a term used to address someone socially or (as an intentional put-down) mentally inferior

27 *unlook'd . . . well* In Shakespeare's day, party hosts considered themselves honored when uninvited guests appeared.

whispered sweet nothings in a beautiful lady's ear
to please her. That's all in the past now, long gone!
You are welcome, gentlemen! Come, musicians, play.

Music plays and they dance.

Clear the hall! Make room! Dance, girls!
Give us more light, you rascals, and get the tables out of   25
   the way.
Put out the fire—the room has grown too hot.
Ah, sir, these party-crashers are welcome.
No, sit down, my good relative Capulet,
for you and I are past our dancing days.
How long has it been since you and I   30
wore a mask?

SECOND CAPULET
I swear, it's been thirty years.

CAPULET
What, it can't be that long, not that long!
It was last at the wedding of Lucentio,
around Pentecost, whenever that comes,   35
some twenty-five years ago that we wore masks.

SECOND CAPULET
No, longer, it was longer ago than that! Lucentio's son is older, sir.
His son is thirty.

CAPULET
How can you say that?
His son was still a minor just two years ago.   40

ROMEO (*to* SERVANT)
Who is the lady who graces the hand
of that gentleman over there?

SERVANT
I don't know, sir.

ROMEO

[handwritten: She beautiful ✓]

O, she doth teach the torches to burn bright!

45 It seems she hangs upon the cheek of night *[handwritten: personification]*

As a rich jewel in an Ethiop's ear; *[handwritten: simile]*

Beauty too rich for use, for earth too dear!

So shows a snowy dove trooping with crows,

As yonder lady o'er her fellows shows.

50 The measure done, I'll watch her place of stand,

And, touching hers, make blessed my rude hand.

Did my heart love till now? Forswear it, sight!

For I ne'er saw true beauty till this night.

TYBALT

This, by his voice, should be a Montague.

55 Fetch me my rapier, boy. What dares the slave

Come hither, cover'd with an antic face,

To fleer and scorn at our solemnity?

Now, by the stock and honour of my kin,

To strike him dead I hold it not a sin.

[handwritten vertical: wants to fight him]

CAPULET

60 Why, how now, kinsman! Wherefore storm you so?

TYBALT

Uncle, this is a Montague, our foe,

A villain that is hither come in spite

To scorn at our solemnity this night.

CAPULET

Young Romeo is it?

TYBALT

                       'Tis he, that villain Romeo.

65

CAPULET

Content thee, gentle coz, let him alone,

'A bears him like a portly gentleman;

And, to say truth, Verona brags of him

To be a virtuous and well-govern'd youth.

70 I would not for the wealth of all this town

Here in my house do him **disparagement**;

Therefore be patient, take no note of him;

It is my will, the which if thou respect,

ROMEO

Oh, she teaches the torches to burn brightly!
She hangs upon the face of night   45
like a rich jewel in an Ethiopian's ear—
her beauty is too rich to be touched, too heavenly for this earth!
She looks like a snow-white dove dancing among crows,
she is so much more beautiful than the other ladies.
When this dance is over, I'll see where she stands,   50
and I'll make my coarse hand blessed by touching her hand.
Did I ever love anyone before now? My eyes will swear
that I never saw real beauty until tonight.

TYBALT (*overhearing* ROMEO)

That man has the voice of a Montague.
Get me my sword, boy. How dare this lowlife   55
come here, disguised by a comic mask,
to mock and scorn our banquet?
Now by my family's good name and reputation,
I wouldn't hold it a sin to kill him.

CAPULET

What's wrong, nephew? Why are you so angry?   60

TYBALT

Uncle, that man is a Montague, our enemy.
He's a villain who has come in hatred
to mock our banquet tonight.

CAPULET

That is young Romeo, isn't it?

TYBALT

Yes, it is the villain Romeo.   65

CAPULET

Calm down, gentle nephew, leave him alone.
He carries himself like a dignified gentleman,
and to tell the truth, Verona's citizens say
that he is a good, well-mannered youth.
I would not for all the riches in this town   70
harm him here in my house.
Be patient and pay no attention to him.
Those are my wishes, which if you'll respect,

Show a fair presence and put off these frowns,
75 An ill-beseeming semblance for a feast.

TYBALT

It fits, when such a villain is a guest.
I'll not endure him.

CAPULET

                              He shall be endur'd.
What, goodman boy! I say he shall; go to!
80 Am I the master here, or you? Go to!
You'll not endure him! God shall mend my soul!
You'll make a mutiny among my guests!
You will set cock-a-hoop! You'll be the man!

TYBALT

Why, uncle, 'tis a shame.

CAPULET

85   Go to, go to;
You are a saucy boy. Is't so, indeed?
This trick may chance to scathe you; I know what.
You must contrary me! Marry, 'tis time.—
Well said, my hearts!—You are a princox; go;
90 Be quiet, or—More light, more light!—for shame!
I'll make you quiet.—What, cheerly, my hearts!

TYBALT

Patience perforce with wilful choler meeting
Makes my flesh tremble in their different greeting.
I will withdraw; but this intrusion shall
95 Now seeming sweet convert to bitt'rest gall.

       [Exit.]

ROMEO   She's important
[to Juliet] If I **profane** with my unworthiest hand
This holy shrine,* the gentle fine is this:

---

98 *holy shrine* Romeo is referring to Juliet. Some scholars think Romeo is disguised
as a pilgrim.

you'll put on a cheery face and stop frowning.
Your frowns aren't proper at a feast. 75

TYBALT

My frowns are fitting when you have a villain for a guest.
I will not tolerate his presence.

CAPULET

You will tolerate him!
What do you mean, boy? I say he shall stay! Be off!
Am I the master here, or are you? Be off! 80
You'll not stand him? By heaven!
You'll disturb the guests!
You'll bring about a riot! You'll play the big hero!

TYBALT

Uncle, this is a disgrace to us.

CAPULET

Enough, enough! 85
You're a rude boy, aren't you? So this is the way it is?
This suggestion of yours may just hurt you. I know what's behind
    this.
You are compelled to contradict me. I swear it's time—
(*to the* DANCERS) Well done, friends.—(*to*
TYBALT) You are impertinent—Go away!
Be quiet, or—(*to* SERVANTS) More light, give us 90
more light! (*to* TYBALT) Shame on you!
I'll shut you up.—(*to* DANCERS) Have fun, friends.

TYBALT

The clash of forced self-control when it meets with anger
makes me shake from the different emotions.
I'll leave, but Romeo's intrusion,
which now seems sweet, will be bitterly regretted. 95

ROMEO (*to* JULIET)

If I abuse with my unworthy hand
your holy shrine, here's the fine I'll pay:

My lips, two blushing pilgrims, ready stand
To smooth that rough touch with a tender kiss.

JULIET   *Not giving enough to him*

100   Good pilgrim, you do wrong your hand too much,
Which mannerly devotion shows in this;
For saints have hands that pilgrims' hands do touch,
And palm to palm is holy palmers' kiss.

ROMEO   *some*

Have not saints lips, and holy palmers too?

JULIET   *to pray*

105   Ay, pilgrim, lips that they must use in prayer.

ROMEO   *— she will be sad if you don't kiss*

O, then, dear saint, let lips do what hands do;
They pray, grant thou, lest faith turn to despair.

JULIET

sonet

Saints do not move, though grant for prayers' sake.

ROMEO

Then move not while my prayer's effect I take.
110   Thus from my lips, by thine, my sin is purg'd.

       [*kissing her*]

JULIET

Then have my lips the sin that they have took.

ROMEO

Sin from my lips? O trespass sweetly urg'd!
Give me my sin again.

       [*kissing her again*]

JULIET

                          You kiss by the book.

NURSE

115   Madam, your mother craves a word with you.

ROMEO

What is her mother?

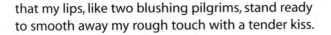

that my lips, like two blushing pilgrims, stand ready
to smooth away my rough touch with a tender kiss.

JULIET

Good pilgrim, your hands are not rough as you say. 100
The touch of your hand is sufficient devotion.
Even saints greet pilgrims by touching hands,
and holding hands is the pilgrim's greeting.

ROMEO

Don't saints have lips, and religious pilgrims, too?

JULIET

Yes, pilgrim. They have lips which they use to pray. 105

ROMEO

Oh, then, dear saint, let lips touch as hands do.
Lips pray, you know, so faith won't turn to despair.

JULIET

Saints do not usually take action, though they may grant favors
prayed for.

ROMEO

Then don't move while I receive what I prayed for.
My lips, by yours, will be cleansed of sin. 110

He kisses her.

JULIET

Now my lips have taken on your sin.

ROMEO

Sin from my lips? That is a sin that is sweetly suggested.
Give me my sin again.

He kisses her again.

JULIET

You kiss as though you researched the subject.

NURSE

Madam, your mother wants to speak with you. 115

ROMEO

Who is her mother?

NURSE

Marry, bachelor,
Her mother is the lady of the house,
And a good lady, and a wise and virtuous.
120 I nurs'd her daughter, that you talk'd withal;
I tell you, he that can lay hold of her
Shall have the chinks.

ROMEO

Is she a Capulet?
O dear account! My life is my foe's debt.

She own him

BENVOLIO

125 Away, be gone; the sport is at the best.

ROMEO

Ay, so I fear; the more is my unrest.

CAPULET

Nay, gentlemen, prepare not to be gone;
We have a trifling foolish banquet towards.
Is it e'en so? Why, then, I thank you all;
130 I thank you, honest gentlemen; good-night.
More torches here! Come on then, let's to bed.
Ah, sirrah, by my fay, it waxes late;
I'll to my rest.

[*All but* JULIET *and* NURSE *begin to go out.*]

JULIET

Come hither, Nurse. What is yond gentleman?

NURSE

135 The son and heir of old Tiberio.

JULIET

What's he that now is going out of door?

NURSE

Marry, that, I think, be young Petruchio.

JULIET

What's he that follows here, that would
not dance?

NURSE

Why, bachelor,
her mother is the lady of this house.
And she is a good lady, as well as being wise and virtuous.
I nursed her daughter with whom you spoke.   120
I tell you, the man who can marry her
will have a lot of money.

ROMEO

Is she a Capulet?
What a costly account! My life is at the mercy of my enemy.

BENVOLIO

Let's go. The party is over.   125

ROMEO

Yes, I'm afraid so; I am worried.

CAPULET

No, gentlemen, don't go.
There's still a modest feast to come.
(They whisper in his ear.) Is that so? Well then, thank you.
Thanks to all of you honest gentlemen. Good night.   130
Bring more torches here! (Maskers leave.) Come on then,
      let's go to bed.
Ah, sir, by my faith, it's late.
I'll go to bed.

> *All but* JULIET *and the* NURSE *leave.*

JULIET

Come here, nurse. Who is that gentleman?

NURSE

The son and heir of old Tiberio.   135

JULIET

Who is that going out the door now?

NURSE

Indeed, I think that's young Petruchio.

JULIET

Who is the one who is following behind—the one who
      would not dance?

NURSE

I know not.

JULIET

140 Go, ask his name.—If he be married,
My grave is like to be my wedding-bed.

NURSE

His name is Romeo, and a Montague;
The only son of your great enemy.

JULIET

My only love sprung from my only hate!
145 Too early seen unknown, and known too late!
Prodigious birth of love it is to me
That I must love a loathed enemy.

NURSE

What's this? What's this?

JULIET

A rhyme I learn'd even now
150 Of one I danc'd withal.

[*One calls within, "Juliet."*]

NURSE

Anon, anon!
Come, let's away; the strangers all are gone.

[*Exeunt.*]

NURSE

I don't know.

JULIET

Go and ask what his name is. (*to herself*) If he is married,   140
my grave will probably be my wedding bed.

NURSE (*leaves and then returns*)

His name is Romeo, Romeo Montague.
He's the only son of your great enemy.

JULIET

My only love springs from my only hate!
I saw him too early when I didn't know him, and now I   145
    realize who he is too late!
This is a horrible beginning to love
that I must love a hated enemy.

NURSE

What is this? What are you saying?

JULIET

A rhyme I just learned from someone
I just danced with.   150

    Someone calls Juliet's name from offstage.

NURSE

We're coming!
Come, let's go; the strangers are all gone.

    They exit.

Act I Review

Discussion Questions

1. What does the first scene of the play reveal about Romeo's behavior? Explain how he changes by the end of Act I.

2. What is your impression of Juliet's father? Describe the relationship between Capulet and his daughter as it is shown during Scene ii.

3. What concepts of love are presented by the female characters in Scene iii?

4. Characterize Mercutio as he appears in Scene iv. What kind of friend is he to Romeo?

5. What do you learn about Tybalt in Scene v?

6. Analyze the behavior of Tybalt, Mercutio, and Benvolio in Act I. Based on your analysis, predict what their roles might be in the rest of the play.

7. Compare Romeo's reaction to Juliet's when each discovers the true identity of the other.

8. Do Romeo's feelings for Juliet seem to be different from his feelings for Rosaline? Explain your answer.

Literary Elements

1. A **foil** is a character who has qualities that are in sharp contrast to another character, thus emphasizing the traits of each. How is Mercutio a foil to Romeo?

2. **Foreshadowing** refers to hints in the text about what will occur later. What examples of foreshadowing do you find in the Prologue and in Scene iv of Act I?

3. **Hyperbole** means obvious exaggeration. Look at Romeo's declaration of love for Rosaline in Act I, Scene i. What examples can you find of hyperbole? Discuss why you think he overstates his feelings.

4. A **pun** is a play on words that have similar sounds but more than one possible spelling or meaning. Scene iv, in which Romeo and his friends banter on the way to the Capulets' masquerade party, is filled with puns. Find a pun in this scene and explain its different meanings and effect.

5. Good drama has **conflict**: struggle between opposing forces. What conflicts are set in motion by events in Scene v?

Writing Prompts

1. Look up the rules for the 14-line form of verse known as a sonnet. Using the rhyme scheme of your choice, write a sonnet of romantic love. Or you may want to write a sonnet that parodies or satirizes the form.

2. Write a description of Romeo based on what you have learned about him so far. Use specific quotes from the play to support your writing.

3. Assume that you write an advice column for a newspaper or magazine. A modern-day Romeo or Juliet writes to you asking for your advice. He or she explains what happened at the party and also mentions the family feud. First write his or her letter, and then write your response.

4. Choose a scene and write a brief summary of its events in one sentence. You may choose to write it in standard English, contemporary slang or street talk, or the language of Shakespeare, Elizabethan English. Or write three summaries; use a separate style in each.

5. Choose a quotation from one of the scenes in Act I that you feel best characterizes that scene. In a paragraph, discuss why you think this quotation is significant and effective at conveying the events or emotions of this scene.

Romeo
and *Juliet* ACT II

Rebecca Callard and Zubin Varin perform the famous balcony scene at
the Open Air Theatre in London. (1993)

"O Romeo, Romeo!
Wherefore art thou Romeo?"

Before You Read

1. Do you think it's possible to fall in love this fast?

2. Be on the lookout for images that appeal to the senses; this kind of language carries a powerful emotional impact.

3. What might be the possible consequences of Romeo and Juliet's marriage?

Literary Elements

1. A **metaphor** makes a direct comparison between things that are not truly alike. In Scene ii, Romeo utters the famous line: "But soft, what light through yonder window breaks? It is the east and Juliet is the sun." The metaphor compares the sun and Juliet.

2. Romeo and Juliet is filled with **imagery**—word pictures that appeal to the five senses (sight, hearing, taste, touch, and smell) and add emotion and power to the writing. Romeo emphasizes the exuberant and uplifting nature of his love for Juliet with this visual image: "With love's light wings did I o'erperch these walls."

3. In drama, a **soliloquy** is a longer speech that reveals the innermost thoughts and feelings of the character who speaks it—just as if the character were speaking to himself or herself. Usually, the character is alone on the stage. If other characters are present, they do not "hear" the speech. One of the most famous soliloquies in drama is Hamlet's "to be or not to be" speech, in which he argues with himself about the value of life.

4. A **malapropism** is a comical mistake uttered by certain characters. For example, Juliet's Nurse uses "confidence" when she means "conference."

5. As noted in Act I, a **pun** is a play on words that have similar sounds but more than one possible spelling or meaning. When the Nurse says of Juliet, "That shall she, marry," she means both "enter into marriage" and "I swear!"

Words to Know

The following vocabulary words appear in Act II in the original text of Shakespeare's play. However, they are words that are still commonly used. Read the definitions here and pay attention to the words as you read the play (they will be in boldfaced type).

chided [chid'st]	criticized; scolded
confounds	confused; obscures
conjure	call up; summon
discourses	talks; speaks
driveling	chattering; jabbering
exposition	display; demonstration
idolatry	worship; adoration
impute	blame; attribute
intercession	asking a favor of; intervention
lamentable	unfortunate; regrettable
perjuries	lies; swearing to what is untrue
rancor [rancour]	hatred; hostility
repose	calm; peacefulness
sallow	sickly; pale

Act Summary

The second act begins with a sonnet describing the obstacles that lie in the way of Romeo and Juliet's love. It offers hope that love will find a way to surmount their difficulties.

Romeo cannot take his mind off Juliet or leave her alone. He climbs over a wall and enters the Capulets' garden to see her. His friends Benvolio and Mercutio search for him in vain. In the famous "balcony scene," Romeo overhears Juliet professing her love for him and responds to her. Both express their love for each other and their hopes to be married.

Romeo sets off for Friar Lawrence's to ask him to perform the marriage ceremony. The Friar agrees, saying he hopes the marriage will end the longtime feud of the Capulets and Montagues.

Mary Anderson (Juliet) and Mrs. Sterling (Nurse), ca. 1885

On the street, Mercutio and Benvolio wonder about Romeo's whereabouts and make fun of his lovesickness. Romeo appears and the friends engage in witty banter. The Nurse finds Romeo and warns him to respect Juliet. Romeo tells her to have Juliet meet him in Friar Lawrence's cell that afternoon for their wedding.

Impatiently, Juliet awaits the Nurse's return and message from Romeo. She finally learns that Friar Lawrence will marry the two lovers that very day.

In Friar Lawrence's cell, Romeo and Juliet express their love for each other and are married by the friar.

PROLOGUE

Enter CHORUS.

CHORUS

Now old Desire doth in his death-bed lie,
   And young Affection gapes to be his heir;
That fair for which love groan'd for and would die,
   With tender Juliet match'd is now not fair.
5   Now Romeo is belov'd and loves again,
   Alike bewitched by the charm of looks,
But to his foe suppos'd he must complain,
   And she steal love's sweet bait from fearful hooks.
Being held a foe, he may not have access
10   To breathe such vows as lovers use to swear;
And she as much in love, her means much less
   To meet her new-beloved anywhere.
But passion lends them power, time means, to meet,
Temp'ring extremities with extreme sweet.

   [*Exit.*]

PROLOGUE

The CHORUS *enters.*

CHORUS
Romeo's old love for Rosaline is now dead,
   and a new love eagerly hopes to win his heart.
That beauty for whom he groaned and wanted to die
   is now no longer beautiful, compared with Juliet.
Romeo is loved and he loves again.   5
   Both have been bewitched by the charm of beauty.
To Juliet, his supposed enemy, he must plead,
   and she must steal love's tempting bait from terrifying hooks.
Since he is considered an enemy, he may not be able
   to use the vows that lovers typically swear.   10
Juliet, just as deeply in love, has even fewer means
   to meet her new beloved anywhere.
However, love gives them power, time gives them the means to
      meet,
and their great problems are softened by great sweetness.

Exit.

ACT II, SCENE I

[A lane by the wall of Capulet's orchard.] Enter ROMEO, *alone.*

ROMEO
Can I go forward when my heart is here?
Turn back, dull earth, and find thy centre out.

[He climbs the wall, and leaps down within it.]

[Enter BENVOLIO with MERCUTIO.]

BENVOLIO
Romeo! My cousin Romeo!

MERCUTIO
      He is wise;
5 And, on my life, hath stol'n him home to bed.

BENVOLIO
He ran this way, and leap'd this orchard wall.
Call, good Mercutio.

MERCUTIO
     Nay, I'll **conjure** too.
Romeo! Humours! Madman! Passion! Lover!
10 Appear thou in the likeness of a sigh!
Speak but one rhyme, and I am satisfied;
Cry but "Ay me," pronounce but "love" and "dove."
Speak to my gossip Venus* one fair word,
One nickname for her purblind son and heir,
15 Young Abraham* Cupid, he that shot so trim,
When King Cophetua* lov'd the beggar-maid!
He heareth not, he stirreth not, he moveth not;
The ape* is dead, and I must conjure him.
I conjure thee by Rosaline's bright eyes,
20 By her high forehead and her scarlet lip,
By her fine foot, straight leg, and quivering thigh,
And the demesnes that there adjacent lie,
That in thy likeness thou appear to us!

---

13 *Venus* Venus is the Roman goddess of love. Cupid is her son, who shoots love's arrows into the breasts of humans to make them fall in love.

15 *Abraham* could mean either "old" (as the biblical Abraham) or "cheating" (an "Abraham man" was a swindler)

ACT 2, SCENE 1

A lane by the wall of Capulet's orchard. ROMEO
enters alone.

ROMEO

How can I leave when my heart is here?
I'll go back and find my heart's delight.

He climbs on the wall, then leaps over it.

BENVOLIO *and* MERCUTIO *enter.*

BENVOLIO

Romeo! My cousin Romeo!

MERCUTIO

He's smart,
so I'll bet on my life that he sneaked home to bed.   5

BENVOLIO

No, he ran this way and jumped over this orchard wall.
Call him, Mercutio.

MERCUTIO

No, I'll conjure him up with an incantation.
Romeo! Moody madman! Passionate lover!
Appear to us in the form of a sigh!   10
Give us just one couplet and I'll be satisfied.
Simply exclaim, "Oh, me!" Just say "love" and "dove."
Say one fair word to my friend Venus,
just one nickname for her totally blind son and heir,
young Adam Cupid. He's the one who shot so well   15
causing King Cophetua to love the beggar maid.
He doesn't hear, he doesn't stir, he doesn't move.
The poor fellow is playing dead and I must conjure him up.
I invoke you by Rosaline's bright eyes,
by her high forehead and her red lips,   20
by her fine foot, straight leg, and quivering thigh,
appear to us as yourself!

---

16   *King Cophetua* a reference to the old ballad "King Ophetus and the Beggar-Maid"

18   *ape* Mercutio compares Romeo to a trained ape that plays dead until the trainer
       gives the command to sit up.

BENVOLIO

An if he hear thee, thou wilt anger him.

MERCUTIO

25   This cannot anger him; 'twould anger him
To raise a spirit in his mistress' circle
Of some strange nature, letting it there stand
Till she had laid it and conjur'd it down.*
That were some spite; my invocation
30   Is fair and honest; in his mistress' name
I conjure only but to raise up him.

BENVOLIO

Come, he hath hid himself among these trees
To be consorted with the humorous night.
Blind is his love and best befits the dark.

MERCUTIO

35   If Love be blind, Love cannot hit the mark.
Now will he sit under a medlar tree
And wish his mistress were that kind of fruit
As maids call medlars,* when they laugh alone.
O, Romeo, that she were, O, that she were
40   An open-[arse], thou a poperin pear!
Romeo, good-night; I'll to my truckle-bed;*
This field-bed is too cold for me to sleep.
Come, shall we go?

BENVOLIO

                Go, then; for 'tis in vain
To see him here that means not to be found.

[*Exeunt* BENVOLIO *and* MERCUTIO.]

26–28   *circle . . . down* Mercutio's metaphor has a second, sexual meaning, as does the rest of this speech.

38   *medlars* an apple-like fruit. Medlars and pears were also vulgar terms for sexual organs in Shakespeare's day.

41   *truckle-bed* This (trundle-bed) is pushed under a regular bed when not in use. Children slept on this kind of bed. Mercutio is saying he will play the innocent and wash his hands of Romeo.

BENVOLIO

If he hears you, he'll be angry.

MERCUTIO

That speech can't anger him. It would anger him   25
to conjure up a spirit of some strange kind
in his lady love's circle and let it stand there until she
   conjured it down.
That would make him mad. My invocation
is proper and respectable—in his lady love's name,   30
I conjure only to raise him up.

BENVOLIO

Come on, he has hidden among these trees
so he can melt into the damp night.
His love is blind, and that best suits the dark.

MERCUTIO

If love is blind, love cannot hit its target.   35
Now he'll sit under an apple tree
and wish his lady love were that kind of fruit
that girls call apples when they're in private.
Oh, Romeo, if only she were that, if she just were
an open unmentionable and you a pear.   40
Romeo, good night. I'm going to my trundle bed.
This ground is too cold for me to sleep on.
Come on, shall we leave?

BENVOLIO

Go on, then. It's useless
to look for him when he does not want to be found.

      BENVOLIO *and* MERCUTIO *exit.*

ACT II, SCENE II

[Capulet's orchard. ROMEO advances from the wall.]

ROMEO

He jests at scars that never felt a wound.

[JULIET appears above at her window.]

But, soft! What light through yonder window breaks?
It is the east, and Juliet is the sun.
Arise, fair sun, and kill the envious moon,
5 Who is already sick and pale with grief
That thou, her maid, art far more fair than she.*
Be not her maid, since she is envious;
Her vestal livery is but sick and green,
And none but fools do wear it; cast it off.
10 It is my lady, O, it is my love!
O, that she knew she were!
She speaks, yet she says nothing; what of that?
Her eye **discourses**; I will answer it.—
I am too bold. 'Tis not to me she speaks.
15 Two of the fairest stars in all the heaven,
Having some business, do entreat her eyes
To twinkle in their spheres till they return.
What if her eyes were there, they in her head?
The brightness of her cheek would shame those stars,
20 As daylight doth a lamp; her eyes in heaven
Would through the airy region stream so bright
That birds would sing and think it were not night.
See how she leans her cheek upon her hand!
O, that I were a glove upon that hand,
25 That I might touch that cheek!

JULIET

                                        Ay me!

ROMEO

                                        She speaks!
O, speak again, bright angel! For thou art

---

6 *she* Romeo is referring to the Roman moon goddess, Diana, in this speech.
Diana demanded that her female followers remain chaste.

ACT 2, SCENE 2

Capulet's orchard. ROMEO *comes from the wall, just having overheard* MERCUTIO *and* BENVOLIO'S *conversation.*

ROMEO
> Mercutio makes fun of scars because he's never felt pain.

> JULIET *appears at her upstairs window, and* ROMEO *sees her.*

> But wait! What light is coming from that window?
> It is the eastern light and Juliet is the sun.
> Rise up, beautiful sun, and make the jealous moon invisible.
> The moon is already sick and pale with grief   5
> because you, Juliet, are more beautiful than she is.
> Don't become one of her virgin followers because she is jealous;
> her virginity is sickly and anemic.
> Only fools wear the uniform of virginity; take off that uniform.
> There stands my lady; oh, she is my love!   10
> If only she could know she is my beloved.
> She speaks, yet she says nothing. What does that matter?
> Her eyes speak; I'll answer them.
> I'm being too confident; she's not speaking to me.
> Two of the most beautiful stars in all the heavens beg her eyes   15
> to twinkle in their orbits while they are gone.
> What if her eyes were in the heavens, and the stars in her head?
> The brightness of her cheek would shame those stars,
> as daylight shames a lamp. If her eyes were stars,   20
> the heavens would shine so brightly
> that the birds would sing because they would think it was day.
> See how she leans her cheek on her hand!
> I wish I were a glove on her hand
> so that I could touch her cheek.   25

JULIET
> Alas!

ROMEO
> She is speaking!
> Oh, speak again, bright angel, for you,

As glorious to this night, being o'er my head,
30 As a winged messenger of heaven
Unto the white-upturned wond'ring eyes
Of mortals that fall back to gaze on him
When he bestrides the lazy-pacing clouds
And sails upon the bosom of the air.

JULIET

35 O Romeo, Romeo! Wherefore art thou Romeo?
Deny thy father and refuse thy name;
Or, if thou wilt not, be but sworn my love,
And I'll no longer be a Capulet.

ROMEO

[*aside*] Shall I hear more, or shall I speak at this?

JULIET

40 'Tis but thy name that is my enemy;
Thou art thyself, though not a Montague.
What's Montague? It is nor hand, nor foot,
Nor arm, nor face, nor any other part
Belonging to a man. O, be some other name!
45 What's in a name? That which we call a rose
By any other word would smell as sweet;
So Romeo would, were he not Romeo call'd,
Retain that dear perfection which he owes
Without that title. Romeo, doff thy name,
50 And for thy name, which is no part of thee,
Take all myself.

ROMEO

I take thee at thy word.
Call me but love, and I'll be new baptiz'd;
Henceforth I never will be Romeo.

JULIET

55 What man art thou that thus bescreen'd in night
So stumblest on my counsel?

ROMEO

By a name
I know not how to tell thee who I am.
My name, dear saint, is hateful to myself,

up there above my head, are as glorious to the night
as is an angel of heaven   30
to the white, upturned, wondering eyes
of humans who stand back to gaze on him
when he rides upon the slow-moving clouds
and sails through the air.

JULIET

Romeo! Romeo! Why are you Romeo?   35
Reject your father and refuse his name.
Or if you will not, just swear to be my love, and I
will no longer be a Capulet.

ROMEO *(to himself)*

Shall I listen to her any longer, or shall I speak to her?

JULIET

Not you, but only your family name is my enemy.   40
You would be Romeo even if you were not a Montague.
What is a Montague? It's not a hand or a foot,
an arm or a face, or any other part
of a man's body. Oh, take some other name!
What's in a name? The thing which we call a rose   45
would smell just as sweet if it had any other name.
So Romeo—even if he weren't called Romeo—
would be just as perfect
without his name. Romeo, get rid of your name,
and in place of that name, which isn't part of you,   50
take me.

ROMEO

I'll take you at your word.
If you'll call me love, I'll be christened again to get a new name
and never again be called Romeo.

JULIET

Who is that, hiding there in the dark,   55
who is eavesdropping on my private thoughts?

ROMEO

If I have to use a name,
I don't know how to tell you who I am.
My name, dear saint, is hateful to me

60   Because it is an enemy to thee;
      Had I it written, I would tear the word.

JULIET

      My ears have yet not drunk a hundred words
      Of thy tongue's uttering, yet I know the sound.
      Art thou not Romeo, and a Montague?

ROMEO

65   Neither, fair maid, if either thee dislike.

JULIET

      How cam'st thou hither, tell me, and wherefore?
      The orchard walls are high and hard to climb,
      And the place death, considering who thou art,
      If any of my kinsmen find thee here.

ROMEO

70   With love's light wings did I o'erperch these walls;
      For stony limits cannot hold love out,
      And what love can do, that dares love attempt.
      Therefore thy kinsmen are no stop to me.

JULIET

      If they do see thee, they will murder thee.

ROMEO

75   Alack, there lies more peril in thine eye
      Than twenty of their swords! Look thou but sweet,
      And I am proof against their enmity.

JULIET

      I would not for the world they saw thee here.

ROMEO

      I have night's cloak to hide me from their eyes;
80   And, but thou love me, let them find me here.
      My life were better ended by their hate,
      Than death prorogued, wanting of thy love.

JULIET

      By whose direction found'st thou out this place?

ROMEO

      By Love, that first did prompt me to inquire;
85   He lent me counsel and I lent him eyes.

because it's the name of your enemy.   60
If I had written it down, I'd tear up the word.

JULIET

I have not listened to even a hundred words
that you've spoken, but I recognize your voice.
Aren't you Romeo—and a Montague?

ROMEO

Neither one, beautiful maiden, if you dislike either.   65

JULIET

How did you get here? Tell me. And why?
The orchard walls are high and hard to climb
and this is a place of death to you—considering who you are—
if any of my relatives should find you here.

ROMEO

I flew over the walls on the wings of love;   70
those strong walls can't keep love out,
and whatever love can do, love will try.
Therefore, your relatives can't keep me out.

JULIET

If they see you, they'll murder you.

ROMEO

I see more danger in your eyes   75
than in twenty of their swords. If you just look sweetly at me,
I'm protected from their hatred.

JULIET

I would not have them find you here for anything in the world.

ROMEO

The dark night will hide me from their eyes,
and if you don't love me, I wish they would find me here. 80
It would be better to be killed by their hate,
than have my death postponed without your love.

JULIET

Who told you how to get here?

ROMEO

Love led me, love who first made me wonder which way to go.
Love gave me advice and I listened.   85

I am no pilot; yet, wert thou as far
As that vast shore wash'd with the farthest sea,
I should adventure for such merchandise.

JULIET

Thou know'st the mask of night is on my face,
90   Else would a maiden blush bepaint my cheek
For that which thou hast heard me speak to-night.
Fain would I dwell on form, fain, fain deny
What I have spoke; but farewell compliment!
Dost thou love me? I know thou wilt say "Ay,"
95   And I will take thy word; yet, if thou swear'st,
Thou mayst prove false. At lovers' **perjuries**,
They say, Jove laughs. O gentle Romeo,
If thou dost love, pronounce it faithfully;
Or if thou think'st I am too quickly won,
100   I'll frown and be perverse and say thee nay,—
So thou wilt woo; but else, not for the world.
In truth, fair Montague, I am too fond,
And therefore thou mayst think my 'haviour light;
But trust me, gentleman, I'll prove more true
105   Than those that have more cunning to be strange.
I should have been more strange, I must confess,
But that thou overheard'st, ere I was ware,
My true love's passion; therefore pardon me,
And not **impute** this yielding to light love,
110   Which the dark night hath so discovered.

ROMEO

Lady, by yonder blessed moon I vow
That tips with silver all these fruit-tree tops—

JULIET

O, swear not by the moon, the inconstant moon,
That monthly changes in her circled orb,
115   Lest that thy love prove likewise variable.

ROMEO

What shall I swear by?

JULIET

Do not swear at all;

I am no ship's pilot, but if you were as far away as
the most distant land on the most distant sea,
I'd risk a voyage there to find you.

JULIET
If the dark didn't hide my face,
you'd see that I am blushing   90
because of what you've heard me say tonight.
I'd gladly stand on formalities—gladly, gladly deny
what you heard me say—but good-bye to proprieties.
Do you love me? I know you'll say "yes."
And I'll believe you. Yet, even if you swear,   95
you could turn out to be a liar. They say even Jove
laughs at the false oaths of lovers! Oh, gentle Romeo,
if you love me, honestly admit it.
Or if you think I am too quickly won by you,
I'll frown and be grouchy and say "no,"   100
so you'll have to court me; but otherwise I wouldn't snub
     you for any reason.
To tell the truth, handsome Montague, I'm too fond of you.
Therefore, you may think my behavior is immodest.
But trust me, gentle sir, I'll be truer
than those who act more clever and pretend coolness.   105
I would have been more coy, I must admit,
but you overheard me before I knew you were here,
my true love. Please forgive me,
and don't think that I fell for you because of a shallow love
which the dark night has revealed.   110

ROMEO
Lady, I swear by the blessed moon
that gives a silver light to the tops of these fruit trees—

JULIET
Oh, don't swear by the moon, the fickle moon
that changes monthly in her circular orbit,
for fear that your love should prove equally changeable.   115

ROMEO
What shall I swear by?

JULIET
Don't swear at all;

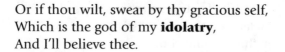

Or if thou wilt, swear by thy gracious self,
Which is the god of my **idolatry**,
120 And I'll believe thee.

ROMEO

                      If my heart's dear love—

JULIET

Well, do not swear. Although I joy in thee,
I have no joy of this contract to-night;
It is too rash, too unadvis'd, too sudden,
125 Too like the lightning, which doth cease to be
Ere one can say it lightens. Sweet, good-night!
This bud of love, by summer's ripening breath,
May prove a beauteous flower when next we meet,
Good-night, good-night! As sweet **repose** and rest
130 Come to thy heart as that within my breast!

ROMEO

O, wilt thou leave me so unsatisfied?

JULIET

What satisfaction canst thou have to-night?

ROMEO

Th' exchange of thy love's faithful vow for mine.

JULIET

I gave thee mine before thou didst request it;
135 And yet I would it were to give again.

ROMEO

Wouldst thou withdraw it? For what purpose, love?

JULIET

But to be frank, and give it thee again.
And yet I wish but for the thing I have.
My bounty is as boundless as the sea,
140 My love as deep; the more I give to thee,
The more I have, for both are infinite.

        [NURSE *calls within.*]

More mature

She wishes she can continue saying)

She loves him

or, if you have to swear, swear by your gracious self.
You're the god I worship
and I'll believe you.   120

ROMEO

If my heart's dear love—

JULIET

Well, don't swear. I'm delighted by you,
but I'm not delighted by our pledges tonight.
Our love is too rash, too unadvised, too sudden,
too like the lightning which has faded   125
before you can even say, "It's lightning." Good night, my sweet!
Our bud of love, ripened by summer's breath,
may have turned into a beautiful flower by the next time we
    meet.
Good night, good night. May sweet rest and peace
come to your heart the way it lies within my breast!   130

ROMEO

Will you leave me so unsatisfied?

JULIET

What satisfaction can you want tonight?

ROMEO

I want you to exchange love's faithful vows with me.

JULIET

I gave you my vow of love before you even asked for it.
I wish I could give it again.   135

ROMEO

Would you take back your vow of love? Why, my love?

JULIET

So I can be generous and give it to you again.
Yet I don't want anything but your love, and I have that.
My desire to give you love is as broad as the sea,
and just as deep; the more love I give you,   140
the more I have to give because my love is infinite.

The NURSE *calls from within.*

I hear some noise within; dear love, adieu!
Anon, good Nurse! Sweet Montague, be true.
Stay but a little; I will come again.

[*Exit, above.*]

ROMEO

145   O blessed, blessed night! I am afeard,
Being in night, all this is but a dream,
Too flattering-sweet to be substantial.

[*Re-enter* JULIET, *above.*]

JULIET

Three words, dear Romeo, and good-night indeed.
If that thy bent of love be honourable,
150   Thy purpose marriage, send me word to-morrow,
By one that I'll procure to come to thee,
Where and what time thou wilt perform the rite;
And all my fortunes at thy foot I'll lay
And follow thee my lord throughout the world.

if he really loves her he would send a messenger

NURSE

155   [*within*] Madam!

JULIET

I come, anon.—But if thou mean'st not well,
I do beseech thee—

NURSE

[*within*] Madam!

JULIET

By and by, I come:—
160   To cease thy suit, and leave me to my grief.
To-morrow will I send.

ROMEO

So thrive my soul—

JULIET

A thousand times good-night!

[*Exit above.*]

I hear a noise inside. Dear love, good-bye!
(to NURSE*)* I'm coming, good nurse.—*(to* ROMEO*)*
    Sweet Montague, be true to me.
Stay here just a little while, and I'll be back.

>   JULIET *exits.*

ROMEO
Oh blessed, blessed night! I'm afraid,   145
since it is night, that this is all a dream,
too flattering and sweet to be real.

>   JULIET *re-enters on the balcony.*

JULIET
Just a few more words, dear Romeo, and then it's definitely
    good night.
If your love is honorable,
and you want to marry me, send me word tomorrow   150
by someone I'll send to you.
Tell me where and what time the wedding will be,
and I'll lay all my wealth at your feet
and follow you as my husband anywhere.

NURSE *(calling)*
Madam!   155

JULIET *(to* NURSE*)*
I am coming right now.—*(to* ROMEO*)* But if you don't have
    honest intentions,
I beg you—

NURSE *(calling)*
Madam!

JULIET *(to* NURSE*)*
Immediately! I'm coming!
(to ROMEO*)*—to stop pursuing me and leave me to my grief.   160
I'll send a messenger tomorrow.

ROMEO
My soul will live for that—

JULIET
Good night a thousand times. (*She exits.*)

ROMEO

A thousand times the worse, to want thy light.
165   Love goes toward love, as schoolboys from their books,
But love from love, toward school with heavy looks.

[*retiring*]

[*Re-enter* JULIET, *above.*]

JULIET

Hist! Romeo, hist! O, for a falconer's voice,
To lure this tassel-gentle back again!
Bondage is hoarse, and may not speak aloud;
170   Else would I tear the cave where Echo* lies,
And make her airy tongue more hoarse than mine,
With repetition of my Romeo's name.
Romeo!

ROMEO

It is my soul that calls upon my name.
175   How silver-sweet sound lovers' tongues by night,
Like softest music to attending ears!

JULIET

Romeo!

ROMEO

      My dear.

JULIET

          What o'clock to-morrow
180   Shall I send to thee?

ROMEO

          By the hour of nine.

JULIET

I will not fail; 'tis twenty year till then.
I have forgot why I did call thee back.

---

170   *Echo* was a Greek nymph who fell in love with Narcissus. She pursued him with
cries until she hid for shame in a cave. There she wasted away until only her
voice was left.

ROMEO

This night is a thousand times worse without your light.

Love is drawn toward love the way schoolboys are drawn   165
away from their books;

but when love is drawn away from love, it's like going to school
with a scowl.

> *He starts to leave.*

> JULIET *re-enters on the balcony.*

JULIET *(Whispers.)*

Romeo! I wish I had a falconer's voice
to lure this male falcon back again!
But being still ruled by others, I can't shout,
or else I would yell until I opened the cave where Echo lies.   170
Then I'd make her silver voice more hoarse than mine
by saying my Romeo's name over and over.
Romeo!

ROMEO

It's my soul that is calling my name.
Lovers' voices sound silver-sweet at night,   175
like soft music to receptive listeners.

JULIET

Romeo!

ROMEO

Yes, my sweet?

JULIET

What time tomorrow
should I send my messenger to you?   180

ROMEO

By nine o'clock.

JULIET

I will not fail. It will be twenty years until then.
I forget why I called you back.

ROMEO

Let me stand here till thou remember it.

JULIET

185   I shall forget, to have thee still stand there,
Rememb'ring how I love thy company.

ROMEO

And I'll still stay, to have thee still forget,
Forgetting any other home but this.

JULIET

'Tis almost morning, I would have thee gone;—
190   And yet no farther than a wanton's bird,
That lets it hop a little from her hand,
Like a poor prisoner in his twisted gyves,
And with a silk thread plucks it back again,
So loving-jealous of his liberty.

ROMEO

195   I would I were thy bird.

JULIET

Sweet, so would I;
Yet I should kill thee with much cherishing.
Good-night, good-night! Parting is such sweet sorrow,
That I shall say good-night till it be morrow.

[*Exit, above.*]

ROMEO

200   Sleep dwell upon thine eyes, peace in thy breast!
Would I were sleep and peace, so sweet to rest!
Hence will I to my ghostly father's cell,
His help to crave, and my dear hap to tell.

[*Exit.*]

[handwritten annotations:]

types of love

Love
- love/hate
- self love
- trust love
- lust
- familial
- paternal
- maternal
- fraternal

- self harm love
- materialism
- soul mate
-

ROMEO

I'll stay here until you remember.

JULIET

I'll forget if you stay here 185
because I'll only remember how much I love your company.

ROMEO

I'll stay so you'll forget everything—
everything except me.

JULIET

It's almost morning. I wish you would go now—
but no farther than a spoiled girl's pet bird 190
which is allowed to hop away from her hand just a little
like a poor prisoner in his twisted chains.
Then with a silk thread, the girl pulls the bird back again,
so loving, and yet so jealous of his freedom.

ROMEO

I wish I were your bird. 195

JULIET

Sweetheart, so do I.
Yet if you were my bird, I'd kill you with too much love.
Good night, good night! Parting is such sweet sorrow
that I could say good night until it's tomorrow.

    JULIET exits.

ROMEO

May you sleep well and feel peaceful inside. 200
I wish I were your sleep and peace to find such a sweet resting
    place.
From here I'll go to my priest
to ask for his help and tell him of my good fortune.

    ROMEO exits.

ACT II, SCENE III

[*Friar Lawrence's cell.* *] Enter FRIAR LAWRENCE,
with a basket.

FRIAR LAWRENCE

The grey-ey'd morn smiles on the frowning night,
Chequ'ring the eastern clouds with streaks of light,
And flecked darkness like a drunkard reels
From forth day's path and Titan's fiery wheels.
5   Now, ere the sun advance his burning eye,
The day to cheer and night's dank dew to dry,

 quote to a womb

I must up-fill this osier cage of ours
With baleful weeds and precious-juiced flowers.
The earth, that's nature's mother, is her tomb;
10   What is her burying grave, that is her womb;
And from her womb children of divers kind
We sucking on her natural bosom find:
Many for many virtues excellent,
None but for some, and yet all different.
15   O, mickle is the powerful grace that lies
In plants, herbs, stones, and their true qualities;
For naught so vile that on the earth doth live   *guidance*
But to the earth some special good doth give,
Nor aught so good but, strain'd from that fair use,
20   Revolts from true birth, stumbling on abuse.
Virtue itself turns vice, being misapplied;
And vice sometimes by action dignified.

Can cause problems if you use it wrong

[*Enter* ROMEO.]

 bad things can help

Within the infant rind of this weak flower
Poison hath residence and medicine power;
25   For this, being smelt, with that part cheers each part;
Being tasted, slays all senses with the heart.
Two such opposed kings encamp them still
In man as well as herbs, grace and rude will;
And where the worser is predominant,
30   Full soon the canker death eats up that plant.

---

* *cell* a monk's house separated from the rest of the monastery by some distance

ACT 2, SCENE 3

Friar Lawrence's cell. FRIAR LAWRENCE *enters with a basket.*

FRIAR LAWRENCE

The grey-eyed morning smiles on the frowning night.
It checkers the eastern clouds with streaks of light,
and the spotted darkness staggers like a drunk
from the path of the day and the sun's fiery wheels.
Now, before the sun can raise his burning eye   5
to cheer up the day and dry up night's dew,
I must fill this wicker basket
with deadly weeds and healing flowers.
The earth, which is the mother of nature, is also a tomb,
both a grave and a womb.   10
And from earth's womb come all kinds of children
who suck from her natural breasts.
Many of earth's children have many excellent uses—
not one child that doesn't have some use—and yet they're all
    different.
Great are the powerful uses that lie   15
in plants, herbs, stones, and in their pure qualities.
For there's nothing that lives on earth that is so bad
that it doesn't give the earth some special good.
And there isn't anything so good that when improperly used,
it stops serving its natural purpose and becomes poisonous.   20
Good can turn to bad when it is misused,
and sometimes evil can be made right by right action.

     ROMEO *enters.*

Within the new bud of this weak flower,
there lies poison and medicinal power.
If you smell this flower, you'll be strengthened all over;   25
but if you taste this flower, you die.
Two opposed kings always live
within man, as well as in herbs—virtue and base lust.
Where evil is predominant,
the cankerworm will soon eat up that plant.   30

ROMEO
Good morrow, father.

FRIAR LAWRENCE
Benedicite!
What early tongue so sweet saluteth me?
Young son, it argues a distempered head
35 So soon to bid good morrow to thy bed.
Care keeps his watch in every old man's eye,
And where care lodges, sleep will never lie;
But where unbruised youth with unstuff'd brain
Doth couch his limbs, there golden sleep doth reign;
40 Therefore thy earliness doth me assure
Thou art up-rous'd with some distemp'rature;
Or if not so, then here I hit it right,
Our Romeo hath not been in bed to-night.

ROMEO
That last is true; the sweeter rest was mine.

FRIAR LAWRENCE
45 God pardon sin! Wast thou with Rosaline?

ROMEO
With Rosaline, my ghostly father? No!
I have forgot that name, and that name's woe.

FRIAR LAWRENCE
That's my good son; but where hast thou been, then?

ROMEO
I'll tell thee ere thou ask it me again.
50 I have been feasting with mine enemy,
Where on a sudden one hath wounded me
That's by me wounded; both our remedies
Within thy help and holy physic lies.
I bear no hatred, blessed man, for, lo,
55 My **intercession** likewise steads my foe.

FRIAR LAWRENCE
Be plain, good son, and homely in thy drift;
Riddling confession finds but riddling shrift.

ROMEO

Good morning, father.

FRIAR LAWRENCE

Bless you!
Who is the early riser who greets me so sweetly?
Young man, you must be very worried to be out of bed so
    early in the morning. 35
Worry is always present in an old man's life,
and where you find worry, you'll never find sleep.
But when the young and the carefree
lie down to rest, then you'll find sleep is king.
So your appearance at this early hour tells me that 40
something is bothering you.
Or if that's not the case, then this must be right—
Romeo, you've not been to bed tonight.

ROMEO

The last statement is true. I had a sweeter rest than bed.

FRIAR LAWRENCE

God forgive your sin! Were you with Rosaline? 45

ROMEO

With Rosaline, father? No!
I've forgotten that name and all the sorrow it brought.

FRIAR LAWRENCE

That's my good boy. But where have you been then?

ROMEO

I'll tell you before you ask me again.
I was dining with my enemies 50
when all of a sudden, one of them wounded me,
whom I in turn wounded. You have the remedy
to help us both with your holy medicine.
I have no hatred, father, for
my request will also benefit my enemy. 55

FRIAR LAWRENCE

Good son, speak clearly and simply.
If you confess in riddles, you'll be forgiven in riddles.

ROMEO

    Then plainly know my heart's dear love is set
    On the fair daughter of rich Capulet.
60   As mine on hers, so hers is set on mine;
    And all combin'd, save what thou must combine
    By holy marriage. When and where and how
    We met, we woo'd, and made exchange of vow,
    I'll tell thee as we pass; but this I pray,
65   That thou consent to marry us to-day.

FRIAR LAWRENCE

    Holy Saint Francis, what a change is here!
    Is Rosaline, that thou didst love so dear,
    So soon forsaken? Young men's love then lies
    Not truly in their hearts, but in their eyes.
70   Jesu Maria, what a deal of brine
    Hath wash'd thy **sallow** cheeks for Rosaline!
    How much salt water thrown away in waste,
    To season love, that of it doth not taste!
    The sun not yet thy sighs from heaven clears,
75   Thy old groans yet ring in mine ancient ears;
    Lo, here upon thy cheek the stain doth sit
    Of an old tear that is not wash'd off yet.
    If e'er thou wast thyself and these woes thine,
    Thou and these woes were all for Rosaline.
80   And art thou chang'd? Pronounced this sentence then:
    Women may fall, when there's no strength in men.

ROMEO

    Thou **chid'st** me oft for loving Rosaline.

FRIAR LAWRENCE

    For doting, not for loving, pupil mine.

ROMEO

    And bad'st me bury love.

FRIAR LAWRENCE

85   Not in a grave,
    To lay one in, another out to have.

ROMEO

Then I'll tell you clearly that the girl I love
is the beautiful daughter of rich Capulet.
Just as my heart is set on her, her heart is set on me, 60
and we're totally united, except by the union
of holy marriage that you must perform. When, where, and how
we met, fell in love, and exchanged our vows,
I'll tell you later, but I ask you this now:
that you agree to marry us today. 65

FRIAR LAWRENCE

Holy Saint Francis! How you have changed!
So, Rosaline, whom you loved so much,
is so quickly forgotten? Then young men's love lies
not in their hearts but in their eyes.
Jesus and Mary, what a lot of salt tears 70
have washed your pale cheeks because of Rosaline!
A lot of salty tears were wasted
to flavor a love that you didn't really feel.
The sun has not yet cleared your signs from the heavens,
and your old groans are still ringing in my old ears. 75
Look, there's still a stain on your cheek
from a tear stain that is not yet washed off.
If ever you were yourself, and that old sorrow was yours,
you and your crying were all for Rosaline.
Have you changed? Say this sentence then: 80
"Women may fall when men don't have the strength to catch
    them."

ROMEO

You often scolded me for loving Rosaline.

FRIAR LAWRENCE

For doting on her, not for loving her, my dear student.

ROMEO

You told me to bury my love.

FRIAR LAWRENCE

Not in a grave 85
where you bury one love to take another one out.

ROMEO

I pray thee, chide me not. Her I love now
Doth grace for grace and love for love allow;
The other did not so.

FRIAR LAWRENCE

90   O, she knew well
Thy love did read by rote that could not spell.
But come, young waverer, come, go with me,
In one respect I'll thy assistant be;
For this alliance may so happy prove
95   To turn your households' **rancour** to pure love.

ROMEO

O, let us hence; I stand on sudden haste.

FRIAR LAWRENCE

Wisely and slow; they stumble that run fast.

[*Exeunt.*]

Rosaline knew his love isnt real,
Juilet fees the same

Lawrence does see it as love

ROMEO

Please, don't scold me. The one I love now
gives me kindness for kindness and love for love.
Rosaline did not.

FRIAR LAWRENCE

Rosaline knew all too well   90
that you were merely repeating words that you didn't mean.
But come, my changeable young man, go with me.
I will help you for just one reason:
this marriage alliance may prove to be so happy
that it will turn the hatred of your two households into love.   95

ROMEO

Let's go. I insist on being quick about this.

FRIAR LAWRENCE

Let's be wise and slow. Those who run too fast stumble.

They exit.

ACT II, SCENE IV

[*A street.*] *Enter* BENVOLIO *and* MERCUTIO.

MERCUTIO
Where the devil should this Romeo be?
Came he not home to-night?

BENVOLIO
Not to his father's; I spoke with his man.

MERCUTIO
Why, that same pale hard-hearted wench, that Rosaline,
5   Torments him so, that he will sure run mad.

BENVOLIO
Tybalt, the kinsman of old Capulet,
Hath sent a letter to his father's house.

MERCUTIO
A challenge, on my life.

BENVOLIO
Romeo will answer it.

MERCUTIO
10   Any man that can write may answer a letter.

BENVOLIO
Nay, he will answer the letter's master, how he dares,
being dared.

MERCUTIO
Alas, poor Romeo! he is already dead; stabb'd with a
white wench's black eye; run through the ear with a love
15   song; the very pin of his heart cleft with the blind bow-
boy's butt-shaft; and is he a man to encounter Tybalt?

BENVOLIO
Why, what is Tybalt?

MERCUTIO
More than prince of cats.* O, he's the courageous captain
of compliments. He fights as you sing prick-song; keeps

---

18   *prince of cats* Tybalt is the name of the prince of the cats in the story "Reynard
the Fox."

ACT 2, SCENE 4

A street. BENVOLIO *and* MERCUTIO *enter.*

MERCUTIO
Where the devil is Romeo?
Didn't he come home last night?

BENVOLIO
Not to his father's house, according to his servant.

MERCUTIO
That pale-hearted witch, Rosaline,
torments him so much that he'll surely go crazy!   5

BENVOLIO
Tybalt, old Capulet's nephew,
sent a letter to Romeo's house.

MERCUTIO
That letter contains a challenge to a duel, I'll bet my life.

BENVOLIO
Romeo will answer it.

MERCUTIO
Any man who can write may answer a letter.   10

BENVOLIO
No, I meant Romeo will answer the writer of the letter. He'll take
   up the challenge to fight a duel.

MERCUTIO
Poor Romeo, he's already dead. He's been stabbed with that
white maid's black eye; shot through the air with a love song;
and the very center of his heart has been split by Cupid's   15
blunt arrow. Is he the kind of man to fight a duel with Tybalt?

BENVOLIO
Why? Who is Tybalt?

MERCUTIO
He's not just the prince of cats. He's the brave master of all the
laws of etiquette. He fights as you would sing from a music sheet,

20   time, distance, and proportion; he rests his minim rests, one, two, and the third in your bosom: the very butcher of a silk button; a duelist, a duelist; a gentleman of the very first house, of the first and second cause. Ah, the immortal *passado!* The *punto reverso!* The *hai!*

BENVOLIO

25   The what?

MERCUTIO

The pox of such antic, lisping, affecting fantasticoes; these new tuners of accent! "By Jesu, a very good blade! A very tall man! A very good whore!" Why, is not this a **lamentable** thing, grandsire, that we should be thus

30   afflicted with these strange flies, these fashion-mongers, these *perdonami's** who stand so much on the new form, that they cannot sit at ease on the old bench? O, their bones,* their bones!

         [*Enter* ROMEO.]

BENVOLIO

Here comes Romeo, here comes Romeo.

MERCUTIO

35   Without his roe, like a dried herring; O flesh, flesh, how art thou fishified! Now is he for the numbers that Petrarch* flowed in. Laura to his lady was a kitchen-wench (marry, she had a better love to be-rhyme her); Dido a dowdy; Cleopatra a gypsy, Helen and Hero hildings and harlots;

40   Thisbe, a grey eye or so, but not to the purpose. Signior Romeo, *bonjour!* There's a French salutation to your French slop.* You gave us the counterfeit fairly last night.

---

31   *perdonami's* "pardon me's" in Italian

33   *bones* a pun on the French word "bon," which means "good"

36–39   *Petrarch . . .* Laura was the subject of the Italian poet Petrarch's sonnets. Queen Dido of Carthage was Aeneas' lover. Cleopatra, ruler of Egypt, captured Antony's and Caesar's affections. Paris' abduction of the beautiful Helen sparked the Trojan War. Hero was Leander's beloved. Thisbe and her lover Pyramus closely compare to Romeo and Juliet.

42   *French slop* a style of French trousers. Romeo has been up all night and is still wearing his costume from the night before.

keeping time, distance, and proportion. He observes 20
even the shortest rests—one, two, and the third is a sword in
your breast. He's the butcher of a silk button on his opponent's
shirt. A duelist, a duelist! He's a gentleman from the best school
of fencing and ready to quarrel over a trifle. He gives the
immortal lunge, the backhanded thrust, the home thrust!

BENVOLIO

The what? 25

MERCUTIO

Damn these grotesque, lisping, snobbish fops, these speakers
of buzz words! "By Jesus, he was a very good swordsman!
A very brave man! A very good fellow!" Isn't it terrible, venerable
sir, that we should be plagued with these strange parasites—
these fashion nuts, these courteous fops who so 30
insist on new fashion that they're not at ease with our old
manners and learning? Oh their bones, their bones!

ROMEO *enters.*

BENVOLIO

Here comes Romeo! Here comes Romeo!

MERCUTIO

Looking like a fish that has spawned—like a dried herring. 35
Oh flesh, flesh how fishy you have become! Now he's ready
to say the kind of poems that Petrarch wrote. But compared
with Rosaline, Petrarch's lady lover was just a kitchen maid
(even if she did have better love poems written to her).
Compared with Rosaline, Dido was a drab woman; Cleopatra,
deceitful; Helen and Hero good-for-nothings and loose women;
Thisbe's shining eyes might be lovely but are not worth 40
mentioning. Sir Romeo, good day! That's a French hello for your
French pants. You certainly gave us the counterfeit last night.

ROMEO

Good morrow to you both. What counterfeit did I give you?

MERCUTIO

45   The slip,* sir, the slip; can you not conceive?

ROMEO

Pardon, good Mercutio, my business was great; and in such a case as mine a man may strain courtesy.

MERCUTIO

That's as much as to say, such a case as yours constrains a man to bow in the hams.

ROMEO

50   Meaning, to curtsy.

MERCUTIO

Thou hast most kindly hit it.

ROMEO

A most courteous **exposition**.

MERCUTIO

Nay, I am the very pink* of courtesy.

ROMEO

Pink for flower.

MERCUTIO

55   Right.

ROMEO

Why, then is my pump well flower'd.

MERCUTIO

Sure wit! Follow me this jest now till thou hast worn out thy pump, that, when the single sole* of it is worn, the jest may remain, after the wearing, solely singular.

ROMEO

60   O single-sol'd jest, solely singular for the singleness!

Word Play

---

45   *slip* besides meaning "escape", also refers to counterfeit coins

53   *pink* means "perfection", "flower", and "a decoration of punched holes"

58   *single sole* means both "weak" and "unique"

ROMEO

Good morning to both of you. What counterfeit did I give you?

MERCUTIO

The slip, sir, the slip! Don't you understand? 45

ROMEO

Excuse me, good Mercutio. I had some serious business to take care of, and in a case such as mine, a man may forget his manners.

MERCUTIO

That's as much as admitting that, in your condition, you have to bow from the hips.

ROMEO

You mean to curtsy. 50

MERCUTIO

You have interpreted quite graciously.

ROMEO

You gave a very polite explanation.

MERCUTIO

Indeed, I am the height of courtesy.

ROMEO

You mean pink for flower.

MERCUTIO

Right. 55

ROMEO

Then my shoe is well-flowered.

MERCUTIO

Touché! Now follow this joke until you have worn out your shoe so that when your single sole is worn out, the joke will be remembered after the telling as unique.

ROMEO

What a weak joke, remarkable only for being so pathetic. 60

MERCUTIO

Come between us, good Benvolio; my wits faint.

ROMEO

Switch and spurs, switch and spurs; or I'll cry a match.

MERCUTIO

Nay, if our wits run the wild-goose chase,* I am done, for
thou hast more of the wild-goose in one of thy wits than,
65   I am sure, I have in my whole five. Was I with you there
for the goose?

ROMEO

Thou wast never with me for anything when thou wast
not there for the goose.*

MERCUTIO

I will bite thee by the ear for that jest.

ROMEO

70   Nay, good goose, bite not.*

MERCUTIO

Thy wit is a very bitter sweeting; it is a most sharp sauce.

ROMEO

And it is not, then, well serv'd into a sweet goose?

Who's smarter?

MERCUTIO

O, here's a wit of cheveril, that stretches from an inch
narrow to an ell* broad!

ROMEO

75   I stretch it out for that word "broad," which added to the
goose, proves thee far and wide a broad goose.

MERCUTIO

Why, is not this better now than groaning for love? Now
art thou sociable, now art thou Romeo, now art thou what

---

63   *wild-goose chase* a game of follow-the-leader on horseback. To catch the goose
was to conclude the chase.

68   *goose* also was slang for "streetwalker"

70   *Nay . . . not.* a proverb meaning "spare me"

74   *ell* equals forty-five inches

MERCUTIO

You'll have to come between us, Benvolio. I can't think of a comeback.

ROMEO

Come on, keep it up, or I'll claim victory!

MERCUTIO

Well, if our wits are on a wild-goose chase, I'm done for. I'm certain you have more wild goose in one of your wits than I have in all five of mine. There—didn't I hit home at the end of the game? 65

ROMEO

You were never with me anywhere if you weren't there looking for a streetwalker.

MERCUTIO

I'll bite you on the ear for that joke!

ROMEO

No, good goose, don't bite me. 70

MERCUTIO

Your wit is like a tart apple: it makes very sharp sauce.

ROMEO

Doesn't such a sauce go well with a sweet goose like you?

MERCUTIO

Oh, here's wit of pliable leather. You stretch a little joke a long way.

ROMEO

I'll stretch my wit to tackle that word "broad," which, when 75 added to goose, proves that you're known far and wide as an out-and-out goose.

MERCUTIO

Now, isn't this better than groaning for love? Now you're being friendly, now you're the Romeo I remember. You're Romeo! Now you are what

80 thou art, by art as well as by nature; for this **driveling** love is like a great natural, that runs lolling up and down to hide his bauble in a hole.

BENVOLIO
Stop there, stop there.

MERCUTIO
Thou desir'st me to stop in my tale against the hair.

BENVOLIO
Thou wouldst else have made thy tale large.*

MERCUTIO
85 O, thou art deceiv'd; I would have made it short; for I was come to the whole depth of my tale, and meant, indeed, to occupy the argument no longer.

ROMEO
Here's goodly gear!

[*Enter* NURSE *and her man* PETER.]

A sail,* a sail!

MERCUTIO
90 Two, two; a shirt and a smock.

NURSE
Peter!

PETER
Anon!

NURSE
My fan, Peter.

MERCUTIO
Good Peter, to hide her face; for her fan's the fairer face.

NURSE
95 God ye good morrow, gentlemen.

---

84 *large* also means "indecent"

89 *sail* The nurse is quite large and is probably wearing a white apron, so Romeo calls her a "sail."

you are, in learning as well as by temperament. This silly
love is like a big idiot running up and down with his   80
tongue hanging out, trying to hide his toy in a hole.

BENVOLIO

Stop! Stop!

MERCUTIO

You want me to stop when I don't want to stop.

BENVOLIO

If I hadn't stopped you, you would have told an overly long story.

MERCUTIO

You're wrong. I'd have kept it short because I said all I'd   85
meant to say, and really didn't intend to continue the discussion
any longer.

ROMEO *(Sees* JULIET's *nurse coming.)*
Here comes some handsome stuff.

    The NURSE *and her servant* PETER *enter.*

A sail, a sail!

MERCUTIO

Two sails! A man and a woman.   90

NURSE

Peter!

PETER

At your service!

NURSE

Give me my fan, Peter.

MERCUTIO

Give it to her, good Peter, so she can hide her face. Her fan is
prettier than her face.

NURSE

Good morning, gentleman.   95

Act 2, Scene 4   131

MERCUTIO

God ye good den, fair gentlewoman.

NURSE

Is it good den?

MERCUTIO

'Tis no less, I tell ye; for the bawdy hand of the dial is
now upon the prick of noon.*

NURSE

100   Out upon you! What a man are you!

ROMEO

One, gentlewoman, that God hath made for himself
to mar.

NURSE

By my troth, it is well said; "for himself to mar," quoth 'a!
Gentlemen, can any of you tell me where I may find the
105   young Romeo?

ROMEO

I can tell you; but young Romeo will be older when you
have found him than he was when you sought him. I am
the youngest of that name, for fault of a worse.*

NURSE

You say well.

MERCUTIO

110   Yea, is the worst well? Very well took i' faith; wisely, wisely.

NURSE

If you be he, sir, I desire some confidence* with you.

BENVOLIO

She will indite* him to some supper.

98–99   *bawdy . . . noon* Mercutio tries to shock the nurse with ribald language.

108   *for fault of a worse* Romeo means "a better name," but the nurse takes him
seriously.

111   *confidence* The nurse really means "conference." She is using a
malapropism—a word similar to the right word but misused and so
(inadvertently) humorous.

112   *indite* a malapropism for "invite." Benvolio is mocking the nurse.

MERCUTIO

Good afternoon, lovely lady.

NURSE

Is it afternoon already?

MERCUTIO

It is, I assure you. The naughty hand on the clock is now on the point of noon.

NURSE

Shame on you! What kind of man are you? 100

ROMEO

He's one, madam, who was made to harm himself.

NURSE

Truly, that was a clever remark. "Made to harm himself," did he say? Gentleman, can any of you tell me where I can find young Romeo? 105

ROMEO

I can tell you. But young Romeo will be older when you have found him than when you started looking for him. I'm the youngest by the name of Romeo, for lack of a worse name.

NURSE

You speak well.

MERCUTIO

Really, is the "worst" good? You're very perceptive, indeed! 110
How intelligent!

NURSE (to ROMEO)

If you're Romeo, sir, I want to have a confidence with you.

BENVOLIO

She'll indite him to supper.

MERCUTIO

A bawd, a bawd, a bawd! So ho!

ROMEO

What hast thou found?

MERCUTIO

115   No hare, sir; unless a hare, sir, in a lenten pie,* that is
something stale and hoar ere it be spent.

[*Sings.*]

> "An old hare hoar,
> And an old hare hoar,
>   Is very good meat in lent;
> 120   But a hare that is hoar
> Is too much for a score,
>   When it hoars ere it be spent."

Romeo, will you come to your father's? We'll to dinner
thither.

ROMEO

125   I will follow you.

MERCUTIO

Farewell, ancient lady; farewell [*singing*] "lady, lady, lady."*

[*Exeunt* MERCUTIO *and* BENVOLIO.]

NURSE

I pray you, sir, what saucy merchant was this, that was so
full of his ropery?

ROMEO

A gentleman, nurse, that loves to hear himself talk, and
130   will speak more in a minute than he will stand to in a
month.

NURSE

An 'a speak anything against me, I'll take him down, an 'a
were lustier than he is, and twenty such Jacks; and if I

---

115   *lenten pie* Lent is a religious period of forty days preceding Easter. Some
Christians do not eat meat during the period (and a Lenten or meat pie would
go stale before it was eaten).

126   *lady, lady, lady* a refrain from an old ballad, "Chaste Susanna"

MERCUTIO

A streetwalker, a streetwalker, a streetwalker! I found her.

ROMEO

What have you found?

MERCUTIO

Not a streetwalker, sir. Unless a streetwalker is 115
   like meat in a pie served during Lent—
stale and old before it is eaten.

> *He sings.*

> An old rabbit harlot,
> Yes, an old rabbit harlot,
>   Is very good meat in Lent.
> But a rabbit that is moldy 120
> Is not good enough to be paid for
>   When it rots before it is eaten.

Romeo, will you come to your father's house? We're going to
dinner there.

ROMEO

Yes, I'll follow you. 125

MERCUTIO *(to* NURSE*)*

Good-bye, old lady. Good-bye. *(Sings.)* "Lady, lady, lady."

> MERCUTIO *and* BENVOLIO *leave.*

NURSE

Tell me sir, what rude fellow was that who had such a fresh
mouth?

ROMEO

He's a gentleman, nurse, who loves to hear himself talk and
who'll say more in a minute than he'll listen to in a month. 130

NURSE

If he says anything bad about me, I'll beat him up—even if he
were bigger than he is and even if there were twenty such rascals

135   cannot, I'll find those that shall. Scurvy knave! I am none of his flirt-gills; I am none of his skains-mates.—And thou must stand by too, and suffer every knave to use me at his pleasure!

PETER

I saw no man use you at his pleasure; if I had, my weapon should quickly have been out. I warrant you, I dare draw
140   as soon as another man, if I see occasion in a good quarrel, and the law on my side.

NURSE

Now, afore God, I am so vex'd that every part about me quivers. Scurvy knave! Pray you, sir, a word: and as I told you, my young lady bid me inquire you out; what she bid
145   me say, I will keep to myself. But first let me tell ye, if ye should lead her into a fool's paradise, as they say, it were a very gross kind of behaviour, as they say; for the gentlewoman is young, and, therefore, if you should deal double with her, truly it were an ill thing to be off'red to
150   any gentlewoman, and very weak dealing.

ROMEO

Nurse, commend me to thy lady and mistress. I protest unto thee—

NURSE

Good heart, and, i' faith, I will tell her as much. Lord, Lord, she will be a joyful woman.

ROMEO

155   What wilt thou tell her, nurse? Thou dost not mark me.

NURSE

I will tell her, sir, that you do protest; which, as I take it, is a gentlemanlike offer.

ROMEO

Bid her devise
Some means to come to shrift this afternoon;
160   And there she shall at Friar Lawrence' cell
Be shriv'd and married. Here is for thy pains.

like him. And if I can't beat him, I'll find someone
who can. Disgusting rascal! I'm not one of his flirting   135
women and I'm not one of his cutthroats. *(to* PETER*)*
And you just stood there and let every rascal use me
as he pleased.

PETER

I didn't see any man use you at his pleasure. If I had, I would
have drawn my weapon quickly. I swear, I'm as quick to
draw my sword as any man, if I see there's a basis for a   140
good quarrel and if the law is on my side.

NURSE

I swear to God, I'm so upset that I am shaking all over.
Disgusting rascal! *(to* ROMEO*)* Sir, I must speak to you.
As I was telling you, my young lady sent me to find you.
What she told me to say, I'll keep to myself. First, let me   145
tell you, if you should seduce her, it would be a terrible
thing to do. My mistress is young, and if you should
two-time her, that would be a terrible thing to do to
any lady and very unmanly behavior.   150

ROMEO

Nurse, give my regards to your lady, your mistress. I vow—

NURSE

Good fellow, truly, I'll tell her so. Lord, lord, she'll be a happy
woman.

ROMEO

What will you tell her, nurse? You didn't listen to me.   155

NURSE

I'll tell her, sir, that you made a vow, which, as I understand it,
is a gentlemanlike offer.

ROMEO

Tell her to find
a way to come to confession this afternoon.
There at Friar Lawrence's cell   160
she shall receive absolution and be married. Here's some
    money for your trouble.

NURSE

No, truly, sir; not a penny.

ROMEO

Go to; I say you shall.

NURSE

This afternoon, sir? Well, she shall be there.

ROMEO

165 And stay, good nurse;—behind the abbey wall
Within this hour my man shall be with thee,
And bring thee cords made like a tackled stair;
Which to the high top-gallant of my joy
Must be my convoy in the secret night.
170 Farewell; be trusty, and I'll quit thy pains.
Farewell; commend me to thy mistress.

NURSE

Now God in heaven bless thee! Hark you, sir.

ROMEO

What say'st thou, my dear nurse?

NURSE

Is your man secret? Did you ne'er hear say,
175 "Two may keep counsel, putting one away"?

ROMEO

I warrant thee, my man's as true as steel.

NURSE *Nurse tells him he shouldn't marry Juliet*

Well, sir; my mistress is the sweetest lady—Lord, Lord!
When 'twas a little prating thing,—O, there is a nobleman
in town, one Paris, that would fain lay knife aboard; but
180 she, good soul, had as lief see a toad, a very toad, as see
him. I anger her sometimes and tell her that Paris is the
properer man; but, I'll warrant you, when I say so, she
looks as pale as any clout in the versal world. Doth not
rosemary* and Romeo begin both with a letter?*

---

184 *rosemary* a fragrant herb that grooms wore at weddings in Shakespeare's time

184 *begin both with a letter* The nurse cannot read, so she does not know one letter
from another.

but he loves her so much he will do whatever

NURSE

No indeed, sir, I won't take a penny.

ROMEO

Not another word! You shall take it.

NURSE

You want her to come this afternoon, sir? Well, she'll be there.

(Starts to leave.)

ROMEO

Good nurse, wait! My servant will come to you   165
within an hour behind the abbey wall
and bring you a rope ladder like those used on ships,
which will be my passageway in the dark night
to the peak of my happiness.
Good-bye. Be trustworthy and I'll reward you.   170
Good-bye. Give my love to your mistress.

NURSE

God in heaven bless you.—Listen, sir.

ROMEO

What did you want to say, dear nurse?

NURSE

Can your servant keep a secret? Didn't you ever hear the saying,
"Two can keep a secret if one is dead?"   175

ROMEO

I assure you that my servant is as trustworthy as steel.

NURSE

Well, sir—my mistress is the sweetest lady. Lord, lord! When
she was just a little chattering thing—Oh, there's a
nobleman in town named Paris who's eager to marry
Juliet. But she, good soul, would as soon see a toad, a real   180
toad, as to see him. I make her angry sometimes and tell
her that Paris is handsomer than you are. But, I swear to you that
when I say that, she looks as pale as any rag in the universe. Don't
rosemary and Romeo begin with the same letter?

ROMEO

185   Ay, nurse; what of that? Both with an *R*.

NURSE

Ah, mocker! That's the dog's name.* *R* is for the—No, I
know it begins with some other letter—and she hath the
prettiest sententious* of it, of you and rosemary, that it
would do you good to hear it.

ROMEO

190   Commend me to thy lady.

NURSE

Ay, a thousand times.

     [*Exit* ROMEO.]

Peter!

PETER

Anon!

NURSE

Before, and apace.

     [*Exeunt.*]

---

186   *dog's name* Dogs were called "R" because their growls sounded like the
        letter.

186–187 *sententious* The nurse means "sentences"; this is another malapropism.

ROMEO

Yes, nurse. So what? Both begin with an *R*. 185

NURSE

You teaser—*R* is a dog's name. *R* is for the—No, I know it begins with some other letter—and she has the prettiest sententious. That letter and you and rosemary. It would do you good to hear them.

ROMEO

Give my love to your lady. 190

NURSE

Yes—a thousand times.

ROMEO *leaves.*

Peter!

PETER

Right away!

NURSE

Go! Go before me and quickly!

They exit.

ACT II, SCENE V

Capulet's orchard. Enter JULIET.

JULIET
> The clock struck nine when I did send the nurse;
> In half an hour she promised to return.
> Perchance she cannot meet him: that's not so.
> O, she is lame! Love's heralds should be thoughts,
> Which ten times faster glide than the sun's beams
> Driving back shadows over louring hills;
> Therefore do nimble-pinion'd doves draw Love,
> And therefore hath the wind-swift Cupid wings.
> Now is the sun upon the highmost hill
> Of this day's journey, and from nine till twelve
> Is three long hours, yet she is not come.
> Had she affections and warm youthful blood,
> She would be as swift in motion as a ball;
> My words would bandy her to my sweet love,
> And his to me;
> But old folks, marry, feign as they were dead,
> Unwieldy, slow, heavy and pale as lead.

[*Enter* NURSE *and* PETER.]

> O God, she comes! O honey nurse, what news?
> Hast thou met with him? Send thy man away.

NURSE
> Peter, stay at the gate.

[*Exit* PETER.]

JULIET
> Now, good sweet nurse,—O Lord, why look'st thou sad?
> Though news be sad, yet tell them merrily;
> If good, thou sham'st the music of sweet news
> By playing it to me with so sour a face.

NURSE
> I am a-weary, give me leave a while.
> Fie, how my bones ache! What a jaunce have I had!

ACT 2, SCENE 5

Capulet's orchard. JULIET *enters.*

JULIET
It was nine o'clock this morning when I sent the nurse;
she promised to return within half an hour.
Maybe she can't find him. No, that can't be.
Oh, she is crippled! Love's messengers should be thoughts,
which can fly ten times faster than the sun's beams   5
driving back shadows over darkening hills.
That's why swift doves pull Venus' chariot,
and that's why Cupid has wings as swift as the wind.
Now, the sun is at the highest spot in the sky.
From nine o'clock to noon   10
is three long hours, and she still hasn't come back.
If she had the emotions and the warm blood of youth,
she'd move as fast as a ball.
My words would speed her to my sweet love,
and his words would speed her back to me.   15
But many old folks move like they are dead—
clumsy, slow, heavy, and pale as lead.

> *The* NURSE *and* PETER *enter.*

Oh God, here she comes! Oh sweet nurse, what's your news?
Did you meet him? Send your servant away.

NURSE
Peter, wait by the gate.   20

> PETER *leaves.*

JULIET
Now, sweet, nurse—Oh Lord, why do you look sad?
Even if the news is sad, tell it happily.
If the news is good, you don't do the music of good news justice
by telling it to me with such a sour face.

NURSE
I'm tired; let me rest awhile.   25
Oh, how my bones ache! What a rough walk I've had!

JULIET

I would thou hadst my bones, and I thy news.
Nay, come, I pray thee, speak; good, good nurse, speak.

NURSE

Jesu, what haste! Can you not stay a while?
30 Do you not see that I am out of breath?

JULIET

How art thou out of breath, when thou hast breath
To say to me that thou art out of breath?
Th' excuse that thou dost make in this delay
Is longer than the tale thou dost excuse.
35 Is thy news good, or bad? Answer to that;
Say either, and I'll stay the circumstance.
Let me be satisfied, is't good or bad?

NURSE

Well, you have made a simple choice; you know not how
to choose a man. Romeo! No, not he. Though his face be
40 better than any man's, yet his leg excels all men's; and for
a hand, and a foot, and a body, though they be not to be
talk'd on, yet they are past compare. He is not the flower
of courtesy, but, I'll warrant him, as gentle as a lamb. Go
thy ways, wench; serve God. What, have you din'd at
45 home?

JULIET

No, no! But all this did I know before. What says he of
our marriage? What of that?

NURSE

Lord, how my head aches! What a head have I!
It beats as it would fall in twenty pieces.
50 My back o' t' other side,—O, my back, my back!
Beshrew your heart for sending me about
To catch my death with jauncing up and down!

JULIET

I' faith, I am sorry that thou art not well. Sweet, sweet,
sweet nurse, tell me, what says my love?

NURSE

55 Your love says, like an honest gentleman, and a courteous,

JULIET

I wish you had my bones and I had your news.
Come on! Please! I beg you tell me good, good nurse. Speak!

NURSE

Jesus, what a hurry you're in! Can't you wait awhile?
Don't you see I'm out of breath?   30

JULIET

How can you be out of breath, when you have breath
to say to me you're out of breath?
The excuse you're giving for this delay
is longer than the story you excused yourself from telling.
Is the news good or bad? Answer that!   35
Say either good or bad, and I'll wait for the details.
Let me be satisfied: is it good or bad?

NURSE

Well, you've made a foolish choice; you don't know how to
choose a man. Romeo! No, not him, though he has the
handsomest face of any man and his leg excels all men's.   40
And for a hand, a foot, and a body—though we won't
discuss them—they're beyond compare. He's not the
most courteous, but I'll swear, he's as gentle as a lamb.
Get along, girl; serve God. Have you already eaten at
home?   45

JULIET

No, no! But I knew all of this before. What does he say about our
marriage? What about that?

NURSE

Lord, how my head aches! What a head I have!
It throbs as if it would split into twenty pieces.
And then my back—Oh, my back, my back!   50
Shame on you for sending me out
to catch my death from jolting up and down!

JULIET

I'm truly sorry you're not well. Sweet, sweet, sweet nurse, tell me,
what does my love say?

NURSE

Your love says, like an honorable gentleman and a courteous,   55

and a kind, and a handsome, and, I warrant, a virtuous,—
Where is your mother?

JULIET

Where is my mother! Why, she is within;
Where should she be? How oddly thou repliest!
60 "Your love says, like an honest gentleman,
'Where is your mother?'"

NURSE

O God's lady dear!
Are you so hot? Marry, come up, I trow;
Is this the poultice for my aching bones?
65 Henceforward do your messages yourself.

JULIET

Here's such a coil!—Come, what says Romeo?

NURSE

Have you got leave to go to shrift today?

JULIET

I have.

NURSE

Then hie you hence to Friar Lawrence' cell;
70 There stays a husband to make you a wife. *excited*
Now comes the wanton blood up in your cheeks;
They'll be in scarlet straight at any news.
Hie you to church; I must another way,
To fetch a ladder, by the which your love
75 Must climb a bird's nest soon when it is dark.
I am the drudge and toil in your delight,
But you shall bear the burden soon at night. *sex*
Go; I'll to dinner; hie you to the cell.

JULIET

Hie to high fortune! Honest nurse, farewell.

[*Exeunt.*]

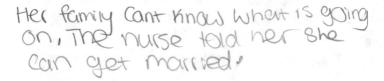

Her family cant know what is going on, The nurse told her she can get married.

kind, handsome, and I swear, a virtuous—where's your mother?

JULIET

Where's my mother? Why, she's inside!
Where else would she be? That's an odd reply,
"Your love says, like an honest gentleman,   60
'Where's your mother?'"

NURSE

By the Virgin Mary!
Are you angry? Come now, slow up.
Is this the medicine for my aching bones?
From now on, deliver your messages yourself.   65

JULIET

Such a fuss! Come on, what does Romeo say?

NURSE

Do you have permission to go to confession today?

JULIET

I have.

NURSE

Then hurry to Friar Lawrence's cell.
There a husband waits to make you a wife.   70
Now the blood has rushed up into your cheeks.
Another scrap of news and you'll turn scarlet.
Hurry to church! I must go another way.
I have to get a ladder by which your love
can climb to your room when it's dark.   75
I'm the slave and laborer for your delight.
But you shall bear the burden tonight.
Go! I'm off to dinner. Hurry to the cell.

JULIET

I'll hurry to my good fortune. Honest nurse, good-bye.

They leave.

ACT II, SCENE VI

[*Friar Lawrence's cell.*] *Enter* FRIAR LAWRENCE *and* ROMEO.

FRIAR LAWRENCE
So smile the heavens upon this holy act,
That after-hours with sorrow chide us not!

ROMEO
Amen, amen! But come what sorrow can,
It cannot countervail th' exchange of joy
That one short minute gives me in her sight.
Do thou but close our hands with holy words,
The love-devouring Death do what he dare;
It is enough I may but call her mine.

FRIAR LAWRENCE
These violent delights have violent ends,
And in their triumph die, like fire and powder,
Which as they kiss consume. The sweetest honey
Is loathsome in his own deliciousness
And in the taste **confounds** the appetite:
Therefore love moderately; long love doth so;
Too swift arrives as tardy as too slow.

[*Enter* JULIET.]

Here comes the lady. O, so light a foot
Will ne'er wear out the everlasting flint.
A lover may bestride the gossamer
That idles in the wanton summer air,
And yet not fall; so light is vanity.

JULIET
Good even to my ghostly confessor.

FRIAR LAWRENCE
Romeo shall thank thee, daughter, for us both.

JULIET
As much to him, else in his thanks too much.

ACT 2, SCENE 6

Friar Lawrence's cell. FRIAR LAWRENCE *and* ROMEO *enter.*

FRIAR LAWRENCE

Heavens smile upon this holy act of marriage
so that sorrow will not come later.

ROMEO

Amen, amen! But whatever sorrow comes,
it cannot equal the joy
that one short minute in her sight gives me.   5
If you will marry us with holy words,
then let love-destroying death do what he dares.
It's enough that I may call her mine.

FRIAR LAWRENCE

Violent passions have violent ends,
and in triumph they die, like fire and gunpowder,   10
which consume one another when they kiss. Even the
    sweetest honey
tastes sickeningly sweet if eaten to excess
and will destroy the appetite.
So love moderately. Love that lasts a long time is moderate.
To push love too fast can be as bad as being too slow to love. 15

> JULIET *enters.*

Here comes the lady. Oh, so light a foot as hers
will never wear out the path.
A lover may ride upon a spider's thread
that waves in the wandering summer breeze,
and yet not fall. So light is earthly love.   20

JULIET

Good evening, father.

FRIAR LAWRENCE

Romeo will kiss you for us both, daughter.

JULIET

The same greeting to Romeo; otherwise he thanks me too much.

ROMEO

    Ah, Juliet, if the measure of thy joy

25   Be heap'd like mine, and that thy skill be more

    To blazon it, then sweeten with thy breath

    This neighbour air, and let rich music's tongue

    Unfold the imagin'd happiness that both

    Receive in either by this dear encounter.

JULIET

30   Conceit, more rich in matter than in words,

    Brags of his substance, not of ornament.

    They are but beggars that can count their worth;

    But my true love is grown to such excess

    I cannot sum up sum of half my wealth.

she needs to understand more of what the love could be

FRIAR LAWRENCE

35   Come, come with me, and we will make short work;

    For, by your leaves, you shall not stay alone

    Till Holy Church incorporate two in one.

       [*Exeunt.*]

ROMEO

Ah, Juliet, if you're as happy
as I am, and if you can   25
sing better than I do, go ahead and sweeten the air with your
  voice,
and let beautiful music
tell the happiness that both
of us feel in meeting each other here.

JULIET

True understanding is deeper in meaning than mere words   30
and is important for its result, not pretty rhetoric.
Those who can verbalize their happiness have little
happiness to speak of. My true love has grown so much that
I can't tell even half of it in words.

FRIAR LAWRENCE

Come! Come with me and we'll make this ceremony short.   35
You shall not be alone,
until the holy church joins you two together.

  They exit.

Act II Review

Discussion Questions

1. What images of light and fire does Juliet inspire in Romeo?

2. After exchanging vows of love in Scene ii, Juliet says, "I have no joy of this contract to-night." What do you think she means by this?

3. What philosophical observations does Friar Lawrence make in Act II, Scene iii?

4. Describe how Romeo and his friends treat the Nurse. Would they treat all women of Verona in the same fashion? Explain.

5. Describe the interview between the Nurse and Romeo in Act II, Scene iv.

6. Why do you think Shakespeare left the wedding ceremony out of the play?

7. Do you approve of the Nurse's and Friar's actions in helping with the secret wedding? Explain why or why not.

Literary Elements

1. A **metaphor** is a direct comparison of unlike things. Find some examples of metaphors in Scene ii. What emotions and attitudes do they help the young lovers express?

2. **Imagery** refers to language that appeals to the five senses (sight, hearing, taste, touch, and smell) and adds emotion and power to the writing. To see how imagery is embedded into the play, find and list the images of light, dark, and fire in Scene ii. What is their dramatic purpose?

3. Shakespeare allows his characters to reveal their innermost thoughts and feelings to the audience through speeches called **soliloquies**. Find soliloquies by Romeo, Juliet, and Friar Lawrence in Act II. What purpose do they serve?

4. A **malapropism** is a comical mistake uttered by certain characters. How are malapropisms used to characterize the Nurse? See if there is anyone else in the play who utters a malapropism.

5. Act II, Scene iv contains a **pun** "free-for-all" among Romeo, Mercutio, and Benvolio. The three engage in a furious war of wits, with many plays on words, and many of those sexual in nature. Find a pun in this scene and consider its double meaning. Why do you think Shakespeare used this form so freely in this particular scene?

Writing Prompts

1. One of this play's most famous quotations is "What's in a name? That which we call a rose by any other word would smell as sweet." Look back at the passage where Juliet speaks this (Act II, Scene ii), and think about the idea Juliet is expressing. Explain how names often get in the way of people knowing each other and getting along. Have you ever known or wanted to know someone who had the "wrong" name? Write about that situation.

2. Write a character description of either the Nurse or Friar Lawrence. What kind of person is she or he? Use quotations from the play to support your ideas.

3. Summarize the action of the play so far. Use one sentence for Act I and one sentence for Act II.

4. Compare Juliet's relationship with the Nurse to her relationship with her mother. Does Juliet seem closer to one woman than the other? Think about the ways she talks and acts around each one. Put your response in writing, using evidence from the play to support your answer.

Romeo and *Juliet* ACT III

Romeo (Leonard Whiting) and Tybalt (Michael York) meet in a fatal fight. (Zeffirelli, 1968)

"A plague o'
both your houses!"

Before You Read

1. Notice how the mood of the play changes during this act.

2. At this point in the play, which character strikes you as more vivid and compelling, Romeo or Juliet? Explain why.

3. Judging from the play, how were gender roles in the Renaissance different from gender roles today?

4. What kind of long-term marriage would you expect Romeo and Juliet to have?

Literary Elements

1. The **theme** of a work of literature is the message about life that the writer wants to convey. The theme of "division" comes up often in *Romeo and Juliet* because it is a play about two feuding families.

2. One of the many ways Shakespeare continues the theme of contrasts in *Romeo and Juliet* is with **oxymorons**. An oxymoron occurs when contradictory words are paired: "O heavy lightness! Serious vanity!"

3. The **repetition** of words and phrases is one of Shakespeare's favorite ways of increasing the tension and emotional impact of a speech or scene. In Scene iii, Romeo repeats the word "banishment" in his conversation with Friar Lawrence, which shows how much he fears the idea of leaving Verona and his dear Juliet behind.

4. As noted earlier, **hyperbole** means obvious exaggeration. After being wounded in a sword fight, Mercutio announces his death with the grimmest image possible: "They have made worms' meat of me."

Words to Know

The following vocabulary words appear in Act III in the original text of Shakespeare's play. However, they are words that are still commonly used. Read the definitions here and pay attention to the words as you read the play (they will be in boldfaced type).

civil	well-mannered; proper
confines	interior; insides
dexterity	skill; proficiency
digressing	getting off of the main topic; deviating
dismembered [dismember'd]	took apart; split
eloquence	expressiveness; verbal facility
garish	gaudy; showy
jocund	cheerful; happy
martial	military; soldierly
monarch	royalty; a king, queen, or emperor
plague	disease; hex
prevails	controls; dominates
reconcile	make peace among
renowned [renown'd]	famous; well-known
usurer	swindler; extortionist

Act Summary

As Romeo is walking home from the secret wedding, he comes upon Benvolio and their mutual friend Mercutio, who is quarreling with Tybalt. Romeo tries but fails to break up the fight between them. Tybalt fatally stabs Mercutio, and, in turn, Romeo avenges his friend's death by killing Tybalt. A furious Prince Escalus bans Romeo from Verona, warning that he will be put to death if he ever returns.

The Nurse gives Juliet the news that Romeo has been banished for

killing Juliet's cousin, Tybalt. At first, Juliet is grief-stricken for Tybalt and angry at Romeo, but her grief soon turns to pain at Romeo's banishment. She learns from the Nurse that she will see Romeo that night.

Romeo tries to commit suicide after learning of his banishment and of Juliet's grief at the events. Friar Lawrence tells Romeo he will make plans for the two newlyweds to spend the night together, before Romeo leaves for Mantua.

The newlyweds separate at dawn. Juliet's mother announces that Juliet must wed Paris, and Juliet refuses, enraging Lord Capulet. She vows to seek the advice of Friar Lawrence.

Romeo and Juliet, painting by Sir Frank Dicksee, 1884

ACT III, SCENE I

[*A public place.*] Enter MERCUTIO, BENVOLIO, *and men.*

BENVOLIO

I pray thee, good Mercutio, let's retire.
The day is hot, the Capulets abroad,
And, if we meet, we shall not 'scape a brawl,
For now, these hot days, is the mad blood stirring.

MERCUTIO

5   Thou art like one of these fellows that, when he enters the
confines of a tavern, claps me his sword upon the table
and says, "God send me no need of thee!" and by the
operation of the second cup draws him on the drawer,
when indeed there is no need.

BENVOLIO

10   Am I like such a fellow?

MERCUTIO

Come, come, thou art as hot a Jack in thy mood as any in
Italy, and as soon moved to be moody, and as soon
moody to be moved.

BENVOLIO

And what to?

MERCUTIO

15   Nay, an there were two* such, we should have none shortly,
for one would kill the other. Thou! Why, thou wilt quarrel
with a man that hath a hair more or a hair less in his
beard than thou hast. Thou wilt quarrel with a man for
cracking nuts, having no other reason but because thou
20   hast hazel eyes. What eye but such an eye would spy out
such a quarrel? Thy head is as full of quarrels as an egg is
full of meat, and yet thy head hath been beaten as addle
as an egg for quarrelling. Thou hast quarrell'd with a man
for coughing in the street because he hath wakened thy
25   dog that hath lain asleep in the sun. Didst thou not fall

---

15 *two* Mercutio is playing on Benvolio's "to."

ACT 3, SCENE 1

A public place. MERCUTIO, BENVOLIO *and* SERVANTS *enter.*

BENVOLIO

Please Mercutio, let's go.
It's hot, the Capulets are around,
and if we meet them, there'll be a fight.
This hot weather makes tempers flare!

MERCUTIO

You're like one of those fellows who enters a bar, throws his 5
sword on the table, and says, "I pray heaven I'll have no reason
to use you!" Then after he has felt the effect of his second cup, he'll
draw his sword on the waiter who brought his wine, for
no reason at all.

BENVOLIO

Am I like that fellow? 10

MERCUTIO

Come on, you're as hot-tempered when you're angry as any
man in Italy. You're quick to get angry, and when you get
angry, you're quick to be moved to—

BENVOLIO

Moved to do what?

MERCUTIO

Really, if there were two like you, we'd soon have none 15
because one would kill the other. You, why, you would quarrel
with a man who has a hair more or a hair less in his beard
than you have. You'll quarrel with a man for cracking hazelnuts
for no other reason than that you have hazel eyes. What kind
of eye, except one like yours, would see the occasion for a 20
quarrel? Your head is as full of quarrels as an egg is full of yolk,
and yet your head has been beaten to a scramble, like an egg,
for quarreling. You've quarreled with a man for coughing in the
street because he woke your dog that was lying asleep in the
sun. Didn't you quarrel with a tailor because he wore his new 25

out with a tailor for wearing his new doublet before
Easter? With another for tying his new shoes with old
riband? And yet thou wilt tutor me for quarrelling!

BENVOLIO

An I were so apt to quarrel as thou art, any man should
30 buy the fee-simple of my life for an hour and a quarter.

MERCUTIO

The fee-simple! O simple!

Enter TYBALT, PETRUCHIO, *and others.*

BENVOLIO

By my head, here comes the Capulets.

MERCUTIO

By my heel, I care not.

TYBALT

Follow me close, for I will speak to them.
35 Gentlemen, good den; a word with one of you.

MERCUTIO

And but one word with one of us?
Couple it with something; make it a word and a blow.

TYBALT

You shall find me apt enough to that, sir, an you will give
occasion.

MERCUTIO

40 Could you not take some occasion without giving?

TYBALT

Mercutio, thou consortest* with Romeo,—

MERCUTIO

Consort! What, dost thou make us minstrels? An thou
make minstrels of us, look to hear nothing but discords.
Here's my fiddlestick; here's that shall make you dance.
45 'Zounds, consort!

---

41 *consort* means both associate and a company of musicians

jacket before Easter? And fought with another man for tying his new shoes with an old lace? And yet you lecture me about quarreling?

BENVOLIO

If I were as likely to quarrel as you, someone who bought my life would own it for about an hour and a quarter. 30

MERCUTIO

Own it? Stupid!

> TYBALT, PETRUCHIO, *and others enter.*

BENVOLIO

I swear by my head, here come the Capulets.

MERCUTIO

I swear by my heel, I don't care.

TYBALT *(to his servants)*

Stay close behind me; I'll speak to them. *(to MERCUTIO and others)*

Gentlemen, good afternoon. I wish to speak a word with one 35 of you.

MERCUTIO

Just one word with one of us?

Add something else to that; make it a word and a punch in the mouth.

TYBALT

I'll be ready enough to do that, sir, if you'll give me a reason to do so.

MERCUTIO

Couldn't you take a reason without my giving you one? 40

TYBALT

Mercutio, you associate with Romeo—

MERCUTIO

Associate? What do you think we are, musicians? If you make musicians of us, you'll hear nothing but sour notes. Here's my fiddlestick! *(He draws his sword.)* This will make you dance! By God, associate! 45

BENVOLIO

We talk here in the public haunt of men.
Either withdraw unto some private place,
Or reason coldly of your grievances,
Or else depart; here all eyes gaze on us.

MERCUTIO

50 Men's eyes were made to look, and let them gaze;
I will not budge for no man's pleasure, I.

Enter ROMEO.

TYBALT

Well, peace be with you, sir; here comes my man.*

MERCUTIO

But I'll be hang'd, sir, if he wear your livery.*
Marry, go before to field, he'll be your follower;
55 Your worship in that sense may call him "man."

TYBALT

Romeo, the love I bear thee can afford
No better term than this: thou art a villain.

ROMEO

Tybalt, the reason that I have to love thee
Doth much excuse the appertaining rage
60 To such a greeting. Villain am I none;
Therefore farewell; I see thou know'st me not.

TYBALT

Boy, this shall not excuse the injuries
That thou hast done me; therefore turn and draw.

ROMEO

I do protest I never injur'd thee,
65 But love thee better than thou canst devise
Till thou shalt know the reason of my love;
And so, good Capulet,—which name I tender
As dearly as mine own,—be satisfied.

MERCUTIO

O calm, dishonourable, vile submission!
70 *Alla stoccata* carries it away.

---

52 "my man" often referred to a servant

53 *livery* the uniform of a servant

162

BENVOLIO
We are talking here in public.
Let's move to a private place,
or coolly discuss your grievances,
or let's leave. Everyone is staring at us here.

MERCUTIO
Men's eyes were made to look, so let them stare.   50
I won't budge for anyone.

      ROMEO *enters.*

TYBALT
Peace be with you, sir. Here comes my man.

MERCUTIO
But I'll be hanged, sir, if he wears your livery.
If you go to the dueling field, he'll certainly follow you.
In that sense, you may call him your follower.   55

TYBALT
Romeo, the love that I feel for you can find
no better word than this—you're a peasant!

ROMEO
Tybalt, the reason that I have for loving you
helps me overcome the anger I should really feel
at such an insult. I'm not a peasant.   60
Therefore, good-bye. I see you don't really know me.

TYBALT
Boy, this will not excuse the wrong
you've done to me. Turn around and draw your sword!

ROMEO
I protest, I've never harmed you.
I love you more than you can understand   65
until you know the reason for my love.
So, good Capulet—a name I value
as dearly as my own—be satisfied.

MERCUTIO
What a calm, dishonorable, disgusting submission to an insult!
Tybalt is getting away with this insult.   70

[*Draws.*]

Tybalt, you rat-catcher, will you walk?

TYBALT

What wouldst thou have with me?

MERCUTIO

Good king of cats, nothing but one of your nine lives; that
I mean to make bold withal, and, as you shall use me
75   hereafter, dry-beat the rest of the eight. Will you pluck
your sword out of his pilcher by the ears? Make haste, lest
mine be about your ears ere it be out.

TYBALT

I am for you.

[*drawing*]

ROMEO

Gentle Mercutio, put thy rapier up.

MERCUTIO

80   Come, sir, your *passado*.

[*They fight.*]

ROMEO

Draw, Benvolio; beat down their weapons.
Gentlemen, for shame, forbear this outrage!
Tybalt, Mercutio, the Prince expressly hath
Forbid this bandying in Verona streets.
85   Hold, Tybalt! Good Mercutio!

[*From under* ROMEO'S *arm,* TYBALT *thrusts*
MERCUTIO *and flees.*]

MERCUTIO

I am hurt.
A **plague** o' both your houses! I am sped. — hurt
Is he gone, and hath nothing? — is tybalt hurt/yes

BENVOLIO

What, art thou hurt?

MERCUTIO

90   Ay, ay, a scratch, a scratch; marry, 'tis enough.

[handwritten margin notes: "Tybalt Stabbed Mercutio" and "wounded"]

164   Romeo and Juliet

He draws his sword.

Tybalt, you ratcatcher, will you cross swords with me?

TYBALT
What do you want of me?

MERCUTIO
Good king of the cats, I want nothing of you except one of your
nine lives. That life I mean to take, and then, depending on
whether you treat me well or badly, I might only thrash your   75
other eight. Will you draw your sword from your scabbard? Hurry,
or my sword will beat your ears before yours is out.

TYBALT
I'm ready for you. *(Draws his sword.)*

ROMEO
Gentle Mercutio, put your sword away.

MERCUTIO
Come on, sir, give your forward thrust.   80

    They fight.

ROMEO
Draw your sword, Benvolio, beat down their weapons.
Gentlemen, this is shameful! Stop this!
Tybalt! Mercutio! The prince has specifically
forbidden fighting in the streets of Verona.
Stop, Tybalt! Please, Mercutio!   85

    ROMEO *reaches to stop them.* TYBALT *sweeps under* ROMEO'S
    arm, stabs MERCUTIO, *and runs away with the rest of his*
    followers.

MERCUTIO
I'm wounded!
A curse on both your houses! I'm mortally wounded.
Is he gone and without even a scrape?

BENVOLIO
Are you hurt?

MERCUTIO
It's just a scratch, a scratch, but it's enough.   90

Where is my page? Go, villain, fetch a surgeon.

[*Exit* PAGE.]

ROMEO

Courage, man; the hurt cannot be much.

MERCUTIO

No, 'tis not so deep as a well, nor so wide as a church
door; but 'tis enough, 'twill serve. Ask for me to-morrow,
95 and you shall find me a grave* man. I am pepper'd, I
warrant, for this world. A plague o' both your houses!
'Zounds, a dog, a rat, a mouse, a cat, to scratch a man to
death! A braggart, a rogue, a villain that fights by the book
of arithmetic! Why the devil came you between us? I was
100 hurt under your arm.

ROMEO

I thought all for the best.

MERCUTIO

Help me into some house, Benvolio,
Or I shall faint. A plague o' both your houses!
They have made worms' meat of me. I have it,
105 And soundly too. Your houses!

[*Exeunt* MERCUTIO *and* BENVOLIO.]

ROMEO

This gentleman, the Prince's near ally,
My very friend, hath got this mortal hurt
In my behalf; my reputation stain'd
With Tybalt's slander,—Tybalt, that an hour
110 Hath been my cousin! O sweet Juliet,
Thy beauty hath made me effeminate
And in my temper soft'ned valour's steel!

Re-enter BENVOLIO.

BENVOLIO

O Romeo, Romeo, brave Mercutio's dead!
That gallant spirit hath aspir'd the clouds,
115 Which too untimely here did scorn the earth.

---

95 *grave* Mercutio is making puns with his last breath. He means "grave" as in
"serious", and also ready for a burial grave.

Where's my page? Go, servant, get a doctor.

The PAGE *exits.*

ROMEO
Be brave, man. The wound cannot be deep.

MERCUTIO
No, it's not as deep as a well, or as wide as a church door.
But it's enough, it will serve. Ask for me tomorrow and you'll   95
find me a grave man. I'm done with this world. A curse on
both your houses! By God, a dog, a rat, a mouse, a cat—he
scratches a man to death! A braggart, a rascal, a villain
who fights according to the manuals. Why the devil did
you come between us? He stabbed me when you tried
to part us.   100

ROMEO
I thought I was doing the right thing.

MERCUTIO
Help me into a house, Benvolio,
or I'll faint. Damn both of your houses!
They have made a corpse of me. I've had it!
Damn your houses!   105

MERCUTIO *and* BENVOLIO *exit.*

ROMEO
Mercutio, the prince's cousin
and my true friend, has been mortally wounded
defending me—my reputation being slandered
by Tybalt's insults—from Tybalt who's been my
cousin for only an hour. Oh sweet Juliet,   110
your beauty has made me act like a woman
and weakened my courage!

BENVOLIO *re-enters.*

BENVOLIO
Oh Romeo, Romeo, brave Mercutio is dead!
His noble soul has climbed to the clouds.
He was too young to leave the earth.   115

ROMEO *Foreshadowing*

    This day's black fate on more days doth depend;
    This but begins the woe others must end. *something others*
                                            have to go through

BENVOLIO

    Here comes the furious Tybalt back again.

        Re-enter TYBALT.

ROMEO

    Alive, in triumph! And Mercutio slain!
120   Away to heaven, respective lenity,
    And fire-eyed fury be my conduct now!
    Now, Tybalt, take the "villain" back again
    That late thou gav'st me; for Mercutio's soul
    Is but a little way above our heads,
125   Staying for thine to keep him company.
    Either thou, or I, or both, must go with him.

TYBALT

    Thou, wretched boy, that didst consort him here,
    Shalt with him hence.

ROMEO

                  This shall determine that.

    [*They fight;* TYBALT *falls.*]

BENVOLIO

130   Romeo, away, be gone!
    The citizens are up, and Tybalt slain.
    Stand not amaz'd; the Prince will doom thee death
    If thou art taken. Hence, be gone, away!

ROMEO

    O, I am fortune's fool!
    bad decision
BENVOLIO

135   Why dost thou stay?

    [*Exit* ROMEO.]

    Enter CITIZENS.

A CITIZEN

    Which way ran he that kill'd Mercutio?
    Tybalt, that murderer, which way ran he?

ROMEO

This day's black fate casts a shadow on the future.
This is only the beginning of the sorrow to come.

BENVOLIO

Here comes the furious Tybalt back again.

> TYBALT *re-enters.*

ROMEO

So, you're living in victory and Mercutio is dead?
Leave thoughtful mercy to the angels—   120
fiery anger will lead me now.
Now, Tybalt, take back that insult
that you gave me just awhile ago. Mercutio's soul
is hovering just over our heads
waiting for your soul to keep him company.   125
Either you, or I, or both will soon join him.

TYBALT

You wretched boy, you who associated with him here,
will soon be near him again.

ROMEO

This fight will decide that!

> *They fight, and* TYBALT *falls.*

BENVOLIO

Romeo, run! Get away!   130
People are starting to gather, and Tybalt is dead!
Don't stand there in shock! The prince will sentence you to death
if you're captured. Go on, run!

ROMEO

I'm a victim of fate.

BENVOLIO

Why are you hanging around?   135

> ROMEO *exits.*

> CITIZENS *enter.*

CITIZEN

Which way did the man run who killed Mercutio?
Which way did that murderer Tybalt go?

BENVOLIO

There lies that Tybalt.

A CITIZEN

Up, sir, go with me;

140   I charge thee in the Prince's name, obey.

Enter PRINCE, MONTAGUE, CAPULET, *their* WIVES, *and all.*

PRINCE ESCALUS

Where are the vile beginners of this fray?

BENVOLIO

O noble Prince, I can discover all
The unlucky manage of this fatal brawl.
There lies the man, slain by young Romeo,

145   That slew thy kinsman, brave Mercutio.

LADY CAPULET   *forgets mercuto killed tybolt*

Tybalt, my cousin! O my brother's child!
O Prince! O cousin! Husband! O, the blood is spilt
Of my dear kinsman! Prince, as thou art true,
For blood of ours, shed blood of Montague.

150   O cousin, cousin!

PRINCE ESCALUS

Benvolio, who began this bloody fray?

BENVOLIO

Tybalt, here slain, whom Romeo's hand did slay!
Romeo that spoke him fair, bid him bethink
How nice the quarrel was, and urg'd withal   *— truthfully*

155   Your high displeasure; all this, uttered
With gentle breath, calm look, knees humbly bow'd,
Could not take truce with the unruly spleen
Of Tybalt deaf to peace, but that he tilts
With piercing steel at bold Mercutio's breast,

160   Who, all as hot, turns deadly point to point
And, with a **martial** scorn, with one hand beats
Cold death aside, and with the other sends
It back to Tybalt, whose **dexterity**
Retorts it. Romeo he cries aloud,

165   "Hold, friends! Friends, part!" and, swifter than his
tongue,

BENVOLIO
Tybalt is lying there.

CITIZEN
Come with me, sir.
I order you in the name of the Prince to obey.   140

> The PRINCE, MONTAGUE, CAPULET, *their wives, and others all*
> *enter.*

PRINCE
Where are the evil people who started this fight?

BENVOLIO
Oh noble Prince, I can reveal
the whole story of this fatal fight.
There lies the man that young Romeo killed.
Tybalt had earlier killed your cousin, Mercutio.   145

LADY CAPULET
Tybalt, my nephew! My brother's child!
Oh prince! Oh nephew! Husband! The blood
of my dear nephew has been shed. Prince, by your honor,
you must execute the Montague who did this!
My nephew! My nephew!   150

PRINCE
Benvolio, who started this fight?

BENVOLIO
Tybalt, who lies here dead, killed by Romeo.
Romeo spoke courteously and urged Tybalt to consider
how trivial their disagreement was, and he told Tybalt
it would rouse your anger. Romeo said all of this   155
with gentleness, calmness, and modesty.
But he could not make peace with hot-tempered
Tybalt, who was deaf to peace. Instead, Tybalt thrusts
his deadly sword at brave Mercutio's breast.
Mercutio, who is just as angry, turns his sword point to   160
    meet Tybalt's,
and with fighting scorn, he beats death away with one hand
and with the other hand, he thrusts
back at Tybalt, who skillfully
returns the thrust. Romeo cries out,
"Stop it, friends! Separate!" And faster than he can say it,   165

His agile arm beats down their fatal points
And 'twixt them rushes; underneath whose arm
An envious thrust from Tybalt hit the life
Of stout Mercutio, and then Tybalt fled;
170   But by and by comes back to Romeo,
Who had but newly entertain'd revenge,
And to 't they go like lightning, for, ere I
Could draw to part them, was stout Tybalt slain,
And, as he fell, did Romeo turn and fly.
175   This is the truth, or let Benvolio die.

LADY CAPULET
He is a kinsman to the Montague; —*Cant tell the truth*
Affection makes him false; he speaks not true.
Some twenty of them fought in this black strife,
And all those twenty could but kill one life.
180   I beg for justice, which thou, Prince, must give;
Romeo slew Tybalt, Romeo must not live.

PRINCE ESCALUS
Romeo slew him, he slew Mercutio;
Who now the price of his dear blood doth owe?

MONTAGUE
Not Romeo, Prince, he was Mercutio's friend;
185   His fault concludes but what the law should end,
The life of Tybalt.

PRINCE ESCALUS
                        And for that offence
Immediately we do exile him hence.
I have an interest in your hate's proceeding,
190   My blood for your rude brawls doth lie a-bleeding;
But I'll amerce you with so strong a fine
That you shall all repent the loss of mine.
I will be deaf to pleading and excuses;
Nor tears nor prayers shall purchase out abuses;
195   Therefore use none. Let Romeo hence in haste,
Else, when he's found, that hour is his last.
Bear hence this body and attend our will.
Mercy but murders, pardoning those that kill.

[*Exeunt.*]

Causing alot of issues

he beats down their weapons with his sword.
Romeo rushes to get between them, but Tybalt
maliciously ran his sword under Romeo's arm and stabbed
brave Mercutio. Then Tybalt fled,
but after a while, he returned to Romeo.   170
Romeo decided he would avenge Mercutio's death,
and as fast as lightning, they were fighting again. Before I
could separate them, brave Tybalt was killed,
and as he fell, Romeo turned and ran.
This is the truth, I swear to you on my life.   175

LADY CAPULET
He is related to the Montagues.
His bias makes him lie—he's not telling the truth.
There were twenty of them fighting in this quarrel,
and all twenty of them could only kill one man.
I beg for justice, which you, Prince, must give.   180
Romeo killed Tybalt; Romeo must not live!

PRINCE
Romeo killed him, but Tybalt killed Mercutio.
Who has to pay the price for Mercutio's death?

MONTAGUE
Not Romeo, Prince. He was Mercutio's friend.
His crime was doing what the law would have done—   185
he killed the murderer Tybalt.

PRINCE
For killing Tybalt,
I immediately exile Romeo.
I have a personal interest in this fight.
My relative Mercutio lies bleeding, thanks to your fight,   190
and I'm going to penalize you with such a heavy fine
that all of you will repent the loss of my cousin.
I'll be deaf to your pleading and excuses.
Neither your tears nor your prayers will buy forgiveness,
so don't even try to use them. Let Romeo leave quickly.   195
Otherwise, if he's found, he'll die within the hour.
Take Tybalt's body and obey my orders.
Mercy only encourages murders when killers are pardoned.

They exit.

ACT III, SCENE II

[Capulet's orchard.] Enter JULIET, *alone.*

JULIET

Gallop apace, you fiery-footed steeds,
Towards Phoebus' lodging; such a waggoner
As Phaeton* would whip you to the west,
And bring in cloudy night immediately.
5   Spread thy close curtain, love-performing night,
That runaways'* eyes may wink, and Romeo
Leap to these arms untalk'd of and unseen!
Lovers can see to do their amorous rites
By their own beauties; or, if love be blind,
10   It best agrees with night. Come, **civil** night,
Thou sober-suited matron, all in black,
And learn me how to lose a winning match,
Play'd for a pair of stainless maidenhoods.
Hood my unmann'd blood, bating in my cheeks,
15   With thy black mantle, till strange love grow bold,
Think true love acted simple modesty.
Come, night; come, Romeo; come, thou day in night;
For thou wilt lie upon the wings of night.
Whiter than new snow on a raven's back.
20   Come, gentle night, come, loving, black-brow'd night,
Give me my Romeo; and, when he shall die,
Take him and cut him out in little stars,
And he will make the face of heaven so fine
That all the world will be in love with night
25   And pay no worship to the **garish** sun.
O, I have bought the mansion of a love,
But not possess'd it, and, though I am sold,
Not yet enjoy'd. So tedious is this day
As is the night before some festival

---

3 *Phaeton* this character from Greek mythology was the son of Phoebus, the sun
god. Phaeton drove his father's chariot of the sun one day. He lost control of the
horses and was killed by Zeus in order to prevent the world's destruction.

6 *runaways'* The meaning of this word is uncertain. Among the interpretations
suggested by scholars are observers, horses (Phoebus' horses), the stars, Phaeton,
and Cupid.

ACT 3, SCENE 2

Capulet's orchard. JULIET *enters alone.*

JULIET
    Gallop quickly, you fiery-footed horses,
    to the sun god's house below the horizon. A driver
    like Phaeton would whip you toward the west,
    and bring night immediately.
    Spread your curtain, love-performing night,   5
    so watchers' eyes may close and Romeo can
    leap into my arms where no one can see and talk about us.
    Lovers can see to make love
    by the light of their own beauty. Or if love is blind,
    it best matches the night. Come, courteous night,   10
    you gravely-dressed woman all in black,
    and teach me how to lose a winning match
    in a game played by two virgins.
    Hide the wild blood fluttering in my cheeks
    with your black robe until unfamiliar love grows bold   15
    and believes that enjoying true love is really a modest act.
    Come, night! Come, Romeo! You're my light in the night.
    You will lie on the wings of night
    even whiter than freshly fallen snow on a raven's back.
    Come, gentle night! Come, loving, black-browed night.   20
    Give me my Romeo. And when he dies,
    take him and cut him out in little stars,
    and he'll make the face of heaven so fine
    that all the world will love the night
    and no longer admire the gaudy sun.   25
    Oh, I have a handsome husband,
    but I have not possessed him yet. Though I am his,
    I've not yet been enjoyed. This day is as long
    as the night before a holiday

30 To an impatient child that hath new robes
And may not wear them.

Enter NURSE, *with cords.*

O, here comes my nurse,
And she brings news; and every tongue that speaks
But Romeo's name speaks heavenly **eloquence**.
Now, nurse, what news? What hast thou there? The cords
35 That Romeo bid thee fetch?

NURSE

Ay, ay, the cords.

[*Throws them down.*]

JULIET
Ay me! What news? Why dost thou wring thy hands?

NURSE
Ah, well-a-day! He's dead, he's dead, he's dead!
We are undone, lady, we are undone!
40 Alack the day! He's gone, he's kill'd, he's dead!

JULIET
Can heaven be so envious?

NURSE
Romeo can,
Though heaven cannot. O Romeo, Romeo!
Who ever would have thought it? Romeo!

JULIET
45 What devil art thou, that dost torment me thus?
This torture should be roar'd in dismal hell.
Hath Romeo slain himself? Say thou but ay,
And that bare vowel "I"* shall poison more
Than the death-darting eye of cockatrice.*
50 I am not I, if there be such an ay;
Or those eyes shut, that makes thee answer ay.
If he be slain, say ay; or if not, no.

---

48 *"I"* (Ay) also Elizabethan for "yes"

49 *cockatrice* a mythical serpent that killed with a glance

to an impatient child who has new clothes   30
but cannot wear them yet.

> *The* NURSE *enters, with ropes. She sits down and wrings her*
> *hands.*

Oh, here comes my nurse.
And she brings news! Every tongue that says
just Romeo's name speaks with heavenly eloquence.
Nurse, what's the news? What do you have there? Are those the
    ropes
that Romeo told you to get?   35

NURSE
Yes, yes, the ropes.

> *She throws them down.*

JULIET
Dear me! What's the news? Why are you wringing your hands?

NURSE
Alas, he's dead, he's dead, he's dead!
We're ruined, lady, we're ruined!
Alas, he's gone, he's killed, he's dead!   40

JULIET
Can heaven be so jealous of me that she has to take him?

NURSE
Romeo can,
though heaven cannot. Oh Romeo, Romeo!
Who would have ever thought it? Romeo!

JULIET
What kind of devil are you that you torment me like this?   45
This torture should be announced in hell.
Has Romeo killed himself? If you say yes,
just the vowel "aye" will be more deadly
than a serpent's death-killing eye.
I'll no longer be an "I" if your answer is yes,   50
or if Romeo's closed eyes make you answer yes.
If Romeo has been killed, say yes. If he hasn't, say no.

Brief sounds determine of my weal or woe.

NURSE

I saw the wound, I saw it with mine eyes,—
55 God save the mark!—here on his manly breast.
A piteous corse, a bloody piteous corse!
Pale, pale as ashes, all bedaub'd in blood,
All in gore-blood; I swounded at the sight.

JULIET

O, break, my heart! Poor bankrupt, break at once!
60 To prison, eyes, ne'er look on liberty!
Vile earth, to earth resign; end motion here;
And thou and Romeo press one heavy bier!

NURSE

O Tybalt, Tybalt, the best friend I had!
O courteous Tybalt! Honest gentleman!
65 That ever I should live to see thee dead!

JULIET

What storm is this that blows so contrary?
Is Romeo slaught'red, and is Tybalt dead?
My dearest cousin, and my dearer lord?
Then, dreadful trumpet,* sound the general doom!
70 For who is living, if those two are gone?

NURSE

Tybalt is gone, and Romeo banished;
Romeo that kill'd him, he is banished.

JULIET

O God! Did Romeo's hand shed Tybalt's blood?

NURSE

It did, it did; alas the day, it did!

JULIET

75 O serpent heart, hid with a flow'ring face!
Did ever dragon keep so fair a cave?
Beautiful tyrant! Fiend angelical!
Dove-feather'd raven! Wolvish ravening lamb!
Despised substance of divinest show!

---

69 *dreadful trumpet* a reference to the religious belief that the sound of a trumpet
will announce Judgment Day, or the end of the world

One brief word will decide if I'm happy or sad.

NURSE

I saw the wound. I saw it with my eyes—
God forbid—here on his manly breast. *(Points.)* 55
A pitiful body! A bloody pitiful body!
He was pale, pale as ashes, and all covered in blood—
all in clotted blood. I fainted at the sight.

JULIET

Oh, break my heart! You are bankrupt! Break at once!
Go to prison, eyes; never look upon freedom! 60
My wretched body will return to earth. I'll end my life here
and Romeo and I can share one grave.

NURSE

Oh Tybalt, Tybalt, the best friend I had.
Oh courteous Tybalt! Honest gentleman!
I didn't think I'd ever live to see you dead. 65

JULIET

What kind of terrible storm is this?
Has Romeo been killed and is Tybalt dead, too?
My dearest cousin and my dearer husband?
Then, dreadful trumpet, announce the end of the world.
Who is living, if these two men are gone? 70

NURSE

Tybalt is dead, and Romeo is banished.
Romeo killed Tybalt, and he is banished.

JULIET

Oh God! Did Romeo kill Tybalt?

NURSE

He did! He did! Alas, he did!

JULIET

Oh, how can he hide such an evil heart with such a 75
    beautiful face?
Did ever an ugly dragon live in such a lovely place?
Beautiful tyrant! Devilish angel!
Dove-feathered raven! Wolf-killing lamb!
Vile creature that looks so beautiful—

80   Just opposite to what thou justly seem'st,
     A damned saint, an honourable villain!
     O nature, what hadst thou to do in hell,
     When thou didst bower the spirit of a fiend
     In mortal paradise of such sweet flesh?
85   Was ever book containing such vile matter
     So fairly bound? O, that deceit should dwell
     In such a gorgeous palace! *There are troubles in him*

NURSE
                              There's no trust,
     No faith, no honesty in men; all perjur'd,
90   All forsworn, all naught, all dissemblers.
     Ah, where's my man? Give me some *aqua vita;*
     These griefs, these woes, these sorrows make me old.
     Shame come to Romeo!

JULIET
                              Blister'd be thy tongue
95   For such a wish! He was not born to shame.
     Upon his brow shame is asham'd to sit;
     For 'tis a throne where honour may be crown'd
     Sole **monarch** of the universal earth.
     O, what a beast was I to chide at him!

NURSE
100 Will you speak well of him that kill'd your cousin?

She regrets, quick reverse in your feelings

JULIET
     Shall I speak ill of him that is my husband?
     Ah, poor my lord, what tongue shall smooth thy name,
     When I, thy three-hours wife, have mangled it?
     But, wherefore, villain, didst thou kill my cousin?
105 That villain cousin would have kill'd my husband.
     Back, foolish tears, back to your native spring;
     Your tributary drops belong to woe,
     Which you, mistaking, offer up to joy.
     My husband lives that Tybalt would have slain;
110 And Tybalt's dead that would have slain my husband.
     All this is comfort; wherefore weep I then?
     Some word there was, worser than Tybalt's death,
     That murd'red me; I would forget it fain;
     But, O, it presses to my memory

just opposite of what you seem. 80
A damned saint! An honorable villain!
Oh nature, what were you doing in hell
when you admitted the devil
into the sweet paradise of the Garden of Eden?
Was there ever such a vulgar book 85
bound with such a beautiful cover? Oh, that deceit should live
in such a gorgeous body!

NURSE

There's no trust,
no faith, no honesty in men. All men are liars,
all break their word, all are wicked, all are phonies. 90
Where's my servant? Get me a drink.
These griefs, these sorrows, these troubles make me old.
Shame on Romeo!

JULIET

I hope your tongue blisters
for saying such a thing! He was not born to feel shame. 95
Shame is ashamed to sit upon his head.
His head is a throne where honor may be crowned
king of the universe.
Oh, what a beast I was to speak against him.

NURSE

Will you speak well of the man who killed your cousin? 100

JULIET

Shall I speak poorly of the man who is my husband?
Alas, my poor husband, what tongue can clear your name
when I, your wife of three hours, have muddied it?
But why, villain, did you kill my cousin?
Because my villainous cousin would have killed my husband! 105
Get back, foolish tears, back to your native spring.
Tear drops are for sorrows,
which you mistakenly offer when I feel happy.
My husband lives whom Tybalt would have killed.
And Tybalt, who would have killed my husband, is dead. 110
This is comforting—why then am I crying?
There was a word, worse than Tybalt's death,
that murdered me. I wish I could forget it,
but it tries to make me remember

115 Like damned guilty deeds to sinners' minds:
     "Tybalt is dead, and Romeo—banished."   *worse*
     That "banished," that one word "banished,"   *the cousins being killed*
     Hath slain ten thousand Tybalts. Tybalt's death
     Was woe enough, if it had ended there;
120 Or, if sour woe delights in fellowship
     And needly will be rank'd with other griefs,
     Why follow'd not, when she said, "Tybalt's dead,"
     "Thy father," or "thy mother," nay, or both,
     Which modern lamentation might have mov'd?   *doesn't want whats worse*
125 But with a rear-ward following Tybalt's death,
     "Romeo is banished," to speak that word,
     Is father, mother, Tybalt, Romeo, Juliet,
     All slain, all dead. "Romeo is banished!"
     There is no end, no limit, measure, bound,
130 In that word's death; no words can that woe sound.
     Where is my father and my mother, Nurse?

NURSE
     Weeping and wailing over Tybalt's corse.
     Will you go to them? I will bring you thither.

JULIET
     Wash they his wounds with tears? Mine shall be spent,   *she wants to kill herself*
135 When theirs are dry, for Romeo's banishment.
     Take up those cords. Poor ropes, you are beguil'd,
     Both you and I, for Romeo is exil'd.
     He made you for a highway to my bed,
     But I, a maid, die maiden-widowed.
140 Come, cords, come, Nurse; I'll to my wedding-bed;
     And death, not Romeo, take my maidenhead!

NURSE
     Hie to your chamber. I'll find Romeo
     To comfort you; I wot well where he is.
     Hark ye, your Romeo will be here at night.
145 I'll to him; he is hid at Lawrence' cell.

JULIET
     O, find him! Give this ring to my true knight
     And bid him come to take his last farewell.

          [*Exeunt.*]

blinded by love

like damning guilty deeds coming to sinners' minds. 115
"Tybalt is dead, and Romeo—banished."
"Banished." That one word "banished"
equals the death of ten thousand Tybalts. Tybalt's death
was sad enough, if that was the end of the bad news.
Or if misery loves company 120
and must be accompanied by other griefs,
why didn't my nurse tell me after she said "Tybalt's dead"
that my father was dead, or my mother, or even both?
Such news would have brought ordinary grief.
But following news of Tybalt's death 125
came the news "Romeo is banished." To say that
is the same as saying father, mother, Tybalt, Romeo, and Juliet
are all killed, all dead! "Romeo is banished!"
There is no end, no limit, no meaning, no boundary
in that word. No words can describe that sorrow. 130
Where are my mother and father, nurse?

NURSE

They are crying and grieving over Tybalt's body.
Will you go to them? I'll take you.

JULIET

Are they washing his wounds with their tears? My tears will
be shed,
when theirs are dry, for Romeo's banishment. 135
Take away those ropes. Poor ropes, you are tricked—
both you and I, for Romeo is exiled.
He wanted you to be a highway to my bed,
but I, a virgin, will die a virgin-widow.
Come, ropes! Come, Nurse! I'll go to my wedding bed. 140
And death, not Romeo, will take my virginity!

NURSE

Hurry to your room! I'll find Romeo
to comfort you. I know where he is.
Listen to me, your Romeo will be here tonight.
I'll go find him. He's hiding at Friar Lawrence's cell. 145

JULIET

Oh, find him! Give this ring to my true knight
and tell him to come to say his last good-bye.

They exit.

Act 3, Scene 2   183

ACT III, SCENE III

[*Friar Lawrence's cell.*] *Enter* FRIAR LAWRENCE,
ROMEO [*following*].

FRIAR LAWRENCE

Romeo, come forth; come forth, thou fearful man:
Affliction is enamour'd of thy parts,
And thou art wedded to calamity.

ROMEO

Father, what news? What is the Prince's doom?
5   What sorrow craves acquaintance at my hand
That I yet know not?

FRIAR LAWRENCE

          Too familiar
Is my dear son with such sour company.
I bring thee tidings of the Prince's doom.

ROMEO

10   What less than dooms-day is the Prince's doom?

FRIAR LAWRENCE

A gentler judgment vanish'd from his lips,
Not body's death, but body's banishment.

ROMEO

Ha, banishment! Be merciful, say "death,"
For exile hath more terror in his look,
15 Much more than death. Do not say "banishment."

FRIAR LAWRENCE

Here from Verona art thou banished.
Be patient, for the world is broad and wide.

ROMEO

There is no world without Verona walls,
But purgatory, torture, hell itself.
20 Hence "banished" is banish'd from the world,
And world's exile is death; then "banished"
Is death mis-term'd. Calling death "banishment,"
Thou cut'st my head off with a golden axe,
And smil'st upon the stroke that murders me.

ACT 3, SCENE 3

Friar Lawrence's cell. Friar Lawrence enters.

FRIAR LAWRENCE
Romeo, come out! Come out, you fearful man!
Pain is in love with you,
and you are married to trouble.

> ROMEO *enters.*

ROMEO
What's the news, father? What is the Prince's sentence?
What sorrow am I going to learn about now   5
that I don't already know?

FRIAR LAWRENCE
You are too familiar
with unhappy things, my dear man.
I bring you news of the Prince's sentence.

ROMEO
What except death can the Prince's sentence be?   10

FRIAR LAWRENCE
He gave a more gentle sentence—
you'll not be executed, just banished.

ROMEO
Banishment! Be merciful! Say "death" instead.
Exile is worse than death,
much worse than death. Don't say "banishment!"   15

FRIAR LAWRENCE
You are banished from Verona.
Be patient. The world is broad and wide.

ROMEO
There's no world outside Verona!
There's only purgatory, torture, and hell itself!
To be banished from Verona is to be banished from the world, 20
and exile from the world is death! So to be banished
means death, in other words. By saying death is banishment,
you cut off my head with a golden axe, and smile upon my
    murder.

FRIAR LAWRENCE

25 O deadly sin! O rude unthankfulness!
Thy fault our law calls death; but the kind Prince,
Taking thy part, hath rush'd aside the law,
And turn'd that black word "death" to "banishment."
This is dear mercy, and thou sees it not.

ROMEO

30 'Tis torture, and not mercy. Heaven is here,
Where Juliet lives; and every cat and dog
And little mouse, every unworthy thing,
Live here in heaven and may look on her;
But Romeo may not. More validity,
35 More honourable state, more courtship lives
In carrion-flies than Romeo; they may seize
On the white wonder of dear Juliet's hand
And steal immortal blessing from her lips,
Who, even in pure and vestal modesty,
40 Still blush, as thinking their own kisses sin;
But Romeo may not; he is banished.
This may flies do, when I from this must fly;
They are free men, but I am banished:
And say'st thou yet that exile is not death?
45 Hadst thou no poison mix'd, no sharp-ground knife,
No sudden mean of death, though ne'er so mean,
But "banished" to kill me?—"Banished"?
O friar, the damned use that word in hell;
Howling attends it. How hast thou the heart,
50 Being a divine, a ghostly confessor,
A sin-absolver, and my friend profess'd,
To mangle me with that word "banished"?

FRIAR LAWRENCE
Thou fond mad man, hear me a little speak.

ROMEO
O, thou wilt speak again of banishment.

FRIAR LAWRENCE
55 I'll give thee armour to keep off that word;

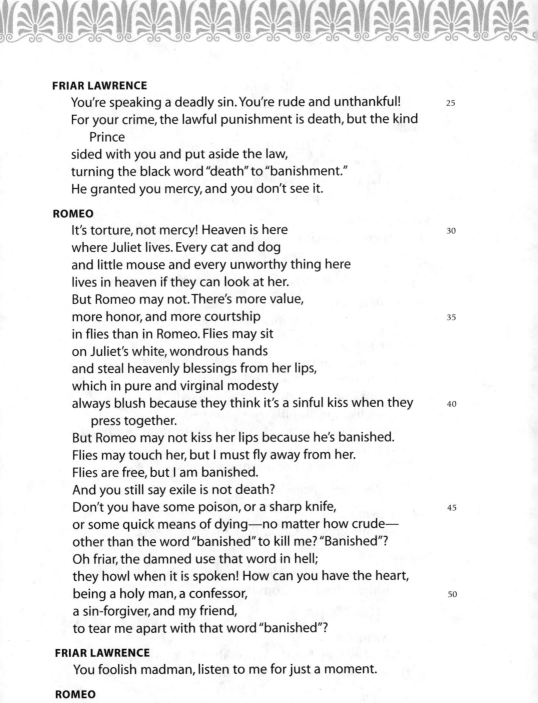

FRIAR LAWRENCE

You're speaking a deadly sin. You're rude and unthankful!   25
For your crime, the lawful punishment is death, but the kind
    Prince
sided with you and put aside the law,
turning the black word "death" to "banishment."
He granted you mercy, and you don't see it.

ROMEO

It's torture, not mercy! Heaven is here   30
where Juliet lives. Every cat and dog
and little mouse and every unworthy thing here
lives in heaven if they can look at her.
But Romeo may not. There's more value,
more honor, and more courtship   35
in flies than in Romeo. Flies may sit
on Juliet's white, wondrous hands
and steal heavenly blessings from her lips,
which in pure and virginal modesty
always blush because they think it's a sinful kiss when they   40
    press together.
But Romeo may not kiss her lips because he's banished.
Flies may touch her, but I must fly away from her.
Flies are free, but I am banished.
And you still say exile is not death?
Don't you have some poison, or a sharp knife,   45
or some quick means of dying—no matter how crude—
other than the word "banished" to kill me? "Banished"?
Oh friar, the damned use that word in hell;
they howl when it is spoken! How can you have the heart,
being a holy man, a confessor,   50
a sin-forgiver, and my friend,
to tear me apart with that word "banished"?

FRIAR LAWRENCE

You foolish madman, listen to me for just a moment.

ROMEO

No. You'll talk again of banishment.

FRIAR LAWRENCE

I'll give you some armor to shield you from that word.   55

Adversity's sweet milk, philosophy,
To comfort thee, though thou art banished.

ROMEO

Yet "banished"? Hang up philosophy!
Unless philosophy can make a Juliet,
60 Displant a town, reverse a prince's doom,
It helps not, it **prevails** not. Talk no more.

FRIAR LAWRENCE

O, then I see that madmen have no ears.

ROMEO

How should they, when that wise men have no eyes?

FRIAR LAWRENCE

Let me dispute with thee of thy estate.

ROMEO

65 Thou canst not speak of that thou dost not feel.
Wert thou as young as I, Juliet thy love,
An hour but married, Tybalt murdered,
Doting like me and like me banished,
Then mightst thou speak, then mightst thou tear thy hair,
70 And fall upon the ground as I do now,
Taking the measure of an unmade grave.

[*knocking within*]

FRIAR LAWRENCE

Arise; one knocks. Good Romeo, hide thyself.

ROMEO

Not I; unless the breath of heart-sick groans,
Mist-like enfold me from the search of eyes.

[*knocking*]

FRIAR LAWRENCE

75 Hark, how they knock! Who's there? Romeo, arise;
Thou wilt be taken.—Stay a while!—Stand up;

[*knocking*]

Run to my study.—By and by!—God's will,
What simpleness is this!—I come, I come!

I'll give you the sweet milk of philosophy
to comfort you, though you are banished.

ROMEO

You say "banished" again? Hang your philosophy—
unless philosophy can make a Juliet,
move Verona, or reverse the Prince's sentence,   60
it won't help, it will be useless. Don't say any more.

FRIAR LAWRENCE

Oh, I see, then, that madmen have no ears.

ROMEO

How can they, when wise men have no eyes?

FRIAR LAWRENCE

Let me discuss your situation with you—

ROMEO

You can't talk about something you can't feel.   65
If you were as young as I am, Juliet your lover,
married only an hour, Tybalt killed,
as deeply in love as I am, and banished like me,
then you could speak. Then you would tear your hair out!
Then you would fall upon the ground, as I do now, and   70
measure your unmade grave.

    There is a knock at the door.

FRIAR LAWRENCE

Get up, Romeo! Someone is knocking. Good Romeo, hide.

ROMEO

No, I won't—not unless the breath from my heartsick groans
wraps me in a mist to hide me from searching eyes.

    There is another knock.

FRIAR LAWRENCE

Listen, they're knocking again. Who's there? Romeo, get up!   75
You'll be arrested! *(to the knocker)* Just a minute! *(to* ROMEO*)*
  Get up!

    Knocking.

Run to my study! *(to the knocker)* I'm coming!

(to ROMEO*)* Why are you acting so foolishly? *(to the knocker)* I'm
  coming, I'm coming!

[knocking]

Who knocks so hard? Whence come you? What's your will?

Enter NURSE.

NURSE

80   Let me come in, and you shall know my errand.
I come from Lady Juliet.

FRIAR LAWRENCE

                        Welcome, then.

NURSE

O holy friar, O, tell me, holy friar,
Where is my lady's lord, where's Romeo?

FRIAR LAWRENCE

85   There on the ground, with his own tears made drunk.

NURSE

O, he is even in my mistress' case,
Just in her case! O woeful sympathy!
Piteous predicament! Even so lies she,
Blubb'ring and weeping, weeping and blubb'ring.

90   Stand up, stand up; stand, an you be a man.
For Juliet's sake, for her sake, rise and stand;
Why should you fall into so deep an O?

ROMEO

Nurse!

NURSE

Ah sir! Ah sir! Death's the end of all.

ROMEO

95   Spak'st thou of Juliet? How is it with her?
Doth not she think me an old murderer,
Now I have stain'd the childhood of our joy
With blood remov'd but little from her own?
Where is she? And how doth she? And what says

100   My conceal'd lady to our cancell'd love?

NURSE

O, she says nothing, sir, but weeps and weeps;
And now falls on her bed; and then starts up,

Knocking.

Who is knocking so hard? Where did you come from? What do you want?

The NURSE enters.

NURSE

Let me come in and I'll tell you what I want.   80
I come from Lady Juliet.

FRIAR LAWRENCE

Welcome, then.

NURSE

Oh, holy friar. Tell me, holy friar,
where's my lady's lord? Where's Romeo?

FRIAR LAWRENCE

He's lying there on the ground, drunk with his own tears.   85

NURSE

He's just like my mistress—
just like her! What a sorrowful echo of Juliet's grief!
It's a pitiful predicament. She lies just like him,
blubbering and crying, crying and blubbering.
Stand up, stand up! Stand if you're a man.   90
For Juliet's sake, for her sake, rise and stand.
Why should you fall into such a fit of grief?

ROMEO *(Rises.)*

Nurse!

NURSE

Alas, sir. Well, death ends everything.

ROMEO

Did you speak of Juliet? How is she?   95
Does she think I am a hardened murderer
now that I have stained the beginning of our joyful marriage
with the blood of her cousin?
Where is she? How is she? What does my
secretly married wife say about our cancelled marriage?   100

NURSE

She says nothing, sir. She just cries and cries
and falls on her bed. Then she gets up

And Tybalt calls; and then on Romeo cries,
And then down falls again.

ROMEO

105   As if that name,
Shot from the deadly level of a gun,
Did murder her, as that name's cursed hand
Murder'd her kinsman. O, tell me, friar, tell me,
In what vile part of this anatomy
110   Doth my name lodge? Tell me, that I may sack
The hateful mansion.

> [*He offers to stab himself, and the Nurse snatches the dagger away.*]

FRIAR LAWRENCE

                      Hold thy desperate hand!
Art thou a man? Thy form cries out thou art;
Thy tears are womanish; thy wild acts denote
115   The unreasonable fury of a beast.
Unseemly woman in a seeming man,
And ill-beseeming beast in seeming both,
Thou hast amaz'd me! By my holy order,
I thought thy disposition better temper'd.
120   Hast thou slain Tybalt? Wilt thou slay thyself,
And slay thy lady that in thy life lives,
By doing damned hate upon thyself?
Why rail'st thou on thy birth, the heaven, and earth?
Since birth, and heaven, and earth,* all three do meet
125   In thee at once, which thou at once wouldst lose.*
Fie, fie, thou sham'st thy shape, thy love, thy wit;
Which, like a **usurer**, abound'st in all,
And usest none in that true use indeed
Which should bedeck thy shape, thy love, thy wit.
130   Thy noble shape is but a form of wax,
Digressing from the valour of a man;
Thy dear love sworn but hollow perjury,
Killing that love which thou hast vow'd to cherish;
Thy wit, that ornament to shape and love,

---

124 *birth, and heaven, and earth* Romeo's family background, soul, and body

125 *at once wouldst lose* Since Friar Lawrence is Catholic, he believes that Romeo
would lose his soul as well as his earthly life if he committed suicide.

and calls Tybalt, and then she cries for Romeo,
and then she falls on her bed again.

ROMEO

It's just like my name   105
is a shot from a deadly gun
that murdered her, as my cursed hand
murdered her cousin. Oh, tell me, friar, tell me,
in what horrible part of my body
does my name lie? Tell me so I can destroy   110
that hateful part.

> ROMEO *tries to stab himself, but the* NURSE *snatches the dagger out of his hand.*

FRIAR LAWRENCE

Stop your desperate hand!
Are you a man? Your body says you are,
but your tears are womanish and your wild actions are like
the irrational actions of an animal.   115
You're like an undignified woman in the body of a man—
an odd animal in seeming to be both man and woman.
You amaze me! By my holy order,
I thought you had a more even-tempered disposition.
Have you killed Tybalt? Will you kill yourself?   120
And will you also kill the lady whose life is your life by killing
　　yourself?
Why are you ranting about your birth, the heavens, and earth?
Birth, heaven, and earth—all three—are joined
in you at the same time. Now you want to desert all of that at   125
　　once.
For shame! You shame your body, your love, and your
　　intelligence.
You're like a moneylender who has countless riches
and yet uses none of that wealth properly
to honor your body, love, and intelligence.
Your handsome body is just a wax model   130
without manly virtues.
The love you have sworn is just a lie
and kills the love which you have vowed to cherish.
Your intelligence, that complement to your body and love,

(margin annotation, left side: First tells him to have sex with her)

135　Mis-shapen in the conduct of them both,
　　Like powder in a skilless soldier's flask,
　　Is set a-fire by thine own ignorance,
　　And thou **dismember'd** with thine own defence.
　　What, rouse thee, man! Thy Juliet is alive,
140　For whose dear sake thou wast but lately dead:
　　There art thou happy. Tybalt would kill thee,
　　But thou slewest Tybalt: there art thou happy.
　　The law that threat'ned death becomes thy friend
　　And turns it to exile: there art thou happy.
145　A pack of blessings light upon thy back;
　　Happiness courts thee in her best array;
　　But, like a misbehav'd and sullen wench,
　　Thou pout'st upon thy fortune and thy love.
　　Take heed, take heed, for such die miserable.
150　Go, get thee to thy love, as was decreed;
　　Ascend her chamber; hence, and comfort her.
　　But look thou stay not till the watch be set,
　　For then thou canst not pass to Mantua,
　　Where thou shalt live till we can find a time
155　To blaze your marriage, **reconcile** your friends,
　　Beg pardon of the Prince, and call thee back
　　With twenty hundred thousand times more joy
　　Than thou went'st forth in lamentation.
　　Go before, Nurse; commend me to thy lady;
160　And bid her hasten all the house to bed,
　　Which heavy sorrow makes them apt unto.
　　Romeo is coming.

(margin annotation, right side: the law was nice to him, why is complaining when he can be dead)

(annotation: Go there)

(annotation below text: by sending Romeo away will make issues better)

NURSE
　　O Lord, I could have stay'd here all the night
　　To hear good counsel. O, what learning is!
165　My lord, I'll tell my lady you will come.

ROMEO
　　Do so, and bid my sweet prepare to chide.

　　　　[NURSE *offers to go in and turns again.*]

poorly directs both of those.   135
Your intelligence is like gunpowder in a novice soldier's
    powder horn—
lit by your own ignorance
and blowing you apart with your own weapon.
Wake up, man! Your Juliet is alive!
It was for her sake that you wanted to be dead just now.   140
You are fortunate. Tybalt wanted to kill you,
but you killed him. You are fortunate.
The law that threatened your death became your friend
and gave you exile. You are fortunate.
A pack of blessings has fallen on your back.   145
Happiness comes to you in her best clothes
but, like a badly behaved and sullen maid,
you frown at your good fortune and your love.
Listen to me, people like you die miserably.
Go, get to your love as your marriage decrees that you   150
    should do.
Climb to her room and comfort her.
But be sure you don't stay until the night guards come on duty,
for then you can't escape to Mantua—
where you will live until we can find a time
to announce your marriage, reconcile your friends,   155
ask the Prince's pardon, and bring you back home
with two million times more joy
than when you left in sorrow.
Go, Nurse. Give my regards to your lady,
and tell her to hurry everyone in the house to bed.   160
Their heavy grief will make them want to go to bed, anyway.
Tell her Romeo is coming.

NURSE

Oh Lord, I could have stayed here all night
to hear such good advice. Oh, learning is wonderful!
My lord, I'll tell my lady you'll come.   165

ROMEO

Do so, and bid my sweet lady to prepare to scold me.

   The NURSE *starts to leave but turns back.*

NURSE

Here, sir, a ring she bid me give you, sir.
Hie you, make haste, for it grows very late.

ROMEO

How well my comfort is reviv'd by this!

[*Exit* NURSE.]

FRIAR LAWRENCE

170 Go hence; good-night; and here stands all your state:
Either be gone before the watch be set,
Or by the break of day disguis'd from hence.
Sojourn in Mantua; I'll find out your man,
And he shall signify from time to time
175 Every good hap to you that chances here.
Give me thy hand; 'tis late. Farewell; good-night.

ROMEO

But that a joy past joy calls out on me,
It were a grief, so brief to part with thee.
Farewell.

[*Exeunt.*]

NURSE

Here's a ring she asked me to give you, sir.
Hurry! Make haste, for it's getting very late.

ROMEO

I'm greatly comforted by this ring.

The NURSE *exits.*

FRIAR LAWRENCE *(to* NURSE*)*

Go, good night. *(to* ROMEO*)* Here's your situation: 170
you must leave before the guards are posted at the gates,
or leave in a disguise at the break of day.
Stay in Mantua. I'll find your servant,
and he'll tell you from time to time
every good thing that occurs here.   175
Give me your hand. It's late. Farewell; good night.

ROMEO

If a joy to surpass all joys did not call me,
it would be sad to leave you so quickly.
Farewell!

They exit.

ACT III, SCENE IV

[*A room in Capulet's house.*] *Enter* CAPULET, LADY CAPULET, *and* PARIS.

CAPULET

Things have fallen out, sir, so unluckily
That we have had no time to move our daughter.
Look you, she lov'd her kinsman Tybalt dearly,
And so did I. Well, we were born to die.
5 'Tis very late, she'll not come down to-night;
I promise you, but for your company,
I would have been a-bed an hour ago.

PARIS

These times of woe afford no times to woo.
Madam, good-night; commend me to your daughter.

LADY CAPULET

10 I will, and know her mind early to-morrow;
To-night she's mewed up to her heaviness.

CAPULET

Sir Paris, I will make a desperate tender
Of my child's love. I think she will be rul'd
In all respects by me; nay, more, I doubt it not.
15 Wife, go you to her ere you go to bed;
Acquaint her here of my son Paris' love;
And bid her—mark you me?—on Wednesday next—
But, soft! What day is this?

PARIS

                         Monday, my lord.

CAPULET

20 Monday! Ha, ha! Well, Wednesday is too soon,
O' Thursday let it be,—o' Thursday, tell her,
She shall be married to this noble earl.
Will you be ready? Do you like this haste?
We'll keep no great ado,—a friend or two;
25 For, hark you, Tybalt being slain so late,
It may be thought we held him carelessly,

ACT 3, SCENE 4

A room in Capulet's house. CAPULET, LADY CAPULET, *and* PARIS *enter.*

CAPULET
Because of recent unhappy events,
we've had no time to talk to our daughter.
You see, she loved her cousin Tybalt dearly,
and so did I. Well, we're all born to die.
It's very late; she won't come down tonight.   5
I assure you, if you had not been here,
I would have been in bed an hour ago.

PARIS
This time of sorrow is not the time to court her.
Madam, good night. Give my regards to your daughter.

LADY CAPULET
I will. And I'll find out what she thinks, tomorrow.   10
Tonight, she's shut up in her room with her grief.

CAPULET
Sir, I'll make a rash offer
of my daughter's love. I think she'll obey me
in everything. No, I don't doubt that she'll listen to me.
Wife, go to her before you go to bed   15
and tell her of Paris' love.
Also tell her—are you listening to me?—that next Wednesday—
Wait! What day is this?

PARIS
Monday, my lord.

CAPULET
Monday! *(laughs)* Well, then Wednesday is too soon.   20
Let it be on Thursday! *(to* LADY CAPULET*)* Tell her that on Thursday
she shall be married to this noble earl.
(to PARIS*)* Can you be ready? How do these speedy arrangements
strike you?
We won't have a big wedding—just a friend or two.
For really, since Tybalt was killed so recently,   25
it could be thought that we didn't care much for him,

Being our kinsman, if we revel much;
Therefore we'll have some half a dozen friends,
And there an end. But what say you to Thursday?

PARIS

30   My lord, I would that Thursday were to-morrow.

CAPULET

Well, get you gone; o' Thursday be it, then.
Go you to Juliet ere you go to bed;
Prepare her, wife, against this wedding-day.
Farewell, my lord. Light to my chamber, ho!
35   Afore me! It is so very late that we
May call it early by and by. Good-night.

[*Exeunt.*]

one of our relatives, if we celebrated too much.
Therefore, we'll invite just a half a dozen friends,
and that will be all. How is Thursday for you, Paris?

PARIS

My lord, I wish Thursday were tomorrow.   30

CAPULET

Well, go now. It will be on Thursday, then. *(to
his wife)* Go to Juliet before you go to bed.
and prepare her for her wedding day. *(to* PARIS*)*
Good-bye, my lord. *(to* SERVANTS*)* Give me a light to my
     bedroom.
By heaven, it's so late,   35
we'll soon have to call it early. Good night.

     They exit.

ACT III, SCENE V

[Capulet's orchard.] Enter ROMEO *and* JULIET, *aloft.*

JULIET
Wilt thou be gone? It is not yet near day.
It was the nightingale, and not the lark,
That pierc'd the fearful hollow of thine ear;
Nightly she sings on yond pomegranate-tree.
5   Believe me, love, it was the nightingale.

ROMEO
It was the lark, the herald of the morn,
No nightingale. Look, love, what envious streaks
Do lace the severing clouds in yonder east.
Night's candles are burnt out, and **jocund** day
10   Stands tiptoe on the misty mountain tops.
I must be gone and live, or stay and die.

JULIET
Yond light is not day-light, I know it, I;
It is some meteor that the sun exhales
To be to thee this night a torch-bearer
15   And light thee on thy way to Mantua;
Therefore stay yet; thou need'st not to be gone.

ROMEO
Let me be ta'en, let me be put to death;
I am content, so thou wilt have it so.
I'll say yon grey is not the morning's eye,
20   'Tis but the pale reflex of Cynthia's brow;
Nor that is not the lark, whose notes do beat
The vaulty heaven so high above our heads.
I have more care to stay than will to go.
Come, death, and welcome! Juliet wills it so.
25   How is't, my soul? Let's talk; it is not day.

JULIET
It is, it is! Hie hence, be gone, away!
It is the lark that sings so out of tune,
Straining harsh discords and unpleasing sharps.
Some say the lark makes sweet division;
30   This doth not so, for she divideth us.

ACT 3, SCENE 5

Capulet's house. ROMEO and JULIET enter on the balcony.

JULIET

    Do you have to go? It isn't day yet.
    It was the nightingale, not the lark,
    that sang in your apprehensive ear.
    She sings every night on the pomegranate tree.
    Believe me, love, it was the nightingale.   5

ROMEO

    It was the lark, the herald of the morning,
    not a nightingale. Look, love, see the envious streaks
    of light that lace the scattering clouds in the east.
    The stars are fading and cheerful day
    stands on tiptoe on the foggy mountaintops.   10
    If I want to live, I must go. If I stay, I will die.

JULIET

    That light is not daylight. I know it.
    It's just a meteor from the sun,
    which will be your torchbearer
    tonight and light your road to Mantua.   15
    Therefore, stay awhile; you don't need to go yet.

ROMEO

    Let them capture me, let them put me to death.
    I'm content if you are satisfied.
    I'll say that the grey I see in the sky isn't morning
    but just a pale reflection of the moon.   20
    It's not the lark I hear singing whose song rises to
    the heavens high above our heads.
    I have more desire to stay than will to go.
    Come, death! Welcome! Juliet wills it.
    How are you, my soul? Let's talk; it's not day.   25

JULIET

    It is! It is! Hurry, go, away!
    It's the lark that sings so out of tune,
    emitting harsh, sour notes and unpleasant sharps.
    Some people say the lark sings a sweet melody,
    but this bird does not because she separates us.   30

Some say the lark and loathed toad change eyes;
O, now I would they had chang'd voices too,
Since arm from arm that voice doth us affray,
Hunting thee hence with hunt's-up to the day.
35 O, now be gone; more light and light it grows.

ROMEO
More light and light; more dark and dark our woes!

Enter NURSE [*from the chamber*].

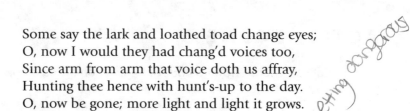

NURSE
Madam!

JULIET
Nurse?

NURSE
Your lady mother is coming to your chamber.
40 The day is broke; be wary, look about.

[*Exit.*]

JULIET
Then, window, let day in, and let life out.

ROMEO
Farewell, farewell! One kiss, and I'll descend.

[*They kiss, and* ROMEO *descends.*]

JULIET
Art thou gone so? Love, lord, ay, husband, friend!
I must hear from thee every day in the hour,
45 For in a minute there are many days.
O, by this count I shall be much in years
Ere I again behold my Romeo!

ROMEO
[*from below*] Farewell!
I will omit no opportunity
50 That may convey my greetings, love, to thee.

JULIET
O, think'st thou we shall ever meet again?

Some people say the lark and the hated toad exchanged eyes.
I wish they'd exchanged voices, too,
since that voice frightens us out of each other's arms
and chases you from here with the song that awakens hunters.
Oh, go now! It grows lighter and lighter. 35

ROMEO
Lighter and lighter means our sorrow grows darker and darker.

The NURSE *enters from the bedroom.*

NURSE
Madam!

JULIET
Nurse?

NURSE
Your mother is coming to your bedroom.
Day is dawning. Be careful; watch out. 40

She exits.

JULIET
Then, window, let day in, and let my life out.

ROMEO
Good-bye, good-bye! One kiss, and I'll descend.

He climbs down.

JULIET
Are you gone? My love, my lord, my husband, and my friend?
I must hear from you every hour of the day,
for just one minute will be like many days. 45
If I count this way, I'll be very old
before I see Romeo again.

ROMEO *(from below)*
Good-bye!
I'll not miss a chance
to send my greetings to you, love. 50

JULIET
Do you think we'll ever meet again?

ROMEO

I doubt it not; and all these woes shall serve
For sweet discourses in our times to come.

JULIET

O God, I have an ill-divining soul!
55 Methinks I see thee, now thou art below,
As one dead in the bottom of a tomb.
Either my eyesight fails, or thou look'st pale.

ROMEO

And trust me, love, in my eye so do you;
Dry sorrow* drinks our blood. Adieu, adieu!

JULIET

60 O Fortune, Fortune! All men call thee fickle;
If thou art fickle, what dost thou with him
That is **renown'd** for faith? Be fickle, Fortune;
For then, I hope, thou wilt not keep him long,
But send him back.

Enter LADY CAPULET.

LADY CAPULET

65   Ho, daughter! Are you up?

JULIET

Who is't that calls? It is my lady mother.
Is she not down so late, or up so early?
What unaccustom'd cause procures her hither?

LADY CAPULET

Why, how now, Juliet?

JULIET

70   Madam, I am not well.

LADY CAPULET

Evermore weeping for your cousin's death?
What, wilt thou wash him from his grave with tears?
An if thou couldst, thou couldst not make him live;
Therefore, have done. Some grief shows much of love,
75 But much of grief shows still some want of wit.

---

59 *dry sorrow* Sorrow was believed to dry up blood and other body fluids.

ROMEO

I'm sure we will. Then all of these sorrows will serve
as sweet conversation in the future.

JULIET

Oh God, I have a feeling of doom!
I think I see you, as you are now,   55
but like a dead person in the bottom of a tomb.
Either my eyesight is failing or you look pale.

ROMEO

Trust me, love. In my eyes, you look pale, too.
Our sorrow makes us pale. Good-bye, good-bye!

JULIET

Oh, Fate. Fate! All men call you fickle!   60
If you're fickle, what business can you have with him
who is known for his faith? Be fickle, Fate.
Then you will not keep him long,
and you'll send him back to me.

              LADY CAPULET *enters.*

LADY CAPULET

Daughter, are you up?   65

JULIET

Who's calling? It's my mother.
Is she up late or up early?
What unusual occurrence brings her here?

LADY CAPULET

How are you, Juliet?

JULIET

Madam, I'm not well.   70

LADY CAPULET

Are you still crying for your cousin's death?
Will your tears wash him out of his grave?
Even if they did, you couldn't make him live.
So quit crying. Some grief reveals deep love,
but too much grief reveals a lack of intelligence.   75

JULIET
Yet let me weep for such a feeling loss.

LADY CAPULET
So shall you feel the loss, but not the friend
Which you weep for.

JULIET
Feeling so the loss,
80   I cannot choose but ever weep the friend.

LADY CAPULET
Well, girl, thou weep'st not so much for his death,
As that the villain lives which slaughter'd him.

JULIET
What villain, madam?

LADY CAPULET
That same villain, Romeo.

JULIET
85   [aside] Villain and he be many miles asunder.—
God pardon him! I do, with all my heart;
And yet no man like he doth grieve my heart.

LADY CAPULET
That is because the traitor murderer lives.

JULIET
Ay, madam, from the reach of these my hands.
90   Would none but I might venge my cousin's death!

LADY CAPULET
We will have vengeance for it, fear thou not;
Then weep no more. I'll send to one in Mantua,
Where that same banish'd runagate doth live,
Shall give him such an unaccustom'd dram
95   That he shall soon keep Tybalt company;
And then, I hope, thou wilt be satisfied.

JULIET
Indeed, I never* shall be satisfied

97-106 *never* . . . Juliet uses double meanings in this speech. She is seconding her
mother's opinion that Romeo should be punished and expressing her devotion
to her lover at the same time.

JULIET
Let me cry over such a deeply felt loss.

LADY CAPULET
Then you'll feel the loss,
but not the friend for whom you weep.

JULIET
Since I feel the loss,
I can't help crying for my friend.   80

LADY CAPULET
Well, girl, you're really not crying for his death,
but for the fact that the villain who killed him still lives.

JULIET
What villain, madam?

LADY CAPULET
The villain Romeo.

JULIET *(to herself)*
There is a big difference between Romeo and a villain.   85
(to LADY CAPULET*)* God forgive him! I forgive him with all my
    heart.
And yet no man grieves my heart more than Romeo.

LADY CAPULET
That's because that traitor and murderer still lives.

JULIET
I wish that only my hands
could avenge my cousin's death.   90

LADY CAPULET
We'll have revenge for his death, don't you fear.
So don't cry anymore. I'll send a message to someone in Mantua
where that banished renegade lives,
and he'll give Romeo so much poison
that he'll soon keep Tybalt company in the grave.   95
Then I hope you'll be satisfied.

JULIET
I'll never be satisfied

With Romeo, till I behold him—dead—
Is my poor heart, so for a kinsman vex'd.
100 Madam, if you could find out but a man
To bear a poison, I would temper it
That Romeo should, upon receipt thereof,
Soon sleep in quiet. O, how my heart abhors
To hear him nam'd, and cannot come to him
105 To wreak the love I bore my cousin Tybalt
Upon his body that hath slaughter'd him!

LADY CAPULET — *wants romeos death*
Find thou the means, and I'll find such a man.
But now I'll tell thee joyful tidings, girl.

JULIET
And joy comes well in such a needy time.
110 What are they, I beseech your ladyship?

LADY CAPULET
Well, well, thou hast a careful father, child;
One who, to put thee from thy heaviness,
Hath sorted out a sudden day of joy
That thou expects not nor I look'd not for.

JULIET
115 Madam, in happy time, what day is that?

LADY CAPULET
Marry, my child, early next Thursday morn
The gallant, young, and noble gentleman,
The County Paris, at Saint Peter's Church, *there gonna get married*
Shall happily make thee there a joyful bride.

JULIET
120 Now, by Saint Peter's Church and Peter too,
He shall not make me there a joyful bride.
I wonder at this haste that I must wed
Ere he that should be husband comes to woo.
I pray you, tell my lord and father, madam,
125 I will not marry yet; and when I do, I swear,
It shall be Romeo, whom you know I hate,
Rather than Paris. These are news indeed!

with Romeo until I see him—dead—
is my poor heart, so upset am I about my cousin's death.
Madam, if you could find a man   100
to take the poison, I would mix it with my own hands so that
as soon as Romeo gets it,
he'll sleep quietly. Oh, how my heart hates
to hear his name and not be able to come to him
to pour the love I bore for Tybalt   105
upon the body of the man who killed him.

LADY CAPULET
You find the poison, and I'll find the poisoner.
But now I'll tell you some joyful news, girl.

JULIET
Joy would be very welcome right now.
What's your news? I beg, your ladyship, tell me.   110

LADY CAPULET
Well, you have a thoughtful father, child.
To help you get over your grief,
he's set a day of joy in the near future
which you did not expect and I did not anticipate.

JULIET
Madam, how fortunate! What day is that?   115

LADY CAPULET
My child, early next Thursday morning,
the brave, young, and noble gentleman,
Count Paris, will make you
a joyful bride at St. Peter's church.

JULIET
By St. Peter's church and St. Peter, too,   120
he won't make me a joyful bride!
I don't understand what's all the rush to force me to marry
my future husband before he even comes to court me.
I beg you, tell my lord and father, madam,
that I'll not marry yet. And when I do get married,   125
it will be to Romeo, whom you know I hate,
rather than to Paris. Now that's a real piece of news!

LADY CAPULET

Here comes your father; tell him so yourself,
And see how he will take it at your hands.

Enter CAPULET *and* NURSE.

CAPULET

130   When the sun sets, the air doth drizzle dew;
But for the sunset of my brother's son
It rains downright.
How now! A conduit, girl? What, still in tears?
Evermore show'ring? In one little body
135   Thou counterfeits a bark, a sea, a wind:
For still thy eyes, which I may call the sea,
Do ebb and flow with tears; the bark thy body is,
Sailing in this salt flood; the winds, thy sighs,
Who, raging with thy tears, and they with them,
140   Without a sudden calm, will overset
Thy tempest-tossed body. How now, wife!
Have you delivered to her our decree?

LADY CAPULET

Ay, sir; but she will none, she gives you thanks.
I would the fool were married to her grave!

CAPULET

145   Soft! Take me with you, take me with you, wife.
How! Will she none? Doth she not give us thanks?
Is she not proud? Doth she not count her blest,
Unworthy as she is, that we have wrought
So worthy a gentleman to be her bride?

JULIET

150   Not proud you have; but thankful that you have.
Proud can I never be of what I hate;
But thankful even for hate that is meant love.

CAPULET

How, how, how, how? Chopped-logic? What is this?
"Proud," and "I thank you," and "I thank you not";

LADY CAPULET

Here comes your father. Tell him yourself,
and see how well he'll take this news from you.

CAPULET *and* NURSE *enter.*

CAPULET

When the sun sets, the air drizzles dew,   130
but the sunset for my brother's son,
is downright rainy.
What's going on? Are you a water pipe, girl? Are you still in
    tears?
Are you always crying? In your one little body,
you imitate a ship, a sea, and a wind.   135
Your eyes, which I might call a sea,
are always ebbing and flowing with tears. The ship is your
body sailing on this salty flood of tears. The winds are your
    sighs,
raging with your tears and your tears raging with those sighs.
If we don't have a sudden calm, the storm will overturn   140
your storm-tossed body. Well, wife?
Have you told her about my decision?

LADY CAPULET

Yes, sir, but she says she won't marry Paris, but thanks you
    anyway.
I wish this fool were married to her grave.

CAPULET

Wait a moment! Let me understand you, wife.   145
What do you mean? She won't? Didn't she thank us?
Isn't she proud? Doesn't she count herself lucky,
unworthy as she is, that we've arranged for
so worthy a gentleman to marry her?

JULIET

I'm not very pleased, but I'm thankful.   150
I can never be proud of what I hate,
but I'm thankful even for something hateful that is meant to
    be a gift of love.

CAPULET

Are you splitting hairs? What is this?
"Proud"? "I thank you"? "I thank you not"

155 And yet "not proud." Mistress minion, you,
Thank me no thankings, nor proud me no prouds,
But fettle your fine joints 'gainst Thursday next,
To go with Paris to Saint Peter's Church,
Or I will drag thee on a hurdle* thither.

160 Out, you green-sickness carrion! Out, you baggage!
You tallow-face!

being a brat

LADY CAPULET

Fie, fie! What, are you mad?

JULIET

Good father, I beseech you on my knees,
Hear me with patience but to speak a word.

CAPULET

165 Hang thee, young baggage! Disobedient wretch!
I tell thee what: get thee to church o' Thursday,
Or never after look me in the face.
Speak not, reply not, do not answer me!
My fingers itch. Wife, we scarce thought us blest

170 That God had lent us but this only child;
But now I see this one is one too much,
And that we have a curse in having her.
Out on her, hilding!

NURSE

God in heaven bless her!

175 You are to blame, my lord, to rate her so.

CAPULET

And why, my lady Wisdom? Hold your tongue,
Good prudence; smatter with your gossips, go.

NURSE

I speak no treason.

CAPULET

O, God ye god-den.

---

159 *hurdle* a sledge or a heavy cart upon which criminals were dragged off to
execution

and "not very pleased"? You spoiled child!   155
Don't thank me with "no thank you" or give me any "not
    prouds."
Just prepare your fine self to be ready next Thursday
to marry Paris at St. Peter's church!
If you don't, I'll drag you there on a cart.
Get out you, you anemic thing! Out, you minx!   160
You waxy-faced girl!

LADY CAPULET

Are you crazy?

JULIET

Good father, I beg you on my knees. *(She kneels.)*
Listen to me with patience. Just let me speak one word.

CAPULET

Hang you, you minx! You disobedient wretch!   165
I'll tell you now: Go to the church on Thursday,
or never look on my face again.
Don't speak, don't reply, don't answer me!
My fingers itch (to hit you). Wife, we really did think we had been
    blessed
when God gave us just this one child.   170
But now I think this one is too much
and that we have been cursed by having her.
Out with her, the wretch!

NURSE

God in heaven bless her!
You're to blame for speaking to her so horribly.   175

CAPULET

What, my Lady Wisdom? Shut your mouth,
Miss Prudence! Go gossip with your old cronies.

NURSE

I'm not speaking treason.

CAPULET

Oh, for God's sake!

NURSE

180   May not one speak?

CAPULET

                       Peace, you mumbling fool!
Utter your gravity o'er a gossip's bowl;
For here we need it not.

LADY CAPULET

                       You are too hot.

CAPULET

185   God's bread! It makes me mad.
Day, night, hour, tide, time, work, play,
Alone, in company, still my care hath been
To have her match'd; and having now provided
A gentleman of noble parentage,
190   Of fair demesnes, youthful and nobly train'd,
Stuff'd, as they say, with honourable parts,
Proportion'd as one's thought would wish a man;
And then to have a wretched puling fool,
A whining mammet, in her fortune's tender
195   To answer, "I'll not wed; I cannot love,
I am too young; I pray you, pardon me."
But, an you will not wed, I'll pardon you.
Graze where you will, you shall not house with me.
Look to 't, think on 't, I do not use to jest.
200   Thursday is near; lay hand on heart, advise.
An you be mine, I'll give you to my friend;
An you be not, hang, beg, starve, die in the streets,
For, by my soul, I'll ne'er acknowledge thee,
Nor what is mine shall never do thee good.
205   Trust to 't, bethink you; I'll not be forsworn.

        [Exit.]

JULIET

    Is there no pity sitting in the clouds,
That sees into the bottom of my grief?
O, sweet my mother, cast me not away!

NURSE

Isn't a person allowed to speak? 180

CAPULET

Quiet, you mumbling fool.
Save your wisdom for the gossipers, for we don't need it here.

LADY CAPULET

You're too angry.

CAPULET

By God's sacrament! It makes me so mad! 185
Day and night, early and late, at work or relaxing,
alone or with others, my one thought has been
to make her a good match. And now I've provided
for you a gentleman from noble parents,
of beautiful estates, youthful and well-trained, 190
full of honor, and as handsome and well-built
as any girl could wish a man to be.
And then to have a wretched, whining fool,
a crying doll, who when offered good fortune,
says, "I won't marry him. I can't love him. 195
I'm too young. I beg you to excuse me."
If you don't marry, I'll "excuse" you to find another home.
Go where you want to—you won't live here.
Take care! Think about it! I'm not one to joke.
Thursday isn't far away. Think about it carefully. 200
If you're my daughter, I'll be giving your hand in marriage
    to my friend.
If you don't marry, you can hang, beg, starve, and die in the
    streets,
for I swear, I'll never recognize you
as my daughter again.
And I'll never give you anything.
Count on that! Think about it. I won't go back on my word. 205

He exits.

JULIET

Is there no pity in heaven
that can understand my grief?
Oh, sweet mother, don't disown me!

Delay this marriage for a month, a week;
210 Or, if you do not, make the bridal bed
In that dim monument where Tybalt lies.

LADY CAPULET

Talk not to me, for I'll not speak a word.
Do as thou wilt, for I have done with thee.

[*Exit.*]

JULIET

Oh God!—O Nurse, how shall this be prevented?
215 My husband is on earth, my faith in heaven;
How shall that faith return again to earth,
Unless that husband send it me from heaven
By leaving earth? Comfort me, counsel me!
Alack, alack, that heaven should practise stratagems
220 Upon so soft a subject as myself!
What say'st thou? Hast thou not a word of joy?
Some comfort, Nurse.

NURSE

                    Faith, here it is.
Romeo is banish'd; and all the world to nothing
225 That he dares ne'er come back to challenge you;
Or, if he do, it needs must be by stealth.
Then, since the case so stands as now it doth,
I think it best you married with the County.
O, he's a lovely gentleman!
230 Romeo's a dishclout to him. An eagle, madam,
Hath not so green, so quick, so fair an eye
As Paris hath. Beshrew my very heart,
I think you are happy in this second match,
For it excels your first; or if it did not,
235 Your first is dead; or 'twere as good as he were
As living here and you no use of him.

JULIET

Speak'st thou from thy heart?

Put off this wedding for a month—a week.
Or if you don't, make my bridal bed   210
in the tomb where Tybalt lies.

LADY CAPULET
Don't talk to me. I won't say a word.
Do as you want to. I'm done with you.

JULIET
Oh God! Nurse, how shall this marriage be prevented?
My husband is on earth. My marriage vow to him was   215
      made in heaven.
How can my heavenly vow be broken
unless my husband's death
makes me a widow? Comfort me, advise me.
Oh God, that heaven should use such tricks
on a person as weak as I am.   220
What do you say? Don't you have a word of comfort?
Give me some comfort, Nurse.

NURSE
Indeed, here it is.
Romeo is banished and I think it's safe to say
that he'll never dare to come back and claim you as his wife. 225
If he does, he'll have to come in secret.
So as the situation now stands,
I think you should marry Count Paris.
Oh, he's a lovely gentleman!
Romeo is a dishrag compared with him. An eagle, madam,   230
doesn't have as green, as quick, or as beautiful an eye
as Paris has. Curse my own heart,
but I think you'll be happy marrying Paris,
for he's better than Romeo. Even if Paris weren't as good as
      Romeo,
your first husband is dead—it comes to the same thing   235
as Romeo still being among the living and you being
      separated from him.

JULIET
Are you speaking from your heart?

NURSE

And from my soul too; else beshrew them both.

JULIET

Amen!

NURSE

240   What?

JULIET

Well, thou hast comforted me marvelous much.
Go in; and tell my lady I am gone,
Having displeas'd my father, to Lawrence' cell,
To make confession and to be absolv'd.

She's leaving and wants to go to Romeo

NURSE

245   Marry, I will; and this is wisely done.

     [*Exit.*]

JULIET

Ancient damnation! O most wicked fiend!
Is it more sin to wish me thus forsworn,
Or to dispraise my lord with that same tongue
Which she hath prais'd him with above compare
250   So many thousand times? Go, counselor;
Thou and my bosom henceforth shall be twain.
I'll to the friar, to know his remedy;
If all else fail, myself have power to die.

     [*Exit.*]

if what happens doesn't happen she will kill herself

NURSE

And from my soul, too. Otherwise, may both be damned.

JULIET

Amen!

NURSE

What? 240

JULIET

Well, you've really comforted me.
Go in and tell my mother I've gone
to Friar Lawrence's cell to confess
and be absolved for having displeased my father.

NURSE

Certainly, I will. Now you're acting wisely. 245

She exits.

JULIET

Damnable old woman! Most wicked devil!
Is it more sinful to wish me to break my vow,
or to condemn my husband with the same tongue
with which she has praised him as above compare
so many times? Go, my adviser! 250
You and my real feelings are separated now forever.
I'll go to the friar and get his advice.
If everything else fails, I'll commit suicide.

She exits.

Act III Review

Discussion Questions

1. Why does Romeo first refuse to fight with Tybalt?

2. Who do you think is to blame for the fight between Mercutio and Tybalt?

3. Explain why Romeo chooses to fight Tybalt after all. In your opinion, was he justified in killing Tybalt? Discuss why or why not.

4. The Nurse advises Juliet to forget about Romeo and marry Paris. Does this advice surprise you? Explain.

5. Compare Juliet's soliloquy of Act II, Scene v, lines 1–19 with her soliloquy of Act III, Scene ii, lines 1–35.

6. Review the Friar's plan in Scene iii. List each step of the plan in the left column of a chart like the one below. Next to each step, write things that could go wrong.

Plan	Things that could go wrong

7. What, if anything, prevents Juliet from simply joining Romeo in Mantua?

8. What occurs in Scene v to alienate Juliet from her family?

Literary Elements

1. A **theme** is the underlying meaning or message of a work of literature. How does Mercutio's speech in Act III ("a plague o' both your houses") reflect one of the major themes of the play?

2. An **oxymoron** occurs when contradictory words are paired. Find examples of oxymorons in this act, especially Scene ii, and consider what they communicate.

3. Shakespeare uses **repetition** to increase the tension and emotional impact of a speech or scene. Review the Friar's speech in Act III, Scene iii, by jotting down the repeated words and phrases you find. What do you think this technique adds to the scene?

4. **Hyperbole** is common in the language of Shakespeare. Find examples of hyperbole in Act III, and explain what you think they add to the play.

Writing Prompts

1. What factor is most responsible for the difficulties facing the two lovers and their families? Write an essay that presents your opinion, supporting it with examples from the play.

2. Reread Act III, Scene iv, noting its many references to time. Write a short essay explaining why you think Shakespeare chose to use this imagery and what effect it might have on the audience.

3. Assume you are a television or radio reporter. Write the story you would deliver about the tragic events that take place in the first scene.

4. The Friar says that Romeo, although banished, has many reasons to be grateful. List these reasons.

Romeo *and* Juliet ACT IV

Olivia Hussey (Juliet) prepares to drink the potion. (Zeffirelli, 1968)

"What if it be a poison . . ."

Before You Read

1. Have your feelings about Romeo changed because of his role in the deaths of Mercutio and Tybalt? Explain.

2. To what lengths do you think Juliet will go to avoid marrying Paris?

3. What contradictory moods are present in the Capulet household?

4. As you read, consider who seems most upset and who seems least upset by Juliet's death.

Literary Elements

1. Shakespeare often adds humorous scenes and characters, or **comic relief**, to an otherwise serious play. The Nurse in *Romeo and Juliet* contributes a great deal of humor and prevents the play from being unbearably tragic.

2. An **allusion** is a reference to a historical or literary figure, happening, or event that is meant to enhance the meaning of the story. In Act IV, Paris tells Friar Lawrence that he has not talked of love with Juliet because she is in mourning for her cousin Tybalt and "Venus smiles not in a house of tears." The reference to Venus—the goddess of love—may be a tactful way to discuss romance with a man of religion.

3. **Dramatic irony** occurs when the audience has important knowledge that a main character lacks. Because of information given in the Prologues to *Romeo and Juliet*, the audience knows many of the events of the play. As a result, we may be more sympathetic to the young lovers, knowing they are doomed.

4. With **personification**, human characteristics are given to nonhuman things. When in Act IV Juliet says to Friar Lawrence, "this bloody knife shall play the umpire," she is saying the knife can decide (play the umpire) whether she should live or die.

Words to Know

The following vocabulary words appear in Act IV in the original text of Shakespeare's play. However, they are words that are still commonly used. Read the definitions here and pay attention to the words as you read the play (they will be in boldfaced type).

arbitrating	deciding; judging
culled [cull'd]	chosen; selected
distraught	upset; distressed
entreat	plead; ask for
immoderately	wastefully; extravagantly
inundation	flood; outpouring
pensive	thoughtful; reflective
prostrate	flat; prone
resolution	solution to a problem
solace	find relief
spited	acted maliciously or with ill will
surcease	suspend; pause
supple	flexible; pliant

Act Summary

Paris asks Friar Lawrence to make arrangements for his wedding to Juliet, but the friar has devised a more daring plan. He directs Juliet to pretend to change her mind and agree to marry Paris. The night before the wedding, however, she must drink a potion that will put her in a death-like state for forty-two hours. The Friar reasons that her body will be taken to the Capulet burial vault. Romeo, who has already left for Mantua, will receive a letter from Friar Lawrence letting him know of the plan and instructing him to arrive at the vault just as Juliet wakes. The two can then leave for Mantua, where they will begin their married life.

Juliet unexpectedly runs into Paris in a production by the Royal Shakespeare Company. (1961)

Alone, Juliet expresses the terror she feels at the thought of awaking in the family burial vault. Finally she drinks the potion that Friar Lawrence has given her.

While the Capulets prepare for the wedding with Paris, the Nurse goes to get Juliet and finds her "dead." Her death is announced, sending everyone into shock and grief. Lord Capulet orders that the wedding preparations be changed to funeral plans. Some comic relief is provided by the musicians, who would like to be paid before they play.

ACT IV, SCENE I

[Friar Lawrence's cell.] Enter FRIAR LAWRENCE *and* PARIS.

FRIAR LAWRENCE
On Thursday, sir? The time is very short.

PARIS
My father Capulet will have it so,
And I am nothing slow to slack his haste.

FRIAR LAWRENCE
You say you do not know the lady's mind.
5   Uneven is the course, I like it not.

PARIS
Immoderately she weeps for Tybalt's death,
And therefore have I little talk'd of love,
For Venus smiles not in a house of tears.
Now, sir, her father counts it dangerous
10   That she do give her sorrow so much sway,
And in his wisdom hastes our marriage
To stop the **inundation** of her tears;
Which, too much minded by herself alone,
May be put from her by society.
15   Now do you know the reason of this haste.

FRIAR LAWRENCE
[aside] I would I knew not why it should be slow'd.
Look, sir, here comes the lady toward my cell.

Enter JULIET.

PARIS
Happily met, my lady and my wife!

JULIET
20   That may be, sir, when I may be a wife.

PARIS
That "may be" must be, love, on Thursday next.

JULIET
What must be shall be.

ACT 4, SCENE 1

Friar Lawrence's cell. FRIAR LAWRENCE
and PARIS *enter.*

FRIAR LAWRENCE
Your wedding is Thursday, sir? That's a very short time away.

PARIS
My new father-in-law Capulet wants it that way,
and I'll not slow his hasty arrangements by being slow myself.

FRIAR LAWRENCE
You say you don't know what the young lady thinks about the
   marriage.
That's unusual. I don't like it.   5

PARIS
She cries all the time over Tybalt's death,
so I haven't talked much about love.
Love is not welcome in the midst of grief.
Her father thinks it's dangerous
that she gives in so much to her sorrow.   10
So in his wisdom, he's rushing the marriage
to stop her grief
which she thinks about too much when she's by herself.
Being around people might help her get over her grief.
So now you know the reason for our haste.   15

FRIAR LAWRENCE *(to himself)*
I wish I didn't know why this wedding must be slowed down.
(to PARIS*)* Look, sir, here comes the lady now.

     JULIET *enters.*

PARIS
How happy I am to see you, my lady and my wife.

JULIET
That may be, sir—when I become your wife.   20

PARIS
Your "may be" will be a "must," my love, on next Thursday.

JULIET
What must be shall be.

FRIAR LAWRENCE

                        That's a certain text.

PARIS

Come you to make confession to this father?

JULIET

25   To answer that, I should confess to you.

PARIS

Do not deny to him that you love me.

JULIET

I will confess to you that I love him.

PARIS

So will ye, I am sure, that you love me.

JULIET

If I do so, it will be of more price,
30   Being spoke behind your back, than to your face.

PARIS

Poor soul, thy face is much abus'd with tears.

JULIET

The tears have got small victory by that,
For it was bad enough before their spite.

PARIS

Thou wrong'st it, more than tears, with that report.

JULIET

35   That is not slander, sir, which is a truth;
And what I spake, I spake it to my face.

PARIS

Thy face is mine, and thou hast slandered it.

JULIET

It may be so, for it is not mine own.
Are you at leisure, holy father, now;
40   Or shall I come to you at evening mass?

FRIAR LAWRENCE

My leisure serves me, **pensive** daughter, now.
My lord, we must **entreat** the time alone.

FRIAR LAWRENCE
That's the truth.

PARIS
Did you come to make your confession to this father?

JULIET
In order to answer that, I'd have to confess to you.   25

PARIS
Don't deny to him that you love me.

JULIET
I'll confess to you that I love him.

PARIS
I'm sure you will confess to him that you love me.

JULIET
If I do, it will mean more
if I say it behind your back rather than to your face.   30

PARIS
Poor soul, your face is very stained with tears.

JULIET
The tears have made little difference
for my face was unattractive enough before I cried.

PARIS
You do more injustice to your face with that statement than
    those tears did.

JULIET
It's not slander, sir, to speak the truth.   35
And what I said, I said to my own face.

PARIS
Your face is mine, and you have slandered it.

JULIET
You may be right because my face is not my own.
Are you free now, holy father,
or should I come to you at evening mass?   40

FRIAR LAWRENCE
I'm free to see you now, my thoughtful daughter.
(to PARIS) My lord, I must beg you to leave us alone.

PARIS

God shield I should disturb devotion!
Juliet, on Thursday early will I rouse ye;
45 Till then, adieu; and keep this holy kiss.

[*Exit.*]

JULIET

O, shut the door! And when thou hast done so,
Come weep with me, past hope, past care, past help!

FRIAR LAWRENCE

O Juliet, I already know thy grief;
It strains me past the compass of my wits.
50 I hear thou must, and nothing may prorogue it,
On Thursday next be married to this County.

JULIET

Tell me not, friar, that thou hear'st of this,
Unless thou tell me how I may prevent it.
If, in thy wisdom, thou canst give no help,
55 Do thou but call my **resolution** wise,
And with this knife I'll help it presently.
God join'd my heart and Romeo's, thou our hands;
And ere this hand, by thee to Romeo's seal'd,
Shall be the label to another deed,
60 Or my true heart with treacherous revolt
Turn to another, this shall slay them both.
Therefore, out of thy long-experience'd time,
Give me some present counsel, or, behold,
'Twixt my extremes and me this bloody knife
65 Shall play the umpire, **arbitrating** that
Which the commission of thy years and art
Could to no issue of true honour bring.
Be not so long to speak; I long to die
If what thou speak'st speak not of remedy.

FRIAR LAWRENCE

70 Hold, daughter! I do spy a kind of hope,
Which craves as desperate an execution
As that is desperate which we would prevent.
If, rather than to marry County Paris,
Thou hast the strength of will to slay thyself,

PARIS

> God forbid that I should disturb a confession.
> Juliet, I'll awaken you early Thursday morning.
> Until then, good-bye, and keep this holy kiss. 45

> *He kisses her and exits.*

JULIET

> Oh, close the door, and when you have done so,
> come cry with me! I'm beyond hope, beyond cure, beyond help!

FRIAR LAWRENCE

> Oh, Juliet, I already know your grief.
> It drives me past my wits' end.
> I hear you must be married to this count 50
> next Thursday and that nothing can postpone it.

JULIET

> Don't tell me that you have heard about this, friar,
> unless you can tell me how to prevent it.
> If even you and your wisdom can't help me,
> just say that my way of solving the problem is wise— 55
> and with this knife, I'll put my plan into action at once.
> God joined my heart and Romeo's and you joined our hands.
> And before this hand, which you joined to Romeo's
> can seal another deal
> or before my faithful heart could turn in treacherous revolt 60
> to another man, this hand will destroy both my hand and my
>   heart.
> Therefore, out of your great experience,
> give me some advice. Otherwise,
> between me and my distress, this bloody knife
> will determine whether I live or die, deciding that 65
> which your experience and skill
> could not honorably resolve.
> Don't wait long to speak. I want to die
> if what you speak can't help me.

FRIAR LAWRENCE

> Wait, daughter! I see some hope. 70
> But it's as dangerous as the danger
> we're trying to prevent.
> If rather than marrying Count Paris,
> you have the strength of will to kill yourself,

75 Then is it likely thou wilt undertake
A thing like death to chide away this shame,
That cop'st with Death himself to 'scape from it;
And, if thou dar'st, I'll give thee remedy.

JULIET

O, bid me leap, rather than marry Paris,
80 From off the battlements of any tower,
Or walk in thievish ways, or bid me lurk
Where serpents are; chain me with roaring bears,
Or hide me nightly in a charnel-house,
O'er-cover'd quite with dead men's rattling bones,
85 With reeky shanks and yellow chapless skulls;
Or bid me go into a new-made grave
And hide me with a dead man in his shroud,—
Things that, to hear them told, have made me tremble;
And I will do it without fear or doubt,
90 To live an unstain'd wife to my sweet love.

*rather die
then mary
Paris*

FRIAR LAWRENCE

Hold, then. Go home, be merry, give consent
To marry Paris. Wednesday is to-morrow.
To-morrow night look that thou lie alone;
Let not the Nurse lie with thee in thy chamber.
95 Take thou this vial, being then in bed,
And this distilled liquor drink thou off;
When presently through all thy veins shall run
A cold and drowsy humour; for no pulse
Shall keep his native progress, but **surcease**;
100 No warmth, no breath shall testify thou livest;
The roses in thy lips and cheeks shall fade
To paly ashes, thy eyes' windows fall,
Like death when he shuts up the day of life;
Each part, depriv'd of **supple** government,
105 Shall, stiff and stark and cold, appear like death:
And in this borrowed likeness of shrunk death
Thou shalt continue two and forty hours,
And then awake as from a pleasant sleep.

Poison

then you'd probably be willing to risk   75
something like death to avoid this shame
that requires you to deal with Death himself in order to escape
    this marriage.
If you have the courage, I'll give you the remedy.

JULIET

Oh, tell me to leap off the top of that tower,
rather than marry Paris.   80
Rather than marry Paris, tell me to walk on a road where
    robbers hide,
or tell me to linger where snakes are, or chain me up with
    roaring bears,
or lock me in a vault with old bones every night,
completely covering me with dead men's rattling bones,
stinking leg bones, and yellow, jawless skulls.   85
Rather than marry Paris, tell me to lie in a newly made grave
and hide me with a dead man in his burial cloth.
Things that, to hear them spoken of have frightened me,
I'll do without fear or doubt,
in order to remain a faithful wife to my sweet love.   90

FRIAR LAWRENCE

All right, then. Go home, be happy, give your consent
to marry Paris. Tomorrow is Wednesday.
Tomorrow night, be sure to sleep alone. Don't let the Nurse
    sleep in your room.
Take this bottle, and when you're in bed,   95
drink this distilled liquor.
Immediately, a cold and quieting liquid
shall run through all your veins. Your pulse will stop.
There'll be no warmth or breath to prove that you're alive.   100
The color in your lips and cheeks will fade
to pale ashes; your eyelids will close
like death when he shuts up the last day of your life.
Each part of your body, stripped of its ability to move,
shall be stiff and rigid and cold, as in death.
And in this imitation of death,   105
you'll remain forty-two hours,
and then you'll awake as if from a pleasant sleep.

Now, when the bridegroom in the morning comes
110   To rouse thee from thy bed, there art thou dead.
Then, as the manner of our country is,
In thy best robes uncovered on the bier
Thou shall be borne to that same ancient vault
Where all the kindred of the Capulets lie.
115   In the mean time, against thou shalt awake,
Shall Romeo by my letters know our drift,
And hither shall he come; and he and I
Will watch thy waking, and that very night
Shall Romeo bear thee hence to Mantua.
120   And this shall free thee from this present shame;
If no inconstant toy, nor womanish fear,
Abate thy valour in the acting it.

JULIET
Give me, give me! O, tell not me of fear!

FRIAR LAWRENCE
Hold; get you gone, be strong and prosperous
125   In this resolve. I'll send a friar with speed
To Mantua, with my letters to thy lord.

JULIET
Love give me strength! And strength shall help afford.
Farewell, dear father!

[*Exeunt.*]

When Paris comes on Thursday morning
to rouse you from your bed, you will seem dead.   110
Then, as is customary,
dressed in your best clothes and with an uncovered face,
    you'll be carried on a bier
to the ancient vault
where all of the Capulets are buried.
In the meantime, before you awake,   115
Romeo will learn through a letter from me what we're doing.
He'll return here, and he and I
will watch for you to awake. Then that very night when you
    do awake,
Romeo will take you to Mantua.
This will let you escape your present shame   120
if no fickle whim or womanish fears
sap your courage to go through with it.

JULIET
Give it to me! Give it to me! Don't talk of fear!

FRIAR LAWRENCE
Enough! Go, and be strong and prosperous
in this plan. I'll send a friar to speed   125
to Mantua with letters to Romeo.

JULIET
Love will give me strength, and strength will help me through.
Good-bye, dear father.

    They exit.

ACT IV, SCENE II

[*Hall in Capulet's house.*] *Enter* CAPULET, LADY
CAPULET, NURSE, *and two or three* SERVING-MEN.

CAPULET

So many guests invite as here are writ.

[*Exit 1.* SERVANT.]

Sirrah, go hire me twenty cunning cooks.

2. SERVANT

You shall have none ill, sir; for I'll try if they can lick their
fingers.

CAPULET

5   How canst thou try them so?

2. SERVANT

Marry, sir, 'tis an ill cook that cannot lick his own fingers;
therefore he that cannot lick his fingers goes not with me.

CAPULET

Go, be gone.

[*Exit 2.* SERVANT.]

We shall be much unfurnish'd for this time.

10   What, is my daughter gone to Friar Lawrence?

NURSE

Ay, forsooth.

CAPULET

Well, he may chance to do some good on her.
A peevish self-will'd harlotry it is.

Enter JULIET.

NURSE

See where she comes from shrift with merry look.

CAPULET

15   How now, my headstrong! Where have you been gadding?

ACT 4, SCENE 2

A hall in Capulet's house. CAPULET, LADY CAPULET, NURSE, *and* SERVANTS *enter.*

CAPULET *(to* SERVANTS*)*
Invite all the guests whose names are written here.

> SERVANT *exits.*

Servant, go and hire twenty skillful cooks.

SECOND SERVANT
You shall have none that aren't good, sir, for I'll test them by
    seeing if they will lick their fingers.

CAPULET
What kind of test is that?   5

SECOND SERVANT
Well, sir, a bad cook won't lick his fingers (because his own
    cooking tastes so bad). Therefore, the cook who won't lick his
    fingers won't be hired by me.

CAPULET
Go, on your way.

> SECOND SERVANT *exits.*

We're not stocked up for this wedding celebration.
Has my daughter gone to Friar Lawrence's?   10

NURSE
Yes.

CAPULET
Well, he may be able to do some good with her.
She's a silly good-for-nothing.

> JULIET *enters.*

NURSE
See! She's coming from confession with a happy look on
    her face.

CAPULET
Hello, my headstrong daughter. Where have you been   15
    running about?

JULIET

Where I have learn'd me to repent the sin
Of disobedient opposition
To you and your behests, and am enjoin'd
By holy Lawrence to fall **prostrate** here
20   And beg your pardon. Pardon, I beseech you!
Henceforward I am ever rul'd by you.

CAPULET

Send for the County; go tell him of this.
I'll have this knot knit up to-morrow morning.

JULIET

I met the youthful lord at Lawrence' cell
25   And gave him what becomed love I might,
Not stepping o'er the bounds of modesty.

CAPULET

Why, I am glad on't; this is well; stand up.
This is as 't should be. Let me see the County;
Ay, marry, go, I say, and fetch him hither.
30   Now, afore God, this reverend holy friar,
All our whole city is much bound to him.

JULIET

Nurse, will you go with me into my closet
To help me sort such needful ornaments
As you think fit to furnish me to-morrow?

LADY CAPULET

35   No, not till Thursday; there is time enough.

CAPULET

Go, Nurse, go with her; we'll to church tomorrow.

    [*Exeunt* JULIET *and* NURSE.]

LADY CAPULET

We shall be short in our provision;
'Tis now near night.

CAPULET

              Tush, I will stir about,
40   And all things shall be well, I warrant thee, wife;
Go thou to Juliet, help to deck up her.

(handwritten margin note: The religious figure cause all the problems)

JULIET

I've been where I learned to repent of the sin
of disobedience
to you and your orders. I've been advised
by holy Friar Lawrence to fall on my knees
and beg your pardon. Please forgive me, I beg you.   20
From now on, I'll be ruled by you.

CAPULET

Send for the count. Tell him about this.
I'll have the wedding tomorrow morning.

JULIET

I met the youthful lord at Friar Lawrence's cell
and gave him the most fitting love I could   25
without overstepping the bounds of modesty.

CAPULET

I'm glad. This is good. Stand up.
This is as it should be. Let me see Count Paris.
Indeed, go and bring him here.
Now, before God, the whole city owes a great deal   30
to this holy reverend father.

JULIET

Nurse, will you go with me to my room
to help me choose the ornaments
that you think are fitting for me to wear tomorrow?

LADY CAPULET

No, not until Thursday. That's soon enough.   35

CAPULET

Go, Nurse, go with her. The wedding will be tomorrow.

> JULIET *and the* NURSE *exit.*

LADY CAPULET

We'll be short of provisions.
It's almost night now.

CAPULET

Nonsense, I'll get busy
and everything will go well, I promise you, wife.   40
Go to Juliet and help dress her up.

I'll not to bed to-night; let me alone;
I'll play the housewife for this once. What, ho!
They are all forth. Well, I will walk myself
45   To County Paris, to prepare up him
Against to-morrow. My heart is wondrous light,
Since this same wayward girl is so reclaim'd.

     [*Exeunt.*]

I won't go to bed tonight! Leave me alone.
I'll play the housewife this one time. Servants!—
They're all gone. Well, I'll go to see
Count Paris myself, to prepare him   45
for tomorrow. My heart is wonderfully light
since this unruly daughter of mine has come to her senses.

    He exits.

ACT IV, SCENE III

[Juliet's chamber.] Enter JULIET *and* NURSE.

JULIET

Ay, those attires are best; but, gentle Nurse,
I pray thee, leave me to myself to-night;
For I have need of many orisons
To move the heavens to smile upon my state,

5   Which, well thou know'st, is cross and full of sin.

Enter LADY CAPULET.

LADY CAPULET

What, are you busy, ho? Need you my help?

JULIET

No, madam; we have **cull'd** such necessaries
As are behoveful for our state to-morrow.
So please you, let me now be left alone,

10   And let the Nurse this night sit up with you;
For, I am sure, you have your hands full all,
In this so sudden business.

LADY CAPULET

                    Good night.
Get thee to bed, and rest; for thou hast need.

[Exeunt LADY CAPULET and NURSE.]

JULIET

15   Farewell! God knows when we shall meet again
I have a faint cold fear thrills though my veins,
That almost freezes up the heat of life.
I'll call them back again to comfort me.
Nurse!—What should she do here?

20   My dismal scene I needs must act alone.
Come, vial.
What if this mixture do not work at all?
Shall I be married then to-morrow morning?
No, no; this shall forbid it. Lie thou there.

[laying down her dagger]

25   What if it be a poison, which the friar

ACT 4, SCENE 3

Juliet's bedroom. JULIET *and the* NURSE *enter.*

JULIET
Yes, those dresses are best, but, gentle nurse,
I beg you, leave me alone tonight.
I must pray many prayers
to move heaven to smile upon my situation,
which, as you well know, is wrong and full of sin.   5

      LADY CAPULET *enters.*

LADY CAPULET
Are you busy? Do you need my help?

JULIET
No, madam. We have gathered those necessities
I'll need for my wedding tomorrow.
So, please, leave me alone now.
Let the nurse sit up with you tonight.   10
I'm sure you have your hands full
since the wedding has been moved up a day.

LADY CAPULET
Good night.
Go to bed and rest; you'll need it.

      LADY CAPULET *and the* NURSE *exit.*

JULIET
Good-bye! God only knows when we'll meet again.   15
I feel a dizzying, cold fear running through my veins
that almost freezes up the warmth of my life.
I'll call them back to comfort me.
Nurse!—But why should she be here?
I'll have to act out this dreadful scene alone.   20
Come, bottle!
What if this mixture doesn't work at all?
Will I be married, then, tomorrow morning?
No! This will see that doesn't happen. Lie there.

     She lays down a dagger.

What if this is a poison which the friar   25

Subtly hath minist'red to have me dead,
Lest in this marriage he should be dishonour'd
Because he married me before to Romeo?
I fear it is; and yet, methinks, it should not,
30   For he hath still been tried a holy man.
How if, when I am laid into the tomb,
I wake before the time that Romeo
Come to redeem me? There's a fearful point!
Shall I not then be stifled in the vault,
35   To whose foul mouth no healthsome air breathes in,
And there die strangled ere my Romeo comes?
Or, if I live, is it not very like
The horrible conceit of death and night,
Together with the terror of the place,—
40   As in a vault, an ancient receptacle,
Where, for this many hundred years, the bones
Of all my buried ancestors are pack'd;
Where bloody Tybalt, yet but green in earth,
Lies fest'ring in his shroud; where, as they say,
45   At some hours in the night spirits resort;—
Alack, alack, is it not like that I,
So early waking,—what with loathsome smells,
And shrieks like mandrakes'* torn out of the earth,
That living mortals, hearing them, run mad;—
50   O, if I wake, shall I not be **distraught**,
Environed with all these hideous fears,
And madly play with my forefathers' joints,
And pluck the mangled Tybalt from his shroud,
And, in this rage, with some great kinsman's bone
55   As with a club, dash out my desperate brains?
O, look! Methinks I see my cousin's ghost
Seeking out Romeo, that did spit his body
Upon a rapier's point. Stay, Tybalt, stay!
Romeo, I come! This do I drink to thee.

[*She falls upon her bed, within the curtains.*]

---

48   *mandrakes'* The root of the mandrake was said to have a humanlike form.
Superstitious belief reported that the mandrake screamed horrible cries when its
roots were pulled out of the ground, driving listeners mad.

has secretly given me to kill me
so that he won't be dishonored by this marriage
since he married me to Romeo earlier?
I'm afraid that's the case. And yet, I don't think so
because he's always shown himself to be a holy man.   30
What if, when I am laid in the tomb,
I awake before Romeo
comes to save me? That's a terrifying thought!
Won't I be stifled in the tomb
where no wholesome air circulates?   35
Won't I suffocate there before my Romeo comes?
Or if I can breathe, isn't it likely that I'll feel
the horrible idea of death and night,
along with the terror of the place?
That vault is an ancient tomb   40
where for hundreds of years the bones
of all my buried ancestors have been stored;
where bloody Tybalt, so recently buried,
lies rotting in his burial cloth; where, so they say,
at some hours in the night, ghosts live.   45
Alas, alas, isn't it likely that waking there,
I'll encounter horrible smells
and shrieks like the uprooted mandrakes'
which drive people insane?
Or if I wake, won't I be driven mad,   50
closed in with all these hideous fears,
and play like a madwoman with my ancestors' bones,
and pluck battered Tybalt from his burial cloth,
and in this fit, take one of my great relative's bones
to use as a club and dash out my desperate brains?   55
Look! I think I see my cousin's ghost
looking for Romeo who stabbed him
with a rapier. Stay there, Tybalt!
Romeo, I'm coming. I drink to you!

She drinks and falls upon her bed, which is enclosed in curtains.

ACT IV, SCENE IV

[*Hall in Capulet's house.*] *Enter* LADY CAPULET *and* NURSE.

LADY CAPULET
Hold, take these keys and fetch more spices, nurse.

NURSE
They call for dates and quinces in the pastry.

Enter CAPULET.

CAPULET
Come, stir, stir, stir! The second cock hath crow'd,
The curfew-bell hath rung, 'tis three o'clock.
5   Look to the bak'd meats, good Angelica;
Spare not for cost.

NURSE
                    Go you cot-quean, go,
Get you to bed. Faith, you'll be sick to-morrow
For this night's watching.

CAPULET
10   No, not a whit! What! I have watch'd ere now
All night for lesser cause, and ne'er been sick.

LADY CAPULET
Ay, you have been a mouse-hunt in your time;
But I will watch you from such watching now.

[*Exeunt* LADY CAPULET *and* NURSE.]

CAPULET
A jealous-hood, a jealous-hood!

Enter three or four SERVING-MEN, *with spits, logs, and baskets.*

15   Now, fellow,
What is there?

1. SERVANT
Things for the cook, sir; but I know not what.

CAPULET
Make haste, make haste.

ACT 4, SCENE 4

A hall in Capulet's house. LADY CAPULET *and the* NURSE *enter.*

LADY CAPULET
  Wait, take these keys and bring me more spices, nurse.

NURSE
  The cooks in the pantry are calling for dates and quinces.

    CAPULET *enters.*

CAPULET
  Come on! Get busy! The second rooster has crowed already.
  The curfew bell has rung. It's three o'clock.
  Check on the meat pies, good Angelica.   5
  Don't worry about the cost.

NURSE *(to* CAPULET*)*
  Go to bed, little housewife.
  Go on, go to bed. Really, you'll be sick tomorrow
  from staying up all night.

CAPULET
  No I won't, not one bit. Why, I've stayed up   10
  all night before for more trivial reasons, and I was never sick.

LADY CAPULET
  Yes, you've been a woman-chaser in your day,
  but I'll see that you don't keep those kinds of late hours anymore.

LADY CAPULET *and the* NURSE *exit.*

CAPULET
  She's a jealous woman, a jealous woman.

    Enter three or four SERVANTS *with cooking rods, logs, and a*
    basket.

  Now, fellow,
    what's that?   15

FIRST SERVANT
  These are things for the cook, sir, but I don't know what they are.

CAPULET
  Hurry up! Hurry up!

[*Exit 1. SERVANT*]

Sirrah, fetch drier logs:
20 Call Peter, he will show thee where they are.

2. SERVANT

I have a head, sir, that will find out logs,*
And never trouble Peter for the matter.

CAPULET

Mass, and well said; a merry whoreson, ha!
Thou shalt be logger-head.

[*Exit 2. SERVANT*]

25 Good faith, 'tis day.
The County will be here with music straight,
For so he said he would. I hear him near.

[*music within*]

Nurse! Wife! What, ho! What, Nurse, I say!

Re-enter NURSE.

Go waken Juliet, go and trim her up;
30 I'll go and chat with Paris. Hie, make haste,
Make haste; the bridegroom he is come already.
Make haste, I say.

[*Exeunt.*]

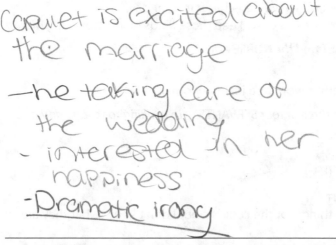

Capulet is excited about
the marriage
— he taking care of
the wedding
— interested in her
happiness
— Dramatic irony

---

21 *logs* The servant's comment reflects humorously on his own head—it is wooden
too.

The FIRST SERVANT *exits.*

Servant, get some drier logs.
Call Peter, he'll show you where they are.   20

SECOND SERVANT
I never have trouble finding logs, sir.
I don't have to bother Peter.

CAPULET
By the mass, that's clever. You're a happy rascal.
You're a blockhead.

> *The* SECOND SERVANT *exits.*

Good heavens, day has dawned!   25
Count Paris will be here with the musicians right away,
as he said he would. I hear him now.

> *Music is heard.*

Nurse! Wife! Where are you? Nurse, I say!

> *The* NURSE *re-enters.*

Go wake Juliet. Go and get her dressed.
I'll go and talk with Paris. Hurry, make haste!   30
Make haste! The bridegroom has already arrived.
Hurry, I say!

> *They exit.*

ACT IV, SCENE V

[*Juliet's chamber.*] *Enter* NURSE.

NURSE
Mistress! What, mistress! Juliet!—Fast, I warrant her, she.—
Why, lamb! Why, lady! Fie, you slug-a-bed!
Why, love! I say, madam! Sweetheart! Why, bride!
What, not a word? You take your penny-worths now;
5   Sleep for a week; for the next night, I warrant,
The County Paris hath set up his rest
That you shall rest but little. God forgive me!
Marry, and amen, how sound is she asleep!
I needs must wake her. Madam, madam, madam!
10   Ay, let the County take you in your bed;
He'll fright you up, i' faith. Will it not be?

[*Draws back the curtains.*]

What, dress'd, and in your clothes! And down again!
I must needs wake you. Lady! Lady! Lady!
Alas, alas! Help, help! My lady's dead!
15   O, well-a-day, that ever I was born!
Some *aqua vitae*, ho! My lord! My lady!

Enter LADY CAPULET.

LADY CAPULET
What noise is here?

NURSE
                 O lamentable day!

CAPULET
What is the matter?

NURSE
20   Look, look! O heavy day!

LADY CAPULET
O me, O me! My child, my only life,
Revive, look up, or I will die with thee!
Help, help! Call help.

Enter CAPULET.

ACT 4, SCENE 5

Juliet's bedroom. The NURSE *enters.*

NURSE
Mistress! Mistress! Juliet—I'll bet she's fast asleep.
Lamb! Lady! For shame, you sleepyhead.
Well, love! I say, madam! Sweetheart! Bride!
What, not a word? Take your little naps now.
Sleep for a week because I'll bet you tonight   5
Count Paris is determined
that you won't rest very much. God forgive me, I shouldn't
    say that.
How sound asleep she is.
I must wake her. Madam, madam, madam!
Are you going to let the Count Paris find you in bed?   10
He'll frighten you, I guarantee. Will nothing wake you?

She draws back the curtains.

What, already dressed and gone back to bed?
I must wake you. Lady, lady, lady!
Alas! Help! Help! My lady is dead!
I wish I'd never been born.   15
Some liquor, here! My lord! My lady!

LADY CAPULET *enters.*

LADY CAPULET
What's all this noise?

NURSE
Oh awful day!

LADY CAPULET
What's the matter?

NURSE
Oh look, look! Oh horrible day!   20

LADY CAPULET
Oh no! Oh no! My child! My only child!
Revive! Look up, or I'll die with you.
Help! Help! Call for help!

CAPULET *enters.*

CAPULET

For shame, bring Juliet forth; her lord is come.

NURSE

25   She's dead, deceas'd, she's dead; alack the day!

LADY CAPULET

Alack the day, she's dead, she's dead, she's dead!

CAPULET

Ha! Let me see her. Out, alas! She's cold;
Her blood is settled, and her joints are stiff;
Life and these lips have long been separated.
30   Death lies on her like an untimely frost
Upon the sweetest flower of all the field.

NURSE

O lamentable day!

LADY CAPULET

O woeful time!

CAPULET

Death, that hath ta'en her hence to make me wail,
35   Ties up my tongue, and will not let me speak.

Enter FRIAR LAWRENCE *and* PARIS, *with*
MUSICIANS.

FRIAR LAWRENCE

Come, is the bride ready to go to church?

CAPULET

Ready to go, but never to return.—
O son! The night before thy wedding-day
Hath Death lain with thy wife. There she lies,
40   Flower as she was, deflowered* by him.
Death is my son-in-law, Death is my heir;
My daughter he hath wedded. I will die
And leave him all; life, living, all is Death's.

PARIS

Have I thought long to see this morning's face,
45   And doth it give me such a sight as this?

---

40   *deflowered* stripped of virginity (and her life)

CAPULET

For shame. Bring Juliet here. Her lord has arrived.

NURSE

She's dead, deceased; she's dead! Curse this day.   25

LADY CAPULET

Horrible day! She's dead. She's dead! She's dead!

CAPULET

Let me see her. Alas, she's cold,
her blood is settled, and her joints are stiff.
Life left her lips a long time ago.
Death lies on her like an untimely frost   30
on the sweetest flower of all the fields.

NURSE

Oh sorrowful day!

LADY CAPULET

Oh woeful time—

CAPULET

Death, who has taken her away to make me cry,
ties up my tongue and will not let me speak.   35

   FRIAR LAWRENCE *and* PARIS *enter with musicians.*

FRIAR LAWRENCE

Is the bride ready to go to the church?

CAPULET

She is ready to go but never to return.
(to PARIS*)* Oh son, the night before your wedding day
Death slept with your wife. See, there she lies,
the flower that she was, deflowered by Death.   40
Death is my son-in-law, Death is my heir;
he has married my daughter. I'll die
and leave Death everything. Life, living—all is Death's.

PARIS

I've thought of nothing else but to see this day dawn.
Why does morning give me such a sight as this?   45

LADY CAPULET

Accurs'd, unhappy, wretched, hateful day!
Most miserable hour that e'er Time saw
In lasting labour of his pilgrimage!
But one, poor one, one poor and loving child,
50 But one thing to rejoice and **solace** in,
And cruel Death hath catch'd it from my sight!

NURSE

O woe! O woeful, woeful, woeful day!
Most lamentable day, most woeful day,
That ever, ever, I did yet behold!
55 O day! O day! O day! O hateful day!
Never was seen so black a day as this.
O woeful day, O woeful day!

over the top / exaggerated

PARIS

Beguil'd, divorced, wronged, **spited**, slain!
Most detestable Death, by thee beguil'd,
60 By cruel, cruel thee quite overthrown!
O love! O life! Not life, but love in death!

CAPULET

Despis'd, distressed, hated, martyr'd, kill'd!
Uncomfortable time, why cam'st thou now
To murder, murder our solemnity?
65 O child! O child! My soul, and not my child!
Dead art thou! Alack! My child is dead;
And with my child my joys are buried.

anger towards death

capital D

FRIAR LAWRENCE

Peace, ho, for shame! Confusion's cure lives not
In these confusions. Heaven and yourself
70 Had part in this fair maid; now heaven hath all,
And all the better is it for the maid.
Your part in her you could not keep from death,
But heaven keeps his part in eternal life.
The most you sought was her promotion,
75 For 'twas your heaven she should be advanc'd;
And weep ye now, seeing she is advanc'd
Above the clouds, as high as heaven itself?

going to a better place

LADY CAPULET

Damned, unhappy, wretched, hateful day!
This is the most miserable hour that Time ever saw
in his ceaseless journey.
Only one—just one, one poor and loving child,
only one child in which to rejoice and find comfort—   50
and cruel Death has snatched her from my sight.

NURSE

Oh, sadness! Sad, sad, sad day!
Most sorrowful day, saddest day,
that I've ever seen!
Oh day! Oh day! Oh hateful day!   55
There's never been such a black day as this!
Oh sad day! Oh sad day!

PARIS

Seduced, divorced, wronged, spited, killed!
You detestable Death, you have seduced her.
You've cruelly destroyed her.   60
Oh, my love! My life!—No longer alive, but at least I'll love
   you in death.

CAPULET

Despised, distressed, hated, martyred, killed!
Discomforting time, why did you come now
to murder our celebration?
Oh, child! Child! My soul, and not my child!   65
You're dead, dead! Alas, my child is dead.
And with you, my child, my joys are buried.

FRIAR LAWRENCE

Peace! For shame! The remedy to disaster is not
in this commotion. Both you and heaven
had a part in this beautiful maiden. Now heaven has all of her,   70
and it's all the better for the maiden.
The body you gave her was mortal and had to die,
but heaven gives her soul eternal life.
The best thing you could think of was to try to marry her
   to a nobleman.
That was your notion of heaven—to see her position raised.   75
So why do you cry now, seeing that she is raised
above the clouds, as high as heaven itself?

O, in this love, you love your child so ill
That you run mad, seeing that she is well.
80 She's not well married that lives married long;
But she's best married that dies married young.
Dry up your tears, and stick your rosemary
On this fair corse; and, as the custom is,
In all her best array bear her to church;
85 For though fond nature bids us all lament,
Yet nature's tears are reason's merriment.

celebrate

CAPULET
All things that we ordained festival,
Turn from their office to black funeral;
Our instruments to melancholy bells,
90 Our wedding cheer to a sad burial feast,
Our solemn hymns to sullen dirges change,
Our bridal flowers serve for a buried corse,
And all things change them to the contrary.

FRIAR LAWRENCE
Sir, go you in; and, madam, go with him;
95 And go, Sir Paris; every one prepare
To follow this fair corse unto her grave.
The heavens do lour upon you for some ill;
Move them no more by crossing their high will.

[*Exeunt* CAPULET, LADY CAPULET, PARIS, *and*
FRIAR.]

1. MUSICIAN
Faith, we may put up our pipes and be gone.

NURSE
100 Honest good fellows, ah, put up, put up;
For well you know, this is a pitiful case.*

[*Exit.*]

1. MUSICIAN
Ay, by my troth, the case may be amended.

---

101 *case* means both situation and a musical case

With this kind of love, you love your child so foolishly
that you go crazy when you know she's better off.
Any woman is not well married when she lives a long   80
    married life.
The woman is best married who dies a young bride.
Dry your tears and pin rosemary
on this lovely corpse. And as is the custom,
dress her in her best clothes and carry her to the church.
For though our foolish human nature tells us all to grieve,   85
reason gives up cause to rejoice that she is in heaven.

CAPULET

Everything that we planned for the wedding feast
will now be used instead for the sad funeral.
The dancing music will become melancholy bells,
our wedding party will become a sad burial feast,   90
our celebration hymns will change to solemn funeral marches,
our wedding flowers will serve as funeral flowers.
Change everything to its opposite (for the funeral).

FRIAR LAWRENCE

Sir, go inside. Madam, go with him.
You, too, Paris. Everyone is to prepare   95
to follow this beautiful corpse to her grave.
The heavens frown on you for some sin you have committed.
Don't anger the heavens more by disobeying their will.

    LADY CAPULET, CAPULET, PARIS, *and* FRIAR LAWRENCE *exit.*

FIRST MUSICIAN

We might as well put away our instruments and leave.

NURSE

Honest fellows, put them away, put them away.   100
You can see that this is a pitiful situation.

    She exits.

FIRST MUSICIAN

Yes, this certainly could be a better case.

Enter PETER.

PETER
Musicians, O, musicians, "Heart's ease,* Heart's ease!"
O, an you will have me live, play "Heart's ease."

1. MUSICIAN
105 Why "Heart's ease"?

PETER
O, musicians, because my heart itself plays "My heart is
full of woe." O, play me some merry dump to comfort me.

1. MUSICIAN
Not a dump we; 'tis no time to play now.

PETER
You will not, then?

1. MUSICIAN
110 No.

PETER
I will then give it you soundly.

1. MUSICIAN
What will you give us?

PETER
No money, on my faith, but the gleek; I will give you the
minstrel.

1. MUSICIAN
115 Then will I give you the serving-creature.

PETER
Then will I lay the serving-creature's dagger on your pate.
I will carry no crotchets;* I'll *re* you, I'll *fa* you. Do you
note me?

1. MUSICIAN
An you *re* us and *fa* us, you note us.

2. MUSICIAN
120 Pray you, put up your dagger, and put out your wit.

---

103 *"Heart's Ease"* or *"My Heart Is Full of Woe"* is an old ballad.

117 *crotchets* means both "whim" and a quarter note in music

PETER *enters.*

PETER
Musicians! Oh, musicians, play "Heart's Ease." "Heart's Ease"! Oh, if you want me to live, play "Heart's Ease"!

FIRST MUSICIAN
Why "Heart's Ease"? 105

PETER
Oh, musicians, because my heart itself is playing, "My heart is full of sorrow." Oh, play me a merry sad song to comfort me.

FIRST MUSICIAN
We're not going to play a sad song! This is no time to play.

PETER
You won't play one then?

FIRST MUSICIAN
No. 110

PETER
Then I'll give it to you good.

FIRST MUSICIAN
What will you give us?

PETER
No money, I swear, but a mocking speech. I'll call you a two-bit player.

FIRST MUSICIAN
Then I'll call you a lackey. 115

PETER
Then I'll crack you over the head with my lackey's dagger. I'll not put up with your whims. I'll "re" you and I'll "fa" you. Understand me?

FIRST MUSICIAN
If you "re" us and "fa" us, you'll set us to music.

SECOND MUSICIAN
Please put away your dagger and use your intelligence. 120

PETER

Then have at you with my wit! I will dry-beat you with an
iron wit, and put up my iron dagger. Answer me like men:
    "When griping griefs the heart doth wound,*
    And doleful dumps the mind oppress,
125   Then music with her silver sound"—

why "silver sound"? Why "music with her silver sound"?
What say you, Simon Catling?*

1. MUSICIAN

Marry, sir, because silver hath a sweet sound.

PETER

Pretty! What say you, Hugh Rebeck?*

2. MUSICIAN

130   I say, "silver sound," because musicians sound for silver.

PETER

Pretty too! What say you, James Soundpost?*

3. MUSICIAN

Faith, I know not what to say.

PETER

O, I cry you mercy; you are the singer; I will say for you.
It is "music with her silver sound," because musicians
135   have no gold for sounding:
    [*Sings*]
        "Then music with her silver sound
        With speedy help doth lend redress."

    [*Exit.*]

1. MUSICIAN

What a pestilent knave is this same!

2. MUSICIAN

Hang him, Jack! Come, we'll in here, tarry for the
140   mourners, and stay dinner.

    [*Exeunt.*]

123–124   *When . . . wound* These are lyrics from Richard Edward's song "In the
        Commendation of Music."

  127   *Catling* Peter calls the musicians a "catstring." Lute strings were made of catgut.

PETER

Then I'll have a go at you with my intelligence. I'll beat you
with an iron intelligence and put away my iron dagger.
Answer me like men. *(Sings.)*

> When terrible griefs wound the heart,
> and sad sorrows trouble the mind.
> Then music with her silver sound— 125

Why "silver sound"? Why "music with her silver sound"?
What do you say, Simon Catling?

FIRST MUSICIAN

Well, sir, because silver has a sweet sound.

PETER

Nicely put! What do you say, Hugh Rebeck?

SECOND MUSICIAN

I say "silver sound" because musicians sound (play) for silver. 130

PETER

That's nicely put, too. What do you say, James Soundpost?

THIRD MUSICIAN

Really, I don't know what to say.

PETER

Oh, well excuse me. You're the singer (and can only sing).
I'll speak for you. The line goes "music with her silver
sounds" because musicians get no gold for playing. 135
(Sings.)

> Then music with her silver sound
> with speedy help gives relief.

He exits singing.

FIRST MUSICIAN

What a pest that rascal is.

SECOND MUSICIAN

Hang him, Jack! Come on, we'll go in here, wait for the
mourners, and stay for dinner. 140

They exit.

---

129   *Rebeck* a three-stringed fiddle

131   *Soundpost* a wooden peg used to brace and support a violin

Act IV Review

Discussion Questions

1. How do you feel about Juliet at the moment when she takes the potion?

2. Why do you think Shakespeare includes the dialogue between Peter and the musicians at the end of Scene v?

3. Compare and contrast Romeo and Paris.

4. Why would Friar Lawrence ask Juliet to carry out a dangerous plan instead of just going to her parents and explaining that she was already married to Romeo?

5. What is your opinion of the Friar's plan? Predict what might go wrong.

6. How has Juliet's relationship with her Nurse changed since the beginning of the play?

7. What differences are there among the reactions of Paris, the Nurse, Lord Capulet, and Lady Capulet to Juliet's "death"?

8. Which characters in Act IV do you have sympathy for? Explain.

Literary Elements

1. Shakespeare often adds **comic relief** to his more serious plays. Where is this element found in Act IV? Discuss what purpose you think it serves.

2. An **allusion** is a reference to a historical or literary figure, happening, or event that is meant to enhance the meaning of the story. Find an allusion in *Romeo and Juliet*. Explain its meaning and how it adds to the play.

3. **Dramatic irony** occurs when the audience knows more than some of the characters in the play. Look for examples of dramatic irony in Act IV. Note two or three examples and explain what makes each ironic.

4. **Personification** means giving human characteristics to nonhuman things or objects. Find some examples of personification in Act IV and explain why you think Shakespeare uses this figure of speech.

Writing Prompts

1. Juliet has changed a great deal since the beginning of the play. Compose an essay explaining these changes.

2. Reread lines 20–40 in Act IV, Scene i, and write down what Juliet might be thinking as she says these words to Paris.

3. Rewrite one scene in this act as a contemporary soap opera. You will want to use up-to-date language and consider differences between Renaissance times and today as to the roles of men and women, and children and parents. You also need to consider how modern technology has made communication much easier than in Romeo and Juliet's day.

4. Compose your own version of Friar Lawrence's letter to Romeo telling him about Juliet's plans. Use the language of Shakespeare in writing the letter.

Romeo *and* Juliet ACT V

Phyllis Neilson-Terry and Vernon Steel

"Eyes, look your last!
Arms, take your last embrace!"

Before You Read

1. How do you think this all will conclude?

2. If the parents of Romeo and Juliet had learned of their children's marriage at the end of Act IV, what do you think they might have done?

3. As you read, note anything in the text that helps create an atmosphere of dread and fear.

Literary Elements

1. A **tragedy** is a serious work of literature that narrates the events leading to the downfall of a **tragic hero**, who is usually of noble birth. This individual's downfall is a result of a **tragic flaw** or fatal character weakness. For example, in Shakespeare's *Macbeth*, the hero's flaw is ambition. In *Othello*, it is jealousy.

2. As noted earlier, with **dramatic irony**, the audience knows something that a character does not. The Act I Prologue alerts us to the outcome of the play, giving us a broader perspective on events than any character could have.

3. A **theme** is the underlying meaning or message of a work of literature. Shakespeare explores many ideas in *Romeo and Juliet*, including the obstacles to young love.

Words to Know

The following vocabulary words appear in Act V in the original text of Shakespeare's play. However, they are words that are still commonly used. Read the definitions here and pay attention to the words as you read the play (they will be in boldfaced type).

abhorred	hated; despised
apprehend	arrest; take into custody
canopy	covering; protection
contempt	scorn; disdain
disperse	scatter; distribute
inexorable	unmovable; relentless
interred [interr'd]	buried; shut in
penury	poverty; destitution
presage	predict; foretell
remnants	remains; leftovers
righteous	virtuous; moral
steeped [steep'd]	soaked; covered in liquid
wretchedness	anguish; torment

Act Summary

Friar Lawrence's plan goes horribly wrong when Romeo does not receive the letter explaining that Juliet's death is false and so believes her dead. Distraught, Romeo buys poison with which to kill himself and then rushes back to Verona to die alongside the body of his young wife.

When he arrives at the vault, however, he learns that he is not alone. Paris, who had planned to marry Juliet, is there placing flowers at her tomb. Romeo fatally wounds Paris, but honors his rival's dying request to be placed in the vault next to Juliet. Romeo then drinks poison and dies just as Juliet is awakening from her deep sleep. With horror, Juliet realizes what has happened, takes Romeo's dagger, and stabs herself.

Word of the deaths spreads quickly along with news of another tragic event—Romeo's mother has died of grief over her son's banishment. The play ends when the heads of the warring households, Lords Montague and Capulet, agree to end their feud and erect a golden monument to their children.

The funeral procession (Zeffirelli, 1968)

ACT V, SCENE I

[Mantua. A street.] Enter ROMEO.

ROMEO

    If I may trust the flattering truth of sleep,

    My dreams **presage** some joyful news at hand.

    My bosom's lord sits lightly in his throne,

    And all this day an unaccustom'd spirit

5   Lifts me above the ground with cheerful thoughts.

    I dreamt my lady came and found me dead—

    Strange dream, that gives a dead man leave to think!—

    And breath'd such life with kisses in my lips

    That I reviv'd and was an emperor.

10   Ah me! How sweet is love itself possess'd,

    When but love's shadows are so rich in joy!

Enter BALTHASAR, *his man, booted.*

    News from Verona!—How now, Balthasar!

    Dost thou not bring me letters from the friar?

    How doth my lady? Is my father well?

15   How fares my Juliet? That I ask again;

    For nothing can be ill, if she be well.

BALTHASAR

    Then she is well, and nothing can be ill.

    Her body sleeps in Capel's monument,

    And her immortal part with angels lives.

20   I saw her laid low in her kindred's vault,

    And presently took post to tell it you.

    O, pardon me for bringing these ill news,

    Since you did leave it for my office, sir.

ROMEO

    Is it even so? Then I defy you, stars!

25   Thou know'st my lodging; get me ink and paper

    And hire post-horses; I will hence to-night.

BALTHASAR

    I do beseech you, sir, have patience.

    Your looks are pale and wild, and do import

    Some misadventure.

ACT 5, SCENE 1

A street in Mantua. ROMEO *enters.*

ROMEO
If I may trust the truth of sleep's illusions,
my dreams predict I'm about to receive some joyful news.
My heart feels light in my breast,
and all day an unusual spirit has
lifted me above the ground with cheerful thoughts.   5
I dreamed my lady came and found me dead—
it's a strange dream that lets a dead man think—
and breathed such life with her kisses
that I revived and became an emperor.
Ah, me, how sweet is real love   10
when just love's images are so joyful.

      BALTHASAR, *his servant, enters.*

News from Verona! Well, Balthasar?
Didn't you bring me letters from the friar?
How's my lady? Is my father well?
How's Juliet? I ask that again   15
because nothing can be bad if she's well.

BALTHASAR
Then she is well, so nothing can be bad.
Her body sleeps in the Capulets' tomb,
and her soul is with the angels.
I saw her laid down in her ancestors' vault,   20
and I immediately hired horses to ride here to tell you.
Oh, forgive me for bringing this bad news,
since you made it my duty, sir.

ROMEO
Is this true? Then I defy you, fate!
(to BALTHASAR*)* You know where I live. Get me some ink   25
    and paper,
and hire me some horses. I'll leave tonight.

BALTHASAR
I beg you sir, be patient.
Your face is pale and wild, and you look like
you're heading for trouble.

ROMEO

30   Tush, thou art deceiv'd:
Leave me, and do the thing I bid thee do.
Hast thou no letters to me from the friar?

BALTHASAR

No, my good lord.

ROMEO

                          No matter; get thee gone
35   And hire those horses; I'll be with thee straight.

        [*Exit* BALTHASAR.]

Well, Juliet, I will lie with thee to-night.
Let's see for means. O mischief, thou art swift
To enter in the thoughts of desperate men!
I do remember an apothecary,—
40   And hereabouts 'a dwells,—which late I noted
In tatt'red weeds, with overwhelming brows,
Culling of simples; meagre were his looks,
Sharp misery had worn him to the bones;
And in his needy shop a tortoise hung,
45   An alligator stuff'd and other skins
Of ill-shap'd fishes; and about his shelves
A beggarly account of empty boxes,
Green earthen pots, bladders and musty seeds,
Remnants of packthread and old cakes of roses
50   Were thinly scattered, to make up a show.
Noting this **penury**, to myself I said,
"And if a man did need a poison now,
Whose sale is present death in Mantua,
Here lives a caitiff wretch would sell it him."
55   O, this same thought did but forerun my need;
And this same needy man must sell it me.
As I remember, this should be the house.
Being holiday, the beggar's shop is shut.
What, ho! Apothecary!

        Enter APOTHECARY.

APOTHECARY

60   Who calls so loud?

ROMEO

Nonsense, you're mistaken. 30
Leave me, and do what I asked you to do.
Don't you have any letters for me from the friar?

BALTHASAR

No, my good lord.

ROMEO

It doesn't matter. Go
and hire the horses. I'll be with you right away. 35

BALTHASAR *exits.*

Well, Juliet, I'll lie with you tonight.
Let's see, what method shall I use? Oh, mischief, you're quick
to enter the thoughts of desperate men.
I remember a pharmacist
who lives near here. I noticed him recently, 40
with his tattered clothes and overhanging eyebrows,
as he sorted medicinal herbs. He was very thin.
Sharp misery had worn him to skin and bones.
In his poor shop hung a tortoise,
a stuffed alligator, and other skins 45
of misshapen fish. On his shelves
were a few empty boxes,
green clay pots, bladders, musty seeds,
bits of twine, and old packets of rose petals—
all thinly scattered for show. 50
Noticing how poor he was, I said to myself,
"If a man should need poison now—
when its sale here in Mantua is punishable by death—
then here lives a miserable wretch who would sell it to him."
This thought came to me before I ever thought about 55
    needing poison,
and this same needy man must sell it to me.
If I remember, this should be his house.
Since this is a holiday, the poor man's shop is closed.
(He calls.) Hello! Pharmacist!

The PHARMACIST *enters.*

PHARMACIST

Who calls so loudly? 60

ROMEO

Come hither, man. I see that thou art poor.
Hold, there is forty ducats. Let me have
A dram of poison, such soon-speeding gear
As will **disperse** itself through all the veins
65 That the life-weary taker may fall dead,
And that the trunk may be discharg'd of breath
As violently as hasty powder fir'd
Doth hurry from the fatal cannon's womb.

APOTHECARY

Such mortal drugs I have; but Mantua's law
70 Is death to any he that utters them.

ROMEO

Art thou so bare and full of **wretchedness**,
And fear'st to die? Famine is in thy cheeks,
Need and oppression starveth in thy eyes,
Contempt and beggary hangs upon thy back;
75 The world is not thy friend nor the world's law,
The world affords no law to make thee rich;
Then be poor, but break it, and take this.

APOTHECARY

My poverty, but not my will, consents.

ROMEO

I pay thy poverty, and not thy will.

APOTHECARY

80 Put this in any liquid thing you will,
And drink it off; and, if you had the strength
Of twenty men, it would dispatch you straight.

ROMEO

There is thy gold, worse poison to men's souls,
Doing more murder in this loathsome world
85 Than these poor compounds that thou mayst not sell.
I sell thee poison; thou hast sold me none.
Farewell! Buy food, and get thyself in flesh.
Come, cordial and not poison, go with me
To Juliet's grave; for there must I use thee.

[*Exeunt.*]

274   Romeo and Juliet

ROMEO

Come here, man. I see that you're poor.
Here are forty gold coins. Let me have
a vial of poison of such quick-working stuff
that it will flow all through the veins
and make the life-weary taker fall dead.   65
Then the body may be discharged of breath
as violently as fired gunpowder
speeds from the deadly cannon's barrel.

PHARMACIST

I have deadly drugs, but Mantua's law
states that anyone who sells them will be executed.   70

ROMEO

You're so poor and wretched—
and yet you're still afraid of death (by execution)?
    There's poverty in your cheeks,
need and oppression starving in your eyes,
and contempt and beggary hangs on your back.
The world is not your friend or the world's law.   75
The world has no law to make you rich.
Then be poor, but break the law and take this gold.

PHARMACIST

My poverty, but not my will, agrees.

ROMEO

Then I'll pay your poverty, not your will.

PHARMACIST

Put this drug in any kind of liquid you wish,   80
and drink it all, and even if you had the strength
of twenty men, it would kill you immediately.

ROMEO

There's your gold—which is a worse poison to men's souls
since it causes more murder in this hateful world
than these poor drugs that you're not allowed to sell.   85
I sell you poison—you haven't sold me any.
Good-bye. Buy food and get some flesh on your bones.
Come, restoring drug, you are not poison. Go with me
to Juliet's grave, for that is where I'll use you.

        ROMEO *and the* PHARMACIST *exit.*

ACT V, SCENE II

[Verona. Friar Lawrence's cell.] Enter FRIAR JOHN.

FRIAR JOHN
Holy Franciscan friar! Brother, ho!

Enter FRIAR LAWRENCE.

FRIAR LAWRENCE
This same should be the voice of Friar John.
Welcome from Mantua! What says Romeo?
Or, if his mind be writ, give me his letter.

FRIAR JOHN
5   Going to find a bare-foot brother out,
One of our order, to associate me,
Here in this city visiting the sick,
And finding him, the searchers of the town,
Suspecting that we both were in a house — *cease*
10   Where the infectious pestilence did reign, *they were*
Seal'd up the doors and would not let us forth, *sick*
So that my speed to Mantua there was stay'd.

FRIAR LAWRENCE
Who bare my letter, then, to Romeo?

FRIAR JOHN
I could not send it,—here it is again,—
15   Nor get a messenger to bring it thee,
So fearful were they of infection.

FRIAR LAWRENCE
Unhappy fortune! By my brotherhood,
The letter was not nice but full of charge
Of dear import, and the neglecting it
20   May do much danger. Friar John, go hence;
Get me an iron crow, and bring it straight
Unto my cell.

FRIAR JOHN
Brother, I'll go and bring it thee.

[Exit.]

ACT 5, SCENE 2

Verona. Friar Lawrence's cell. FRIAR JOHN *enters.*

FRIAR JOHN

Holy Franciscan friar! Brother, hello!

FRIAR LAWRENCE *enters.*

FRIAR LAWRENCE

That voice should be Friar John's.
Welcome back from Mantua. What did Romeo say?
Or if he wrote, give me his letter.

FRIAR JOHN

I went to find another friar   5
from our order to accompany me.
He was here in the city visiting the sick.
I found him, but the health officials of the town,
suspecting that we both were in a house
where plague victims lived,   10
sealed the doors and would not let us leave.
So my journey to Mantua to see Romeo was stopped.

FRIAR LAWRENCE

Who took my letter to Romeo, then?

FRIAR JOHN

I couldn't send it. Here it is.
I couldn't find a messenger to bring it to you   15
because they were so afraid of the plague.

FRIAR LAWRENCE

Unhappy fate! By the Franciscans,
this was not just a trivial letter but one full of news
of great importance. Failure to deliver it
could do much damage. Friar John, go and   20
get me a crowbar and bring it here right away
to my cell.

FRIAR JOHN

Brother, I'll go get it and bring it to you.

He exits.

FRIAR LAWRENCE

    Now must I to the monument alone;

25   Within this three hours will fair Juliet wake.

    She will beshrew me much that Romeo

    Hath had no notice of these accidents;

    But I will write again to Mantua,

    And keep her at my cell till Romeo come;

30   Poor living corse, clos'd in a dead man's tomb!

    [*Exit.*]

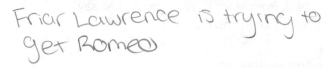

Friar Lawrence is trying to get Romeo

FRIAR LAWRENCE

Now I must go to the tomb alone.
Within three hours, beautiful Juliet will awake.   25
She'll blame me that Romeo
hasn't been told about what's going on.
But I'll write another letter to Mantua
and keep her at my cell until Romeo comes.
Poor living body, shut up in a dead man's tomb!   30

He exits.

ACT V, SCENE III

[*A churchyard; in it a tomb belonging to the Capulets.*]
Enter PARIS *and his* PAGE *with flowers and sweet water
and a torch.*

PARIS

    Give me thy torch, boy. Hence, and stand aloof.
    Yet put it out, for I would not be seen.
    Under yond yew-tree lay thee all along,
    Holding thine ear close to the hollow ground;
5   So shall no foot upon the churchyard tread,
    Being loose, unfirm, with digging up of graves,
    But thou shalt hear it. Whistle then to me,
    As signal that thou hear'st something approach.
    Give me those flowers. Do as I bid thee, go.

PAGE

10 [*aside*] I am almost afraid to stand alone
    Here in the churchyard; yet I will adventure.

       [*Retires.*]

PARIS

    Sweet flower, with flowers thy bridal bed I strew,—
    O woe! Thy **canopy** is dust and stones—
    Which with sweet water nightly I will dew,
15 Or, wanting that, with tears distill'd by moans.
    The obsequies that I for thee will keep
    Nightly shall be to strew thy grave and weep,

       [*The PAGE whistles.*]

    The boy gives warning something doth approach.
    What cursed foot wanders this way to-night,
20 To cross my obsequies and true love's rite?
    What, with a torch! Muffle me, night, a while.

       [*Retires.*]

    Enter ROMEO *and* BALTHASAR, *with a torch, a
    mattock, and a crow of iron.*

ACT 5, SCENE 3

A churchyard with the Capulet family tomb. PARIS *and his* PAGE
enter with flowers, perfumed water, and a torch.

PARIS
Give me your torch, boy. Go stand over there.
Put out the torch, for I don't want to be seen.
Go lie under that yew tree,
and keep your ear close to the ground.
No foot will walk about the churchyard—   5
since the soil is loose and not firm due to the digging of graves—
that you won't be able to hear. Whistle
to signal me if you hear someone coming.
Give me those flowers. Do as I tell you. Go!

PAGE *(to himself)*
I'm almost afraid to be alone   10
here in this churchyard, but I'll chance it.

> *He hides.*

PARIS
Sweet Juliet, my flower, with these flowers, I'll cover your
    bridal bed.

> *He scatters flowers around the tomb.*

Oh, sorrow! Your bed is dust and stones—
which I'll sprinkle with perfume every night.
Or if I don't have perfume, I'll use tears mixed with my moans.   15
The funeral rites that I'll keep for you
every night will be to sprinkle flowers on your grave and weep.

> *The* PAGE *whistles.*

That's the boy's signal that someone is approaching.
What damned foot wanders this way tonight
to interrupt the ritual for my true love?   20
What—someone with a torch? Hide me, night, for a while.

> *He hides.*

> ROMEO *and* BALTHASAR *enter with a torch, a pickaxe, and a*
> *crowbar.*

ROMEO

Give me that mattock and the wrenching iron.
Hold, take this letter; early in the morning
See thou deliver it to my lord and father.
25 Give me the light. Upon thy life I charge thee,
Whate'er thou hear'st or seest, stand all aloof,
And do not interrupt me in my course.
Why I descend into this bed of death
Is partly to behold my lady's face,
30 But chiefly to take thence from her dead finger
A precious ring, a ring that I must use
In dear employment; therefore hence, be gone.
But if thou, jealous, dost return to pry
In what I farther shall intend to do,
35 By heaven, I will tear thee joint by joint
And strew this hungry churchyard with thy limbs.
The time and my intents are savage-wild,
More fierce and more **inexorable** far
Than empty tigers or the roaring sea.

BALTHASAR

40 I will be gone, sir, and not trouble ye.

ROMEO

So shalt thou show me friendship. Take thou that;
Live, and be prosperous; and farewell, good fellow.

BALTHASAR

[*aside*] For all this same, I'll hide me hereabout.
His looks I fear, and his intents I doubt.

[*Retires.*]

ROMEO

45 Thou detestable maw, thou womb of death,
Gorg'd with the dearest morsel of the earth,
Thus I enforce thy rotten jaws to open,
And, in despite, I'll cram thee with more food!

[*Opens the tomb.*]

ROMEO

Give me that pickaxe and the crowbar.
Wait! Take this letter and deliver it
to my lord and father early in the morning.
Give me the light. Upon your life, I order you,   25
whatever you hear or see, to stand aside
and don't try to stop me.
I'm going into this tomb
partly to see my lady's face,
but mostly to take from her dead finger   30
a precious ring—a ring that I must use
in important business. Therefore, go away!
But if you become curious and return to pry
into what I intend to do,
by heaven, I'll tear you limb from limb   35
and cover this hungry churchyard with your body.
The time and my plans are savage and wild,
far more fierce and more relentless
than hungry tigers or the roaring sea.

BALTHASAR

I'll go, sir, and not bother you.   40

ROMEO

By doing so, you'll prove you're my friend. Take this. *(Gives him money.)*
Live and be prosperous. Good-bye, good fellow.

BALTHASAR *(to himself)*

Despite what he said, I'll hide close by.
His looks are frightening, and I am suspicious about what he intends to do.

> *He hides.*

ROMEO *(looking at the tomb)*

You detestable stomach. You womb of death.   45
You are gorged with the dearest morsel on earth.
So I'll force your rotten jaws to open,
and to spite you, I'll cram you with more food!

> *Opens the tomb.*

PARIS

This is that banish'd haughty Montague,

50 That murd'red my love's cousin, with which grief,

It is supposed, the fair creature died;

And here is come to do some villainous shame

To the dead bodies. I will **apprehend** him.

[*Comes forward.*]

Stop thy unhallowed toil, vile Montague!

55 Can vengeance be pursued further than death?

Condemned villain, I do apprehend thee.

Obey, and go with me; for thou must die.

ROMEO

I must indeed; and therefore came I hither.

Good gentle youth, tempt not a desperate man.

60 Fly hence, and leave me; think upon these gone.

Let them affright thee. I beseech thee, youth,

Put not another sin upon my head

By urging me to fury: O, be gone!

By heaven, I love thee better than myself;

65 For I come hither arm'd against myself.

Stay not, be gone; live, and hereafter say

A madman's mercy bid thee run away.

PARIS

I do defy thy conjurations

And apprehend thee for a felon here.

ROMEO

70 Wilt thou provoke me? Then have at thee, boy!

[*They fight.*]

PAGE

O Lord, they fight! I will go call the watch.

[*Exit.*]

PARIS

O, I am slain! [*Falls.*] If thou be merciful,

Open the tomb, lay me with Juliet.

[*Dies.*]

PARIS

There's that banished, haughty Montague
who murdered my love's cousin. It was from grieving for Tybalt, 50
it's said, that my beautiful love died.
And now he's come to do some villainous dishonor to
the dead bodies. I'll stop him.

He comes forward.

Stop your unholy work, evil Montague!
Can you demand any further revenge than death? 55
Condemned villain, I'll stop you.
Obey and go with me, for you must die.

ROMEO

I must die, indeed, and that is why I came here.
Good gentle youth, don't tempt a desperate man.
Fly away and leave me. Think about those who are dead. 60
Let them frighten you. I beg you, youth,
don't lay another sin on my head
by making me angry. Go away!
By heaven, I love you better than I love myself,
for I came here with weapons to hurt myself. 65
Don't stay; go! Live, and later you can say that
a madman's mercy told you to run away.

PARIS

I reject your appeals,
and I arrest you as a criminal.

ROMEO

You want to start something? Then take that, boy. 70

They fight.

PAGE

Oh Lord, they're fighting! I'll go call the guards.

He exits.

PARIS

Oh, I'm dying. *(He falls.)* If you are merciful,
open the tomb and lay me beside Juliet!

He dies.

ROMEO

75

80

85

In faith, I will. Let me peruse this face.
Mercutio's kinsman, noble County Paris!
What said my man, when my betossed soul
Did not attend him as we rode? I think
He told me Paris should have married Juliet.
Said he not so? Or did I dream it so?
Or am I mad, hearing him talk of Juliet,
To think it was so? O, give me thy hand,
One writ with me in sour misfortune's book!
I'll bury thee in a triumphant grave.
A grave? O, no! A lantern,* slaughter'd youth,
For here lies Juliet, and her beauty makes
This vault a feasting presence full of light.
Death, lie thou there, by a dead man **interr'd**.

[Laying PARIS *in the tomb.]*

90

95

100

105

How often when men are at the point of death
Have they been merry! Which their keepers call
A lightning before death. O, how may I
Call this a lightn'ing? O my love! My wife!
Death, that hath suck'd the honey of thy breath,
Hath had no power yet upon thy beauty.
Thou art not conquer'd; beauty's ensign yet
Is crimson in thy lips and in thy cheeks,
And death's pale flag is not advanced there.
Tybalt, li'st thou there in thy bloody sheet?
O, what more favour can I do to thee,
Than with that hand that cut thy youth in twain
To sunder his that was thine enemy?
Forgive me, cousin! Ah, dear Juliet,
Why art thou yet so fair? Shall I believe
That unsubstantial Death is amorous,
And that the lean **abhorred** monster keeps
Thee here in dark to be his paramour?
For fear of that, I still will stay with thee,
And never from this palace of dim night
Depart again. Here, here will I remain

---

84 *lantern* a room on top of a tower designed with many windows to admit light and air

ROMEO

Truly, I will. Let me look at his face.
This is Mercutio's relative, the noble Count Paris!   75
What was it my servant said when my disturbed soul
did not listen to him as we rode? I think
he told me Paris was supposed to have married Juliet.
Isn't that what he said? Or did I dream it?
Or am I crazy, hearing him talk of Juliet,   80
to believe it? Oh, give me your hand.
We've both been written about in sour misfortune's book.
I'll bury you in a triumphant grave.
A grave? Oh, no, rather a lantern, slain youth,
because Juliet lies here, and her beauty makes   85
this tomb a state banquet hall full of light.
Dead man, lie there, buried by a dead man.

He lays PARIS *in the tomb.*

Often when men are at the point of death,
they have been happy. Their nurses call this
a revival before death. Oh, how may I   90
call this a revival? Oh, my love! My wife!
Death, that has sucked the honey from your breath,
has no power yet over your beauty.
You are not conquered. Beauty's flag is
still crimson in your lips and cheeks,   95
and death's pale flag has not advanced there.
Tybalt, is that you lying there in your bloody sheet?
Oh, what greater favor can I do for you
than, with this hand that killed you,
kill the one who was your enemy?   100
Forgive me, cousin.—Ah, dear Juliet,
why are you still so beautiful? Shall I believe
that the phantom Death is passionate
and that the thin, hateful monster keeps
you here in the dark to be his mistress?   105
For fear of that, I'll stay with you
and never again leave this palace of
dim night. Here, here I'll remain

With worms that are thy chamber-maids; O, here
110 Will I set up my everlasting rest,
And shake the yoke of inauspicious stars
From this world-wearied flesh. Eyes, look your last!
Arms take your last embrace! And, lips, O you
The doors of breath, seal with a **righteous** kiss
115 A dateless bargain to engrossing death!
Come, bitter conduct, come, unsavoury guide!
Thou desperate pilot, now at once run on
The dashing rocks thy sea-sick weary bark!
Here's to my love! [*Drinks.*] O true apothecary!
120 Thy drugs are quick. Thus with a kiss I die.

[*Dies.*]   Dramatic
Irony

Enter FRIAR LAWRENCE, *with lantern, crow, and spade.*

He doesn't know she is waking up

FRIAR LAWRENCE
Saint Francis be my speed! How oft tonight
Have my old feet stumbled at graves!* Who's there?

BALTHASAR
Here's one, a friend, and one that knows you well.

FRIAR LAWRENCE
Bliss be upon you! Tell me, good my friend,
125 What torch is yond, that vainly lends his light
To grubs and eyeless skulls? As I discern,
It burneth in the Capels' monument.

BALTHASAR
It doth so, holy sir; and there's my master,
One that you love.

FRIAR LAWRENCE
130   Who is it?

BALTHASAR
                                   Romeo.

FRIAR LAWRENCE
How long hath he been there?

---

122 *stumbled at graves* This was considered a bad omen.

with worms that are your servingmaids. Oh, here
I'll take my eternal rest.   110
and shake off the grip of unkind fate
from my world-wearied body. Eyes, take your last look!
Arms, take your last embrace! And lips—Oh, you lips
that are the doors of breath—seal with a fitting kiss
an eternal bargain to all-consuming death!   115
Come, bitter poison, come distasteful guide.
You desperate pilot, crash my seasick, tired body
against the dashing rocks at once.
Here's to my love! *(He drinks the poison.)* Oh, faithful pharmacist!
Your drugs are quick. With this kiss, I die.   120

ROMEO *kisses* JULIET *and dies.*

FRIAR LAWRENCE *enters with a lantern, a crowbar, and a spade.*

FRIAR LAWRENCE
Saint Francis, help me! How often tonight
have my old feet stumbled over graves. Who's there?

BALTHASAR
A friend and one who knows you well.

FRIAR LAWRENCE
Bless you. Tell me, my friend,
what torch is that over there that vainly lights up   125
the worms and eyeless skulls? As best as I can see,
it burns in the Capulets' tomb.

BALTHASAR
It does, holy sir; and that's where my master is,
one that you love.

FRIAR LAWRENCE
Who's that?   130

BALTHASAR
Romeo.

FRIAR LAWRENCE
How long has he been there?

BALTHASAR

Full half an hour.

FRIAR LAWRENCE
Go with me to the vault.

BALTHASAR
135   I dare not, sir.
My master knows not but I am gone hence,
And fearfully did menace me with death
If I did stay to look on his intents.

FRIAR LAWRENCE
Stay, then; I'll go alone. Fear comes upon me:
140   O, much I fear some ill unthrifty thing.

BALTHASAR
As I did sleep under this yew tree here,
I dreamt my master and another fought,
And that my master slew him.

FRIAR LAWRENCE
Romeo!

[*Advances.*]

145   Alack, alack, what blood is this, which stains
The stony entrance of this sepulchre?
What mean these masterless and gory swords
To lie discolour'd by this place of peace?

[*Enters the tomb.*]

Romeo! O, pale! Who else? What, Paris too?
150   And **steep'd** in blood? Ah, what an unkind hour
Is guilty of this lamentable change!
The lady stirs.

[JULIET *rises.*]

JULIET
O comfortable friar! Where is my lord?
I do remember well where I should be,
155   And there I am. Where is my Romeo?

[*noise within*]

BALTHASAR

At least half an hour.

FRIAR LAWRENCE

Go with me to the tomb.

BALTHASAR

I don't dare, sir. 135
My master doesn't know that I haven't left.
With frightening words, he threatened me with death
if I stayed to see what he did.

FRIAR LAWRENCE

Stay here then; I'll go alone. I'm beginning to feel frightened.
I'm afraid something terribly unlucky has happened. 140

BALTHASAR

As I slept under this yew tree here,
I dreamed my master and another man fought,
and that my master killed him.

FRIAR LAWRENCE

Romeo!

He advances toward the tomb.

Alas, alas, whose blood is this that stains 145
the stone entrance of this tomb?
What's the meaning of these unclaimed, bloody swords
that lie here, stained with blood, in this peaceful place?

He enters the tomb.

Romeo! How pale he is! Who else is here? What, Paris, too?
And he's covered in blood? The hour that saw this 150
sad turn of events occur is tragic, indeed!
The lady is waking up.

JULIET rises.

JULIET

Oh, comforting friar, where is my lord?
I remember quite well where I am supposed to be,
and here I am. But where is my Romeo? 155

There is a noise.

FRIAR LAWRENCE

I hear some noise—Lady, come from that nest
Of death, contagion, and unnatural sleep.
A greater power than we can contradict
Hath thwarted our intents. Come, come away.
160 Thy husband in thy bosom there lies dead;
And Paris too. Come, I'll dispose of thee
Among a sisterhood of holy nuns.
Stay not to question, for the watch is coming;
Come, go, good Juliet. [*noise again*] I dare no longer stay.

[*Exit* FRIAR LAWRENCE.]

JULIET

165 Go, get thee hence, for I will not away.
What's here? A cup, clos'd in my true love's hand?
Poison, I see, hath been his timeless end.
O churl! Drunk all, and left no friendly drop
To help me after? I will kiss thy lips;
170 Haply some poison yet doth hang on them,
To make me die with a restorative.
Thy lips are warm.

Enter WATCH, *with the* PAGE *of Paris.*

1. WATCH

Lead, boy; which way?

JULIET

Yea, noise? Then I'll be brief. O happy dagger!

[*snatching* ROMEO'S *dagger*]

175 This is thy sheath. [*Stabs herself.*] There rust, and let
me die.

[*Falls on* ROMEO'S *body and dies.*]

PAGE

This is the place; there, where the torch doth burn.

1. WATCH

The ground is bloody—search about the churchyard.
Go, some of you, whoe'er you find, attach.

[*Exeunt some.*]

FRIAR LAWRENCE

I hear some noise. Lady, come from that bed
of death, contamination, and unnatural sleep.
A greater power than we can argue with
has ruined our plans. Come, come away.
Your dear husband lies dead—   160
and Paris, too. Come, I'll hide you
in a convent of nuns.
Don't stop to ask questions because the guards are coming.
Come, let's go, good Juliet. *(The noise is heard again.)* I don't
    dare stay any longer.

> FRIAR LAWRENCE *exits.*

JULIET

Go, go away. I'll stay.   165
What's this? A bottle, clutched in my true love's hand?
Poison, I see, has brought him to his untimely end.
Oh, the rascal drank it all and didn't leave one good drop
to help me follow him. I'll kiss your lips, then.
Perhaps some drop of poison still hangs on them   170
to make me die from that life-giving kiss.
Your lips are warm!

> GUARDS *and Paris's* PAGE *enter.*

FIRST GUARD

Lead the way, boy. Which direction?

JULIET

Noise! Then I'll be brief. What luck—a dagger!

> *She snatches* ROMEO'S *dagger.*

This is your holder. *(She stabs herself.)* Rest there and let   175
    me die.

> JULIET *falls on* ROMEO's *body and dies.*

PAGE

That's the place—there where the torch burns.

FIRST GUARD

The ground is bloody. Search the churchyard.
Go, some of you, and whoever you find, arrest.

> *Some of the* GUARDS *exit.*

180 Pitiful sight! Here lies the County slain;
And Juliet bleeding, warm, and newly dead,
Who here hath lain this two days buried.
Go, tell the Prince; run to the Capulets;
Raise up the Montagues; some others search.

[Exeunt others.]

185 We see the ground whereon these woes do lie;
But the true ground of all these piteous woes
We cannot without circumstance descry.

Re-enter some of the WATCH, *with* BALTHASAR.

2. WATCH

Here's Romeo's man; we found him in the churchyard.

1. WATCH

Hold him in safety till the Prince come hither.

Re-enter another WATCHMAN, *with* FRIAR
LAWRENCE.

3. WATCH

190 Here is a friar, that trembles, sighs, and weeps.
We took this mattock and this spade from him,
As he was coming from this churchyard's side.

1. WATCH

A great suspicion. Stay the friar too.

Enter the PRINCE *and Attendants.*

PRINCE ESCALUS

What misadventure is so early up,
195 That calls our person from our morning rest?

Enter CAPULET, LADY CAPULET, *and others.*

CAPULET

What should it be, that they so shriek abroad?

LADY CAPULET

Oh! The people in the street cry Romeo,
Some Juliet, and some Paris; and all run,
With open outcry, toward our monument.

This is a pitiful sight! Here lies Count Paris, killed. 180
And there lies Juliet, bleeding, warm and just dead,
though she has lain here buried for two days.
Go, tell the Prince. Run to the Capulets.
Wake up the Montagues. Others of you, search the area!

> *Other* GUARDS *exit.*

We see the ground where these sorrows lie. 185
But the true cause of all these pitiful sorrows
we can't tell without more details.

> *Some of the* GUARDS *re-enter with* BALTHASAR.

SECOND GUARD
Here's Romeo's servant. We found him in the churchyard.

FIRST GUARD
Keep him under guard until the Prince comes.

> *Another* GUARD *re-enters with* FRIAR LAWRENCE.

THIRD GUARD
Here's a friar who shakes, sighs, and weeps. 190
We took this pickaxe and this spade from him,
as he was coming from the side of this churchyard.

FIRST GUARD
This is very suspicious. Keep the friar, too.

> *The* PRINCE *and* ATTENDANTS *enter.*

PRINCE
What trouble is up so early
that wakes me from my morning sleep? 195

> CAPULET, LADY CAPULET, *and others enter.*

CAPULET
What could it be that people are shouting in the streets?

LADY CAPULET
The people in the streets shout "Romeo,"
some shout "Juliet," and some shout "Paris." And all of them
    are running
with noisy shouts toward our tomb.

PRINCE ESCALUS

200   What fear is this which startles in our ears?

1. WATCH

Sovereign, here lies the County Paris slain;
And Romeo dead; and Juliet, dead before,
Warm and new kill'd.

PRINCE ESCALUS

Search, seek, and know how this foul murder comes.

1. WATCH

205   Here is a friar, and slaughter'd Romeo's man,
With instruments upon them, fit to open
These dead men's tombs.

CAPULET

O heavens! O wife, look how our daughter bleeds!
This dagger hath mista'en,—for, lo, his house
210   Is empty on the back of Montague,—
And it mis-sheathed in my daughter's bosom!

LADY CAPULET

O me! This sight of death is as a bell,
That warns my old age to a sepulchre.

Enter MONTAGUE *and others.*

PRINCE ESCALUS

Come, Montague; for thou art early up
215   To see thy son and heir more early down.

MONTAGUE

Alas, my liege, my wife is dead to-night;
Grief of my son's exile hath stopp'd her breath.
What further woe conspires against mine age?

PRINCE ESCALUS

Look, and thou shalt see.

MONTAGUE

220   O thou untaught! What manners is in this,
To press before thy father to a grave?

PRINCE ESCALUS

Seal up the mouth of outrage for a while,

PRINCE

What news has alarmed everyone? 200

FIRST GUARD

Your majesty, here lies Count Paris, killed.
Romeo is also dead, and Juliet, who was dead before,
is still warm and newly killed.

PRINCE

Search, investigate, and find out how this foul murder happened.

FIRST GUARD

Here's a friar, and Romeo's servant, 205
carrying tools that could be used to open
these dead men's tombs.

CAPULET

Oh heavens! Wife, see how our daughter bleeds!
This dagger has missed the right victim. See, Romeo's dagger
sheath
is empty, and the dagger has been 210
mistakenly placed in our daughter's breast.

LADY CAPULET

Alas! This sight of death is like a bell
that summons my aged body to my grave.

MONTAGUE *and others enter.*

PRINCE

Come, Montague. You are up early
to see your son and heir who just retired even earlier. 215

MONTAGUE

Alas, Prince, my wife died tonight!
Grief over my son's exile killed her.
What further sorrow schemes against me in my old age?

PRINCE

Look and you will see.

MONTAGUE

Oh, you rude boy. What kind of manners is this 220
to hurry before your father to a grave?

PRINCE

No more of your violent grieving for a while

Till we can clear these ambiguities,
And know their spring, their head, their true descent;
225 And then will I be general of your woes
And lead you even to death. Meantime forbear,
And let mischance be slave to patience.
Bring forth the parties of suspicion.

FRIAR LAWRENCE

I am the greatest, able to do least,
230 Yet most suspected, as the time and place
Doth make against me, of this direful murder;
And here I stand, both to impeach and purge
Myself condemned and myself excus'd.

best person to tell the story

PRINCE ESCALUS

Then say at once what thou dost know in this.

FRIAR LAWRENCE

235 I will be brief, for my short date of breath
Is not so long as is a tedious tale.
Romeo, there dead, was husband to that Juliet;
And she, there dead, that Romeo's faithful wife.
I married them; and their stol'n marriage-day
240 Was Tybalt's dooms-day, whose untimely death
Banish'd the new-made bridegroom from this city,
For whom, and not for Tybalt, Juliet pin'd.
You, to remove that siege of grief from her,
Betroth'd and would have married her perforce
245 To County Paris. Then comes she to me,
And, with wild looks, bid me devise some mean
To rid her from this second marriage,
Or in my cell there would she kill herself.
Then gave I her, so tutor'd by my art,
250 A sleeping potion; which so took effect
As I intended, for it wrought on her
The form of death. Meantime I writ to Romeo,
That he should hither come as this dire night
To help to take her from her borrowed grave,
255 Being the time the potion's force should cease.
But he which bore my letter, Friar John,

Humble brag

everyone woes wrong caused by making her do something she don't want

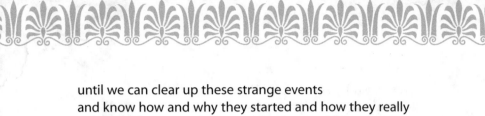

until we can clear up these strange events
and know how and why they started and how they really
   occurred.
Then I'll be your leader in mourning   225
and lead you even to death. But in the meantime, no more.
Bear your sorrows with patience.
Bring here the people under suspicion.

FRIAR LAWRENCE
I'm the most important suspect, least likely to do something
   wrong,
yet I'm most suspected since the time and place   230
stands as evidence against me and seems to prove me guilty
   of this shocking murder.
And here I stand, both to charge myself and clear myself,
condemn myself and excuse myself.

PRINCE
Then tell us at once what you know about this.

FRIAR LAWRENCE
I'll be brief because the span of my remaining years   235
is not as long as a long tale.
Romeo, who lies dead there, was Juliet's husband.
And she, who lies dead there, was Romeo's faithful wife.
I married them, and their secret wedding day
was Tybalt's last day. His untimely death   240
banished the new bridegroom from this city.
It was for him—not for Tybalt—that Juliet grieved.
You, Lord Capulet, to shake her out of her depression,
arranged for her to marry Count Paris   245
right away. Then she came to me,
and with wild looks, begged me to think of some way
to get her out of this second marriage.
If I didn't, she said she'd kill herself there in my cell.
Then I gave her, from my knowledge of medicine,
a sleeping potion. It worked   250
as I intended it to do since it made her
seem like she was dead. Meanwhile, I wrote to Romeo
that he should come here tonight
to help free her from this borrowed grave,
as tonight was the time the potion would wear off.   255
But Friar John, who was to take my letter to Romeo,

Was stay'd by accident, and yesternight
Return'd my letter back. Then all alone
At the prefixed hour of her waking,
260   Came I to take her from her kindred's vault;
Meaning to keep her closely at my cell,
Till I conveniently could send to Romeo;
But when I came, some minutes ere the time
Of her awak'ning, here untimely lay
265   The noble Paris and true Romeo dead.
She wakes; and I entreated her come forth
And bear this work of heaven with patience.
But then a noise did scare me from the tomb;
And she, too desperate, would not go with me,
270   But, as it seems, did violence on herself.
All this I know; and to the marriage   *he is laying*
Her nurse is privy; and, if aught in this
Miscarried by my fault, let my old life
Be sacrific'd, some hour before his time,
275   Unto the rigour of severest law.

PRINCE ESCALUS

We still have known thee for a holy man.
Where's Romeo's man? What can he say to this?

BALTHASAR

I brought my master news of Juliet's death;
And then in post he came from Mantua
280   To this same place, to this same monument.
This letter he early bid me give his father,
And threat'ned me with death, going in the vault,
If I departed not and left him there.

PRINCE ESCALUS

Give me the letter; I will look on it.
285   Where is the County's page, that rais'd the watch?
Sirrah, what made your master in this place?

PAGE

He came with flowers to strew his lady's grave;
And bid me stand aloof, and so I did.

was detained by accident, and last night,
he brought my letter back. Then all alone,
at the time I estimated Juliet would awaken,
I came to take her from her relatives' tomb. 260
I intended to keep her hidden in my cell
until I could conveniently get word to Romeo.
But when I came some minutes before
she was to awaken, here lay
the noble Paris and faithful Romeo, dead before their time. 265
Juliet awoke and I begged her to come out
and patiently accept these events willed by heaven.
But then a noise scared me away from the tomb,
and she, too deep in despair, wouldn't go with me.
She stayed, and it seems she committed suicide. 270
This is all I know. Her nurse was in on the secret
about Juliet's marriage. And if any of this
went wrong because of me, let my old life
be sacrificed, some hour before my time,
according to the severity of the strictest laws. 275

PRINCE
I've always known you to be a holy man.
Where's Romeo's servant? What can he add to this?

BALTHASAR
I brought my master news of Juliet's death.
And then, in haste, he came from Mantua
to this same place and this same tomb. 280
He told me to deliver this letter to his father early in the
    morning,
and as he went into the tomb, he threatened me with death
if I didn't go away and leave him there.

PRINCE
Give me the letter; I want to look at it.
Where is Count Paris' page—the one who called the guards? 285
Servant, what made your master come to this place?

PAGE
He came with flowers to scatter at his lady's grave.
He asked me to stay away, so I did.

Anon comes one with light to ope the tomb,
290 And by and by my master drew on him;
And then I ran away to call the watch.

PRINCE ESCALUS

This letter doth make good the Friar's words,
Their course of love, the tidings of her death.
And here he writes that he did buy a poison
295 Of a poor 'pothecary, and therewithal
Came to this vault to die, and lie with Juliet.
Where be these enemies? Capulet! Montague!
See what a scourge is laid upon your hate,
That Heaven finds means to kill your joys with love.
300 And I for winking at your discords too
Have lost a brace of kinsmen. All are punish'd.

CAPULET

O brother Montague, give me thy hand.
This is my daughter's jointure, for no more
Can I demand.

MONTAGUE

305   But I can give thee more;
For I will ray* her statue in pure gold;
That whiles Verona by that name is known,
There shall no figure at such rate be set
As that of true and faithful Juliet.

CAPULET

310 As rich shall Romeo's by his lady's lie,
Poor sacrifices of our enmity!

PRINCE ESCALUS

A glooming peace this morning with it brings;
The sun, for sorrow, will not show his head.
Go hence, to have more talk of these sad things;
315 Some shall be pardon'd, and some punished:
For never was a story of more woe
Than this of Juliet and her Romeo.

          [*Exeunt.*]

---

306 *ray* dress, or array

Soon, someone came with a light to open the tomb.
After a while, my master drew his sword on him,　　　290
and I ran away to call the guard.

PRINCE

This letter proves the truth of the friar's words.
It tells the course of their love and the news of her death.
Here he writes of how he bought poison
from a poor pharmacist and then　　　295
came to this tomb to die and lie with Juliet.
Where are these enemies? Capulet, Montague!
See what a curse is laid upon your hatred.
Heaven finds the means to kill your joys with love.
And I, for overlooking your feud,　　　300
have lost two relatives, too. We've all been punished.

CAPULET

Oh, my brother Montague, give me your hand.
This is my daughter's dowry, for I can ask
for nothing more.

MONTAGUE

But I'll give you more,　　　305
for I'll put up a statue to her in pure gold.
So as long as Verona is called Verona,
there'll be no other figure valued
more than the true and faithful Juliet.

CAPULET

I'll put up an equally rich statue of Romeo beside Juliet's.　　　310
They are poor sacrifices of our feud.

PRINCE

This morning brings a cloudy peace.
The sun, out of sorrow, will not show its head.
Go! We'll talk more about these sad things.
Some of you will be pardoned and some of you will be　　　315
　　punished.
There was never a story of more sorrow
than this one of Juliet and her Romeo.

　　　They exit.

Act V Review

Discussion Questions

1. Summarize Romeo's last soliloquy in Scene iii.

2. Do you think that fate or the characters themselves are more responsible for the outcome of the play? Explain.

3. Why do you think Balthasar ignores Romeo's threats and stays near the vault?

4. Why does Paris challenge Romeo in the churchyard?

5. Friar Lawrence runs from the tomb after Juliet awakens. Decide whether or not this action is "in character." Why might Shakespeare have him do this?

6. Why do you think Shakespeare includes the deaths of Paris and Lady Montague in Act V?

7. Do you think the feud of the Capulets and the Montagues is really over? Explain your answer.

8. In what way are the adults responsible for the fate of Romeo and Juliet? Name some of the things they could have done differently.

Literary Elements

1. A **tragedy** tells of the defeat of a **tragic hero.** His or her downfall is a result of a **tragic flaw** or fatal character weakness. Decide who is the tragic hero of *Romeo and Juliet.* What is that person's tragic flaw?

2. What is **ironic** about Romeo's opening soliloquy in Act V, Scene i?

3. Name some of the **themes** addressed by events in the last act. From reading *Romeo and Juliet,* what would you say Shakespeare believes about family conflicts and the courtship of young people?

Writing Prompts

1. Choose any scene from Act V and rewrite it. Using the translation on the right side as your guide, make the language even more contemporary, complete with slang and up-to-date references. Explain what you think is lost and gained in the translation.

2. Pretend you write obituaries for the main newspaper in Verona. Write an obituary for either Romeo or Juliet. Include all of the relevant facts. Try to word it in such a way that it will not disturb the newly created truce between the families.

3. What if Romeo and Juliet had not died? Think about what their married life might have been like fifteen years later. Now, write a scene portraying that relationship.

4. What happens afterward? Shakespeare based his story on *The Tragicall Historye of Romeus and Juliet,* a poem by Arthur Brooke. At the end of his poem, Brooke tells what happens to several characters after the lovers' deaths. For example, the Apothecary is hanged for selling poison. Write your own description of the fate of the characters who remain alive, especially the Nurse, Lord Capulet, and the Friar.

The Play in Review

Discussion and Analysis

1. Identify some situations in today's world where two lovers might find obstacles because of their membership in feuding groups.

2. Cite some of the ways popular stories of romantic love have remained unchanged since *Romeo and Juliet* was written. In what ways have they changed? Discuss some examples.

3. In the original source material for *Romeo and Juliet*, the action of the drama took place over 9 months, whereas in Shakespeare's play, less than 5 days elapse. What do you think is Shakespeare's purpose in compressing time so intensely? Discuss how he manages to "squeeze" time and why he would want to do so.

4. Some critics believe that Shakespeare shows the love of Romeo and Juliet ending in tragedy because they married against their parents' wishes. Do you believe that this is the message that Shakespeare wishes to convey with this play? Cite evidence from the play to support your opinion.

5. What kind of person is the Nurse? Explain some of the aspects of her character and her role in *Romeo and Juliet*. Do you think she acts like a caricature (an exaggerated portrayal) or more like a flesh-and-blood character? Explain.

6. Love and hate exist side by side in this play. Talk about the many ways in which one affects the other.

Literary Elements

1. A work as complex as a Shakespeare play will generally have more than one **theme**. With your classmates, discuss all of the themes found in *Romeo and Juliet*.

2. *Romeo and Juliet* is rich in **conflicts**—struggles among characters and forces in the play that move the plot along. Name one conflict that contributes to the tragedy. How would you rate its importance in bringing about the death of the young couple?

3. *Romeo and Juliet* is famous for its **lyric poetry**, poetry which allows the characters to express their emotions in a powerful, almost musical way. Find some examples of language in the play that you find emotionally powerful because of their rhyme and/or rhythm.

4. With **personification**, human characteristics are given to nonhuman things, for example, in the Prologue in Act II, the lines, "Now old Desire doth in his death-bed lie / and young Affection gapes to be his heir." Why do you think Shakespeare personifies Desire and Affection? Explain your answer.

5. **Dramatic irony** occurs when the audience knows more about what is happening on the stage than at least one of the characters or when what is said contrasts with what has happened already. Go through the play and find examples of dramatic irony. What do you think a playwright gains using this technique?

6. The rich **diction**, or word choice, in *Romeo and Juliet* has provided English with many well-known phrases and expressions. You are probably acquainted with "parting is such sweet sorrow" and "what's in a name?" Alone or with a partner, find as many lines or phrases from the play as you can that sound familiar to you.

Writing Prompts

1. Write a short parody of *Romeo and Juliet*.

2. Imagine that it is ten years or more after the deaths of Romeo and Juliet. Pretend that you are either the Nurse or Friar Lawrence, and write your memoirs. Consider how you view the tragedy and its aftermath at this point, and describe what impact it has had on your own life.

3. Several characters express their philosophy of life in this play. Whom would you choose for an adviser—the Nurse, Juliet, Mercutio, or Friar Lawrence? Write an essay commenting on how that character influences others in the play and why that character's philosophy appeals to you.

4. Argue that Romeo and Juliet are either a) tragic figures or b) pathetic figures (you may decide that one is tragic and one is pathetic). Research definitions of each term. Then state your position and support it with examples from each play.

5. Go back in time many generations before the birth of Romeo and Juliet. Write a one-act dramatic scene that shows the conflict that started the terrible feud between the Capulets and the Montagues.

Multimodal and Group Activities

1. As a class, perform a choral reading of the Prologue to Act I. This will introduce you to the flow of Shakespearean language (especially in his formal sonnets), the plot, and the characters of the play. As you read it, think about what words, images, and ideas are introduced. Notice how "two" is repeated, including not only the word itself but also paired items, concepts, and even sounds. What is gained by this repetition of "two"?

2. Discuss how insults are an intrinsic part of arguments and feuds. Note how Shakespeare starts the play with a fight scene, building up the drama with a verbal slugfest between the Capulet and Montague families. Next, using a Shakespearean Insult Sheet (which you can find at a Shakespeare Web site), create some insults in Elizabethan English.

After memorizing your insults, get on your feet and conduct a verbal duel by hurling your insults at your classmates (with vigor, not violence!).

3. Choose one of the dreams from the play and illustrate it with a collage, a maze, or an illustration in the form of a puzzle. Combine design elements from photography, drawing, fabric, computer art, or any other resources. Then discuss how dreams play a part in *Romeo and Juliet*. In real life, what part do dreams play?

4. Divide into two teams, affirmative and negative, and debate one of the following resolutions.

   Resolved: Arranged marriages are a good way to find your lifelong partner.

   Resolved: Free will is a stronger force than fate.

5. At the end of the play, the Capulets and Montagues declare that they will commission statues of gold in memory of their beloved children. In small teams, come up with a design of such a work. You might want to incorporate a quote from the play in the sculptures, show Romeo and Juliet at any point in their courtship, or imagine how they might have looked if they had lived. When you're finished, display your design to the class and explain the thinking behind it.

6. Who is really guilty of the deaths of Romeo and Juliet? Explore characters who have secondary responsibility for escalating the action. After assigning a judge, jury, and prosecution and defense attorneys, as well as witnesses, conduct a trial that assesses who instigated their deaths, who did not act responsibly in trying to save them, and what the consequences should be.

7. Play a version of the TV game show *Family Feud*. With your teacher as the game show host and scorekeeper, divide into two "family" teams: the Capulets and the Montagues. A bell or handheld buzzer is passed down the row from student to student. When a question about the play is asked, the family member who rings first gets to answer. If correct, the family gets the points. If not, the other family gets a chance to answer.

Shakespeare's Life

Many great authors can be imagined as living among the characters in their works. Historical records reveal how these writers spoke, felt, and thought. But Shakespeare is more mysterious. He never gave an interview or wrote an autobiography—not even one of his letters survives. What we know about his life can be told very briefly.

Shakespeare was born in April 1564. The exact date of his birth is unknown, but he was baptized on April 26 in the Stratford-upon-Avon church. His father, John, was a prominent local man who served as town chamberlain and mayor. Young William attended

grammar school in Stratford, where he would have learned Latin—a requirement for a professional career—and some Greek.

In 1582, William married Anne Hathaway. He was 18; she was 26. At the time of their marriage, Anne was already three months pregnant with their first daughter, Susanna. In 1585, the couple had twins, Judith and Hamnet. Hamnet died before reaching adulthood, leaving Shakespeare no male heir.

Even less is known about Shakespeare's life between 1585 and 1592. During that time, he moved to London and became an actor and playwright. He left his family behind in Stratford. Although he surely visited them occasionally, we have little evidence about what Shakespeare was like as a father and a husband.

Several of his early plays were written during this time, including *The Comedy of Errors*, *Titus Andronicus*, and the three parts of *Henry VI*. In those days, working in the theater was rather like acting in soap operas today—the results may be popular, but daytime serials aren't recognized as serious art. In fact, many people were opposed to even allowing plays to be performed. Ministers warned their congregations of the dangers of going to plays.

Queen Elizabeth I

But Shakespeare and his friends were lucky. Queen Elizabeth I loved plays. She protected acting companies from restrictive laws and gave them her permission to perform. Shakespeare wrote several plays to be performed for the queen, including *Twelfth Night*.

After Elizabeth's death in 1603, Shakespeare's company became known as the King's Men. This group of actors performed for James I, who had ruled Scotland before becoming the King of England. Perhaps to thank James for his patronage, Shakespeare wrote *Macbeth*, which included two topics of strong interest to the king—Scottish royalty and witchcraft.

Unlike many theater people, Shakespeare actually earned a good living. By 1599, he was part owner of the Globe, one of the newest theaters in London. Such plays as *Othello*, *Hamlet*, and *King Lear* were first performed there.

In 1610 or 1611, Shakespeare moved back to the familiar surroundings of Stratford-upon-Avon. He was almost 50 years old, well past middle age by 17th-century standards. Over the years, he'd invested in property around Stratford, acquiring a comfortable estate and a family coat of arms.

But Shakespeare didn't give up writing. In 1611, his new play *The Tempest* was performed at court. In 1613, his play *Henry VIII* premiered. This performance was more dramatic than anyone expected. The stage directions called for a cannon to be fired when "King Henry" came on stage. The explosion set the stage on fire, and the entire theater burned to the ground.

Shakespeare died in 1616 at the age of 52. His gravestone carried this inscription:

> **Good friend for Jesus sake forbear**
> **To dig the dust enclosed here!**
> **Blest be the man that spares these stones,**
> **And curst be he that moves my bones.**

This little verse, so crude that it seems unlikely to be Shakespeare's, has intrigued countless scholars and biographers.

Anyone who loves Shakespeare's plays and poems wants to know more about their author. Was he a young man who loved Anne Whateley but was forced into a loveless marriage with another Anne? Did he teach school in Stratford, poach Sir Thomas Lucy's deer, or work for a lawyer in London? Who is the "dark lady" of his sonnets?

But perhaps we are fortunate in our ignorance. Orson Welles, who directed an all-black stage production of *Macbeth* in 1936, put it this way: "Luckily, we know almost nothing about Shakespeare . . . and that makes it so much easier to understand [his] works . . . It's an egocentric, romantic, 19th-century conception that the artist is more interesting and more important than his art."

In Shakespeare's world, there can be little question of which is truly important, the work or the author. Shakespeare rings up the curtain and then steps back into the wings, trusting the play to a cast of characters so stunningly vivid that they sometimes seem more real than life.

Shakespeare's Theater

In Shakespeare's London, a day's entertainment often began with a favorite amusement, bearbaiting. A bear would be captured and chained to a stake inside a pit. A pack of dogs would be released, and they would attack the bear. Spectators placed bets on which would die first. Admission to these pits cost only a penny, so they were very popular with working-class Londoners.

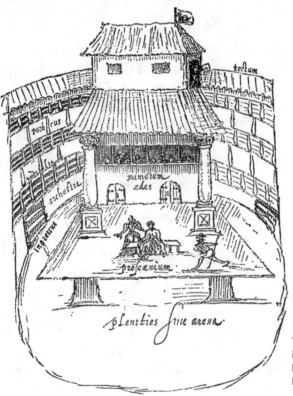

The Swan Theatre in London, drawn by Arend van Buchell in 1596

After the bearbaiting was over, another penny purchased admission to a play. Each theater had its own company of actors, often supported by a nobleman or a member of the royal family. For part of his career, Shakespeare was a member of the Lord

Chamberlain's Men. After the death of Queen Elizabeth I, King James I became the patron of Shakespeare's company. The actors became known as the King's Men.

As part owner of the Globe Theatre, Shakespeare wrote plays, hired actors, and paid the bills. Since the Globe presented a new play every three weeks, Shakespeare and his actors had little time to rehearse or polish their productions. To complicate matters even more, most actors played more than one part in a play.

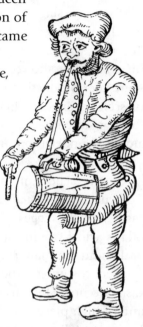

Richard Tarleton, comedian

Boys played all the female roles. Most acting companies had three or four youths who were practically raised in the theater. They started acting as early as age seven and played female roles until they began shaving. Shakespeare had a favorite boy actor (probably named John Rice) who played Cleopatra and Lady Macbeth. Actresses would not become part of the English theater for another 50 years.

The audience crowded into the theater at about 2 p.m. The cheapest seats weren't seats at all but standing room in front of the stage. This area, known as the "pit," was occupied by "groundlings" or "penny knaves," who could be more trouble to the actors than they were worth. If the play was boring, the groundlings would throw rotten eggs or vegetables. They talked loudly to their friends, played cards, and even picked fights with each other. One theater was set on fire by audience members who didn't like the play.

The theater was open to the sky, so rain or snow presented a problem. However, the actors were partially protected by a roof known as the "heavens," and wealthier patrons sat in three stories of sheltered galleries that surrounded the pit and most of the main stage.

The main stage, about 25 feet deep and 45 feet wide, projected into the audience, so spectators were closely involved in the action. This stage was rather bare, with only a few pieces of furniture. But this simplicity allowed for flexible and fluid staging. Unlike too many later productions, plays at the Globe did not grind to a halt for scene changes. When one group of actors exited through one doorway and a new group entered through another, Shakespeare's audience understood that a new location was probably being represented.

So the action of the plays was exciting and swift. The first Prologue of *Romeo and Juliet* speaks of "the two hours' traffic of our stage," which suggests a rate of performance and delivery that today's actors would find nearly impossible.

Behind the main stage was the "tiring-house" where the actors changed costumes. Above the stage was a gallery that, when it wasn't occupied by musicians or wealthy patrons, could suggest any kind of high place—castle ramparts, a cliff, or a balcony. Although *Romeo and Juliet* was written too early to have been first presented at the Globe, it surely appeared in a theater with many of the same characteristics. In the play's famous "balcony scene," Juliet must have stood in such a gallery. There was possibly also a recessed, curtained area below this gallery where characters could be "revealed"—for example, the sleeping Juliet in the Capulet crypt.

Special effects were common. A trap door in the main stage allowed ghosts to appear. Even more spectacularly, supernatural beings could be lowered from above the stage. For added realism, actors hid bags of pig's blood and guts under their stage doublets. When pierced with a sword, the bags spilled out over the stage and produced a gory effect. This effect would have added excitement to the duels in *Romeo and Juliet*.

All these staging methods and design elements greatly appealed to Elizabethan audiences and made plays increasingly popular. By the time Shakespeare died in 1616, there were more than 30 theaters in and around London.

The New Globe Theatre, London

What would Shakespeare, so accustomed to the rough-and-tumble stagecraft of the Globe, think of the theaters where his plays are performed today? He would probably miss some of the vitality of the Globe. For centuries now, his plays have been most often performed on stages with a frame called the "proscenium arch," which cleanly separates the audience from the performers. This barrier tends to cast a peculiar shroud of privacy over his plays so that his characters do not seem to quite enter our world.

But with greater and greater frequency, Shakespeare's plays are being performed out-of-doors or in theaters with three- or four-sided stages. And a replica of the Globe Theatre itself opened in London in 1996, only about 200 yards from the site of the original. This new Globe may prove an exciting laboratory where directors and actors can test ideas about Elizabethan staging. Their experiments may change our ideas about how Shakespeare's plays were performed and give new insights into their meaning.

The Globe Theatre Layout

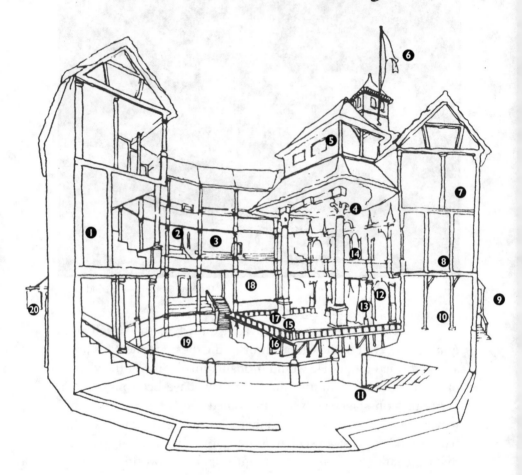

1 **Corridor** A passageway serving the middle gallery.

2 **Entrance** Point leading to the staircase and upper galleries.

3 **Middle Gallery** The seats here were higher priced.

4 **The Heavens** So identified by being painted with the zodiac signs.

5 **Hut** A storage area that also held a winch system for lowering characters to the stage.

6 **Flag** A white flag above the theater meant a show that day.

7 **Wardrobe** A storage area for costumes and props.

8 **Dressing Rooms** Rooms where actors were "attired" and awaited their cues.

9 **Tiring-House Door** The rear entrance or "stage door" for actors or privileged spectators.

10 **Tiring-House** Backstage area providing space for storage and business.

11 **Stairs** Theatergoers reached the galleries by staircases enclosed by stairwells.

12 **Stage Doors** Doors opening into the Tiring-House.

13 **Inner Stage** A recessed playing area often curtained off except as needed.

14 **Gallery** Located above the stage to house musicians or spectators.

15 **Trap Door** Leading to the Hell area where a winch elevator was located.

16 **Hell** The area under the stage, used for ghostly comings and goings or for storage.

17 **Stage** Major playing area jutting into the Pit, creating a sense of intimacy.

18 **Lords Rooms** or private galleries. Six pennies let a viewer sit here, or sometimes on stage.

19 **The Pit** Sometimes referred to as "The Yard," where the "groundlings" watched.

20 **Main Entrance** Here the doorkeeper collected admission.

IMAGE CREDITS